MARKETING
AND
CONSUMER
RESEARCH
IN THE
PUBLIC
INTEREST

MARKETING AND CONSUMER RESEARCH IN THE PUBLIC INTEREST

HF
5415.2
.M3542
1996

RONALD PAUL HILL
EDITOR

SAGE Publications
International Educational and Professional Publisher
Thousand Oaks London New Delhi

For information address:

SAGE Publications, Inc.
2455 Teller Road
Thousand Oaks, California 91320
E-mail: order@sagepub.com

SAGE Publications Ltd.
6 Bonhill Street
London EC2A 4PU
United Kingdom

SAGE Publications India Pvt. Ltd.
M-32 Market
Greater Kailash I
New Delhi 110 048 India

Printed in the United States of America

Library of Congress Cataloging-in-Publication Data

Main entry under title:

Marketing and consumer research in the public interest / [edited by] Ronald Paul Hill.
  p.   cm.
  Includes bibliographical references (p.   ).
  ISBN 0-8039-7190-7 (cloth: alk. paper).—ISBN 0-8039-7191-5 (pbk.: alk. paper)
  1. Marketing research—Social aspects. 2. Advertising—Social aspects. 3. Consumer behavior. 4. Public interest. 5. Consumer education. I. Hill, Ronald Paul.
HF5415.2.M3542 1995
658.8′3—dc20   95-36413

This book is printed on acid-free paper.

96 97 98 99 00 10 9 8 7 6 5 4 3 2 1

Sage Production Editor: Astrid Virding
Sage Typesetter: Andrea D. Swanson

Contents

Introduction

There comes a time in a man's life when to get where he has to go—if there are no doors or windows—he walks through a wall.

Bernard Malamud

FEW IN THE field of marketing in general or consumer behavior in particular doubt that the scholars whose chapters are contained in this book follow something close to Malamud's maxim as a guiding philosophy of their professional (and sometimes personal) lives. We were "raised" in a profession dominated by economic (i.e., rational consumer) and cognitive psychological (e.g., information processing) models of behavior that were most often applied to the selling of mundane consumer products rather than to the understanding of complex social issues. The latter types of investigation were rare (see Andreasen, 1975, for an exception) and typically were viewed as the domain of other social scientists such as urban sociologists.

Recently, however, a major change has taken place within the field. Social marketing remains an important component (Andreasen, 1994), but our profession now views topics such as addiction (Hirschman, 1992), compulsive buying (Faber & O'Guinn, 1992), homelessness (Hill, 1991), and idealized images in advertising (Richins, 1991) as acceptable terrain. The purpose of this book is to expand our thinking along these lines and provide some of the leading social and public policy scholars in our field with an opportunity to express their opinions regarding their research areas.

Part I contains two chapters that discuss controversial yet cutting-edge theoretical approaches to investigating the public interest. In the first chapter, "Uniting Critical Theory and Public Policy to Create the Reflexively Defiant Consumer" by Julie Ozanne and Jeff Murray, the authors use Jürgen Habermas's theory of communicative competence to explore traditional notions of consumer education. They present an alternative vision of critical consumers who must become *reflexively defiant* by questioning the economic, political, and social structures that attempt to bind and control their consumption behaviors. The second chapter, by Julia Bristor and Eileen Fischer, titled "Exploring Simultaneous Oppressions: Toward the Development of Consumer Research in the Interest of Diverse Women," argues that to develop public policies that will work in the interests of diverse female consumers, it is imperative to recognize how sexism intersects with racism, classism, and heterosexism.

Part II examines the troublesome consumption issues of addiction, grief and the marketplace interface, and consumer behavior and the poor. The chapter by Elizabeth Hirschman, "Professional, Personal, and Popular Culture Perspectives on Addiction," weaves together *professional* theorization regarding addiction, *popular culture* narratives representative of current cultural understandings of addiction, and *personal* perspectives of the author regarding the phenomenon of addiction. "Social Support for Decision Making During Grief Due to Death" by Jim Gentry and Cathy Goodwin summarizes, synthesizes, and extends Gentry's work on how grieving consumers cope with the vagaries of the marketplace. Finally, Linda Alwitt, in "Marketing and the Poor," provides five remedies designed to correct the imbalance that exists between marketers and poor consumers by strengthening the ethical foundation of the exchange relationship.

Part III contains media issues. The authors examine target marketing, social comparison, and portrayals of minority groups. Debra Ringold summarizes and extends her work on the marketing of controversial products in her chapter titled "Social Criticisms of Target Marketing: Process or Product?" In this chapter, she discusses the widely accepted practice of target marketing as it applies to vulnerable populations and to products such as alcohol and tobacco.

In "Materialism, Desire, and Discontent: Contributions of Idealized Advertising Images and Social Comparison," Marsha Richins explores the impact that idealized images in advertising have on consumers' perceptions of their lives, particularly with respect to their material possessions. The final chapter in this section, "Portrayals of African, Hispanic, and Asian Americans in Magazine Advertising" by Ray Taylor, Ju Lee, and Barbara Stern, presents the results of a content analysis of advertising portrayals of Americans who are members of minority groups.

Part IV explores legislative and social marketing issues. In the first chapter, titled "Alcohol Warning Label Effects: Socialization, Addiction, and Public Policy Issues," Craig Andrews and Rick Netemeyer broaden the discussion of the effectiveness of warning labels by drawing on several bodies of research including cigarette warning research, fear appeal literature, the alcohol socialization process, and studies of addictive behavior. Jeff Stoltman and Fred Morgan, in "Expanding the Perspective on Consumer Product Safety," promote a reevaluation of the adequacy of information-based solutions to product safety problems and introduce a new perspective to the issue of consumer safety. In the final chapter, L. J. Shrum, Tina Lowrey, and John McCarty present their work titled "Using Marketing and Advertising Principles to Encourage Pro-Environmental Behaviors." In their presentation, the researchers provide an overview of past research and suggestions of how research on green buying can be applied to encourage green buying practices.

Although this book covers a lot of ground, it does not include all of the issues that are currently being investigated by scholars in the marketing and consumer behavior fields. Nonetheless, these chapters are fairly representative of the areas in which researchers are doing work that is recognized by leading journals and national conferences, and they exemplify the kinds of investigation that will take place in the future.

I would like to take this opportunity to thank the authors for their important contributions. Special thanks go to the members of the review board: Bill Bearden, Marv Goldberg, Morris Holbrook, Brian Ratchford, Peter Reingen, Randy Rose, Debbie Scammon, John Schouten, Debra Stephens, and Craig Thompson.

References

Andreasen, A. R. (1975). *The disadvantaged consumer*. New York: Free Press.

Andreasen, A. R. (1994). Social marketing: Its definition and domain. *Journal of Public Policy & Marketing, 13,* 108-114.

Faber, R. J., & O'Guinn, T. C. (1992). A clinical screener for compulsive buying. *Journal of Consumer Research, 19,* 459-469.

Hill, R. P. (1991). Homeless women, special possessions, and the meaning of "home": An ethnographic case study. *Journal of Consumer Research, 18,* 298-310.

Hirschman, E. C. (1992). The consciousness of addiction: Toward a general theory of compulsive consumption. *Journal of Consumer Research, 19,* 155-179.

Richins, M. L. (1991). Social comparison and the idealized images of advertising. *Journal of Consumer Research, 18,* 71-83.

PART I

THE FIELDS of marketing and consumer behavior have a tradition of "borrowing" theoretical constructs and paradigms from various social sciences, especially economics, psychology, and sociology. Although this tactic has resulted in major advances in our thinking, it has inadvertently caused the subsequent utilization of positivist approaches that often were employed in previous studies of these constructs outside of our domain. A small group of scholars emerged in the mid-1980s, however, to challenge this dominant paradigm, and what are now referred to as "post-positivist" methods have an accepted place in the discipline.

The two chapters contained in Part I take this developing perspective one step further by *advocating* critical approaches that examine the way previous research and practice has created a marketing system that oppresses certain groups within society. Researchers are urged to question the fundamental bases for these oppressions. Further, we are charged to change the way we view and treat those we study, eliminating the "shackles" associated with the role of "subject" and researcher "objectivity." Instead, our informants become co-creators of new knowledge, with the ultimate goal of our research being to change the system to empower them.

Additional Readings

Bristor, J. M., & Fischer, E. (1993). Feminist thought: Implications for consumer research. *Journal of Consumer Research, 19,* 518-537.

Hirschman, E. C. (1989). *Interpretive consumer research.* Provo, UT: Association for Consumer Research.

Murray, J. B., & Ozanne, J. L. (1991). The critical imagination: Emancipatory interests in consumer research. *Journal of Consumer Research, 18,* 129-144.

1

Uniting Critical Theory and Public Policy to Create the Reflexively Defiant Consumer

JULIE L. OZANNE
JEFF B. MURRAY

IN A POSTMODERN society, people maneuver through an information-rich environment in which their relationships with other people are increasingly being mediated by forces such as television, VCRs, computers, and information highways. This *hyperreality* creates new cultural spaces that shape our understanding of ourselves and our environment, and may require different adaptive skills (Kincheloe & McLaren, 1994). The marketplace is one example of the changing cultural spaces that we face. The explosion of information technology means that late 20th-century consumers can shop from their televisions, scan their bank checking cards at grocery stores, and order merchandise at home using their computers. As consumers make choices in this mediascape, information technology facilitates the tracking, recording, and storing of information about their behavior at unprecedented levels. What are the implications of this new marketplace—and

AUTHORS' NOTE: The authors would like to thank Ron P. Hill for having a dream.

how should consumers respond in the face of these new cultural forms? A more insurgent consumer may be needed in order to challenge and contest the role of the postmodern marketplace in defining and fulfilling consumer needs.

The purpose of this chapter is to suggest a point of convergence between critical theory and public policy. This convergence suggests a different type of consumer, one that is empowered to reflect on his or her social conditions in order to decide how to live. This decision may result in informed participation in the consumer culture, the reflexive defiance of this lifestyle, or a creative combination of these two strategies.

Critical theory is the term that is often used to describe the work of the group of researchers who coalesced around the Frankfurt Institute beginning in the early 1920s (Held, 1980). The early theorists—who included Max Horkheimer, Theodor Adorno, Leo Lowenthal, Herbert Marcuse, and Friedrich Pollack—wanted to use interdisciplinary approaches to study the link between the individual and society. Contemporary social theorists have extended and revitalized the ideas of the Frankfurt School. These extensions make critical theory relevant to a postmodern marketplace that is characterized by an explosion of information and increasingly abstract symbolism. For example, Habermas expresses the emancipatory interest in terms of a theory of communication. And Baudrillard takes the Frankfurt School's theory of one-dimensional society to a higher level by utilizing the semiological theory of the sign to describe the world of commodities (Kellner, 1989). These theorists seek to critique society systematically in order to help people envision new forms of social organization (Adorno, 1973; Baudrillard, 1981; Habermas, 1971; Horkheimer, 1972; Jay, 1973). Thus, both critical theorists and public policy analysts share the common goal of trying to improve the quality of people's lives that are shaped by social structures such as laws and public policy (Forester, 1985a; Murray & Ozanne, 1991).

Although critical theory and public policy both emphasize theory-directed social change in the public interest, their research traditions have stressed different parts of this theory-practice equation. Public policy research generally emphasizes the practice side of this equation (e.g., studying the impact of deregulation on marketing and consumer welfare, changing perspectives at the FTC and FDA, consumption of alcohol and cigarettes, advertising practices, consumer education, etc.). Critical theorists, on the other hand, emphasize the theory side of this equation. These researchers live in an abstract world of ideas such as materialism (as a proposed solution to Cartesian interactive dualism), immanent critique (as a proposed solution to problems associated with foundationalism), functional ethical relativism, dialectics, ideal speech situations, and so forth (Murray & Ozanne, 1991). Because the two traditions are emphasizing different elements of the same theory-practice equation, or what the critical theorists would refer to as *praxis,* they each have something to offer the other. For example, critical theory's long-standing commitment to creating forms of social organization that make possible freedom, justice, and reason could usefully guide public policy making. Similarly, the policy analysts' focus on concrete policies could help with critical theory's ongoing struggle to translate theory into meaningful action (Forester, 1985b).

The work of the Frankfurt Institute, together with contemporary critical and postmodern theorists, spans many decades and covers a wide range of topics and therefore cannot be presented as a single, unified approach. Critical theory was meant to be an unfinished, ongoing, and open-ended project so it could be adapted to explore social contexts not yet realized (Jay, 1973; Murray & Ozanne, 1991, 1994). In addition, the problems critical theory selects to analyze are so penetrating and integral to the social system that solutions *do not* come easily and may never be found. Yet critical theory explores many issues that are of potential interest to public policy making. For example, critical methodology highlights the connections between an individual's interpretation of policies and social structures, or what Morrow (1994) refers to as *interpretive structuralism.* This method may contribute to different aspects of public policy research. Similarly, critical theory's systematic and historical analysis of various forms of domination could help inform and broaden public policy research aimed at protecting consumer rights and broader social interests.

Here, rather than attempt to cover the broad scope of critical theory, we have chosen to focus on Jürgen Habermas's recent attempts to revitalize critical social research (Habermas, 1971, 1975, 1989). Specifically, Habermas's theory of communicative competence has much to contribute to the area of consumer education. We also draw on Jean Baudrillard's (1981) extension of Marx in *For a Critique of the Political Economy of the Sign*. First, we review traditional ideas about the need for education to create critical consumers. Next, Habermas's theory of communicative competence is briefly introduced. Finally, the implications of both Habermas and Baudrillard are considered for informing our ideas on what it means to be a *reflexively defiant* consumer.

The Traditional Notion of the Informed Consumer

Different scholars have noted various rights of buyers and sellers during marketplace exchanges. For example, although sellers have the right to bring products to the market, and the right to price, promote, and distribute these products, buyers have the right to refuse to buy products, to expect products to be safe, and to expect products to perform as claimed (e.g., President Kennedy's 1962 statement of consumers' rights).

Across different marketplaces and times, we have had various ideas about what skills and understandings are needed to be a critical consumer in marketplace exchange. For example, during the most recent wave of consumerism beginning in the 1960s, consumer groups and the government saw an imbalance in this buyer-seller exchange and attempted to improve the rights of consumers. Bloom and Greyser (1981) suggest that this wave of consumerism sought to "help people get satisfaction in the marketplace" (p. 131) because products were increasingly complex, services (which are intangible) were growing, and new forms of retailing (such as self-service) were growing. Seeking to protect consumers through legislation, their successes included the Truth in Packaging, the Truth in Lending, and the Consumer Product Safety acts.

Although consumers can always refuse to buy products, consumer advocates and public policy makers have argued that unless consumers are educated and informed, they will not choose wisely. Thus, the importance of complete information and of protecting consumers from questionable products and marketing practices have been stressed. For instance, consumers have the right to know the real cost per unit of a brand, the ingredients in a product, accurate nutritional information, and truthful claims in advertising. Consumers are provided more information and improved skills through a range of strategies: legislation, consumer education, information services, redress assistance, and consumer representation. To summarize, the traditional view from a public policy perspective has been that if consumers are informed and educated, then they can make rational choices (Bloom & Greyser, 1981).

The focus by many consumer researchers on problems of processing information fits clearly within this view of the well-informed consumer. Not only must we be concerned about whether or not consumers get enough information, but can they get this information in the form and amount that they can process? (e.g., the information overload debate is an exemplar of this concern [Jacoby, 1984; Jacoby, Speller, & Kohn, 1974; Malhotra, 1984; Summers, 1974; Wilkie, 1974]).

Habermas's Theory of Communicative Competence

Habermas is also concerned with understanding various forms of distorted communications that exist throughout contemporary society. Distorted communication occurs in a variety of ways; for example, blind adherence to tradition, presenting ethical or marketing problems as scientific ones, using authority or experts as guides, or accepting knowledge claims at face value. All these instances involve the potential for people to act in ways that maintain or endorse a social system that may not be in their own self-interest. If people blindly follow authority—for instance, within their organization—they may unknowingly reproduce a dominant-submissive relationship that legitimizes and reinforces their subordination. The communication that is involved in this reproduction is therefore *distorted* from the point of view of the repressed.

To develop his theory of distorted communication, Habermas first identifies the core expectations that must exist for reciprocal, everyday communication to take place. By identifying these expectations, Habermas develops a benchmark against which all forms of distorted communication can be compared. Habermas reasons that as we enter into dialogue with others, we anticipate that (a) others will speak so we can understand them (i.e., the norm of comprehensibility), (b) they will communicate their true intentions (i.e., the norm of sincerity), (c) they will communicate based on a shared normative context (i.e., the norm of legitimacy), and (d) they will speak the truth (i.e., the norm of truthfulness). These shared expectations are Habermas's universal norms of pragmatics; they are the competence that we must share if we are to communicate successfully without distortion (Forester, 1985a; Grahame, 1985). Further, Habermas states that a rational consensus can be reached only if there is a "symmetrical distribution of chances to select and employ speech acts" (Habermas, quoted in McCarthy, 1978, p. 306). *General symmetry* refers to a situation in which all people have an equal opportunity to engage in discourse unconstrained by authority, tradition, or dogma. This condition of symmetrical free speech is Habermas's ideal speech situation.

Habermas's identification of an ideal speech situation provides the grounds for the critique of distorted communication. Distorted communication reproduces those belief systems that "could not be validated if subjected to rational discourse" (Schroyer, 1973, p. 163). Because of unacknowledged social forces in the self-formation process, humans may not be cognizant of distorted communication. Through critique and dialogue, unquestioned assumptions and claims can be challenged in order to reconstruct a communicative competence that, in turn, leads to a rational consensus. Thus, the ideal speech situation anticipates an ideal social structure that makes possible freedom, justice, and reason (Murray & Ozanne, 1991).

Habermas's theory provides the basis for a broad critique of society. Many failures to communicate are used to legitimize existing structures in society. Those people who benefit from the existing structures and forces of production may use communication to legitimate their power so it has a taken-for-granted status. They may attempt to narrow the domain of communication to exclude the interests of others. They may raise scientific and technical evidence as having the legitimacy to solve moral problems. And they may narrow political participation to exclude those issues that threaten existing patterns of power. Thus, Habermas's analysis of communication at the interpersonal level becomes the basis for analysis of social and political structures (Forester, 1985a).

The Critical Consumer

How can Habermas's theory of communicative competence be used to inform our notions about being a critical consumer? Habermas's ideal speech situation is clearly an unrealizable goal; nevertheless, its power lies as an axiology that can guide actions toward a particular vision (Murray & Ozanne, 1991). It might therefore be useful to identify where in the marketplace an exchange exists that most closely approaches this ideal. Although public policy has given the consumer more power, the buyer-seller exchange does not exhibit general symmetry because sellers have the upper hand: Sellers control the information that is exchanged, have resources to test their claims empirically, and have access to mass media to promote their products.

Perhaps the growing number of publications like *Consumer Reports* more closely approximates the goal of ideal speech. Here, we have a third party that is fairly independent of the buyer-seller exchange (norm of sincerity). This organization has the resources to substantiate product claims empirically and then report them to the public in a fairly inexpensive form (greater general symmetry). Potential goods and services are compared in matrices in which relevant attributes across different brands are compared (norm of truthfulness) under a variety of conditions (norm of legitimacy). Generally, this format does not give preferential treatment to a product and instead allows each consumer to compare and contrast products in the ways that they desire (norm of comprehensibility). Thus, embodied in the structure of the report is the attempt to avoid a single, authoritative reading of the text (Grahame, 1985).

Although *Consumer Reports* approximates Habermas's ideal speech situation, it implicitly assumes that the consumer is going to evaluate alternatives in a consideration set and make a choice. In other words, it assumes participation in a consumer culture. It does not encourage reflection on the origins of this culture and which groups in society benefit from this system. In other words, from a traditional public policy perspective, the informed consumer is critical within the bounds of the existing society.

For example, when consumerists, market researchers, and public policy analysts focus primarily on informing and educating the consumer to improve decision making, in many ways consumer education has become appropriated by the dominant system. Consumer resistance is one more form of opposition that is incorporated by the system. The promise of consumerist movements is that the consumer will become an active, critical consumer. And to the extent that people become better decision makers the promise *appears* to have been delivered. But this form of criticalness serves to recreate the existing system by more firmly entrenching people in their primary role in life as consumers: "consumers are undone by their very preoccupation with consumption" (Grahame, 1985, p. 166). Consumers become motivated not by dreams of justice, truth, or ideal speech, but by stepping up to the next level of neighborhood, house, furniture, automobile, or accessory (Murray & Ozanne, 1994; Waters, 1994). The structure and function of the marketplace may be refined and improved, but its role in satisfying consumers' needs is given and fixed—at no time is the role of the marketplace questioned.

The Reflexively Defiant Consumer

Let us return to the format of *Consumer Reports* and dig deeper into the underlying assumptions implicit in such a document. The *Report* assumes the existence of an underlying need that can be fulfilled by acquiring the product, that the choice problem involves a rational weighing of attributes, that performance criteria can be made empirical, and that these criteria can be objectively rated.

For example, if consumers were to evaluate a wood-cleaning product along the lines suggested by *Consumer Reports,* they would read about the ratings of various product attributes, then—using a compensatory process—make a decision as to the most effective brand for cleaning wood. Motivating and underlying this process is the sign value (symbolism created by the ensemble of objects) of particular interior designs that communicate taste, image, history, prestige, and social status. Choosing objects on the basis of sign value comes not from a rational compensatory or noncompensatory decision-making process but from enculturation (i.e., the consumer internalizes the "consumption code" through the process of socialization). Although the consumer may not be consciously aware of the consumption code, continual interpretation of the sign value of literally hundreds of products each day is necessary in order to construct a place within the social system—to "fit" in. From this perspective, acquisition and consumption can be considered *productive activity*, requiring socialization, education, and effort. This productive activity is necessary for social integration and, therefore, for the development of self and identity.

This point of view suggests that consumption does not merely arise in response to fundamental human needs or use values (utility); it is *social activity* that integrates consumers into a specific social system and commits them to a particular social vision. In other words, consumption does not stem from the realm of nature (i.e., the primordial satisfaction of needs) but from the realm of culture. Consumption is a *cultural code* that expresses the logic of differentiation and creates a social structure (Baudrillard, 1981; Bourdieu, 1984; Jameson, 1991; Kellner, 1989). According to Baudrillard (1981), as individuals consume the code, they reproduce the system: "Through objects a stratified society speaks and, if like the mass media, objects seem to speak to everyone, it is in order to keep everyone in a certain place" (p. 38). Thus, as individuals are socialized by the institutions of late capitalism, they find themselves challenged by a system of needs where satisfaction reproduces their own social domination (Kellner, 1989).

To refuse to reproduce this social domination means that the consumer must rebel against the "code" or seek new consumption styles. Thus, a more radical notion of the informed consumer would involve consumers forming a different relationship to the marketplace in which they identify unquestioned assumptions and challenge the status of existing structures as natural. Through reflection, consumers may choose to defy or resist traditional notions of consumption, become more independent from acquisition and disposition systems, or define their own needs independent from the marketplace. Critical theory's emphasis on abstract theory has encouraged reflection on the social totality as only one of many possibilities. Questioning the hegemonic control of the groups in power is a different form of being critical that is consistent with Habermas's suggestion to explore taken-for-granted assumptions in order to reconstruct communicative competence (Murray & Ozanne, 1991, 1994).

If *reflexively defiant* consumers consciously choose to dissociate themselves from consumption patterns, this estrangement is not alienating because it is a reflexive act. In fact, Baudrillard (1981) would argue that nonreflexive, unconscious consumption is alienating because the objects (things) dominate the subjects (people). Conscious estrangement from "normal" consumption empowers consumers by removing their dependence on the code and the asymmetry between buyers and sellers. By removing dependence and asymmetry, consumers have the opportunity to better approximate Habermas's ideal speech situation. At this point, individuals are no longer defined externally by society as consumers but instead define themselves. As a condition of ideal speech, people must reclaim their own voices and become the architects of their own history. The understanding and expression of "need" would then come from individual citizens rather than from the marketplace.

The reflexively defiant consumer may still acquire products but alter their sign value in the usage situation to signify antagonism and opposition. For example, the defiant consumer may still purchase computers but use networks to better integrate and organize oppositional groups. Or, clothes and various forms of body adornment may be used to signify opposition to establishment values. Because products mark distinction and therefore signify identity and standing, oppositional consumption develops the critical imagination (see Hebdige, 1979; Willis, 1978).

> Capital . . . can commodify music and use it to sell records and concerts, whereas individuals may use it to circulate subversive messages, thereby giving rise to new values and visions of life which may be antithetical to existing capitalist societies. (Kellner, 1989, p. 37)

Because oppositional signs can be quickly appropriated by capital and marketing management, reflexively defiant consumption takes place in subcultures acting as insurgent movements. As soon as the symbol is marketed, it loses its critical force and the subculture must change the signifier. Other forms of defiance may seek and discover alternatives to acquisition (e.g., borrowing, recycling, self-production, customizing, and various forms of self-sufficiency).

It is the full development of consumer culture beginning in the late 1940s that makes the concept of a reflexively defiant consumer relevant and meaningful. Just as rural populations were indoctrinated into industrial labor throughout the 19th century, 20th-century consumers are indoctrinated into systematic and organized consumption (Baudrillard, 1988; Kellner, 1989). "The same process of rationalization of productive forces which took place in the nineteenth century in the production sector, is accompanied, in the twentieth century, in the consumption sector" (Baudrillard, 1988, p. 50). From this perspective, production and consumption are part of the same logical process. After shaping the masses into a labor force, the industrial system was not complete until the masses were also shaped into a consumption force.

Given that current consumers are generally unaware and unorganized, and given the ease with which capital can seize oppositional symbols, few critical or postmodern theorists view the active manipulation of signs as a theory of agency (Baudrillard, 1981; Kellner, 1989). Yet various forms of mass refusal do have potential for social change. Just as public policy aided labor to become aware (i.e., class conscious) and organized, this process may also aid consumers in their attempts to become *code conscious.* Only an organized movement of reflexively defiant consumers has the potential to act as agent; public policy can encourage this organization. It is in this way that critical theory and public policy can stand together—a quid pro quo.

Conclusion

During the late middle ages, as the newly emerging merchant class started to challenge the social fabric of feudalism, it began to emulate the consumption habits of the landed class. According to Ewen (1988), "Although the merchants' fortunes were a product of commercial enterprise, their consumption patterns were designed to obtain the imagistic trappings of landed heritage" (p. 27). This consumption eventually led to *sumptuary laws* designed to preserve class distinctions with sign value (e.g., it was against the law for the new merchant class to wear velvet). Thus, during the first stage of capitalism, public policy was used to preserve the traditional feudal estate. But later, as the monarchy lost power, public policy aided the merchant class in its attempts to revolutionize the social system.

During industrialization, or the second stage of capitalism, a large rural population became indoctrinated into industrial labor. Here both conservative and critical analyses focused on production (i.e., labor). Again, public policy served both to preserve class distinctions and to help labor become aware and organized in its attempts to revolutionize society.

World War I, the Depression, and World War II kept full-fledged consumer capitalism at bay. In the late 1940s and the 1950s, however, capitalism engulfed American culture in full force. Here both optimistic interpretations of postmodernism and critiques focus on consumption and consumer culture. More than anything else, it is the transition from an analysis of production (with labor as the agent) to consumption (with the consumer as the agent) that marks the postmodern movement (Kellner, 1989). If critical theory and public policy have a future together, they must work hand in hand to embrace the idealism of a true democracy and empower the consumer to become reflexively defiant.

References

Adorno, T. W. (1973). *Negative dialectics*. New York: Continuum.

Baudrillard, J. (1981). *For a critique of the political economy of the sign*. St. Louis, MO: Telos.

Baudrillard, J. (1988). Consumer society. In *Jean Baudrillard selected writings* (pp. 29-56). Stanford, CA: Stanford University Press.

Bloom, P. N., & Greyser, S. A. (1981, November-December). The maturing of consumerism. *Harvard Business Review*, pp. 130-139.

Bourdieu, P. (1984). *Distinction: A social critique of the judgement of taste*. Cambridge, MA: Harvard University Press.

Ewen, S. (1988). *All consuming images*. New York: Basic Books.

Forester, J. (1985a). Critical theory and planning practice. In J. Forester (Ed.), *Critical theory and public life* (pp. 202-227). Cambridge: MIT Press.

Forester, J. (1985b). The policy analysis. In J. Forester (Ed.), *Critical theory and public life* (pp. 258-280). Cambridge: MIT Press.

Grahame, P. (1985). Criticalness, pragmatics, and everyday life: Consumer literacy as critical practice. In J. Forester (Ed.), *Critical theory and public life* (pp. 147-174). Cambridge: MIT Press.

Habermas, J. (1971). *Knowledge and human interests*. Boston: Beacon.

Habermas, J. (1975). *Legitimation crisis*. Boston: Beacon.

Habermas, J. (1989). *The structural transformation of the public sphere*. Cambridge: MIT Press.

Hebdige, D. (1979). *Subculture: The meaning of style*. London: Routledge & Kegan Paul.

Held, D. (1980). *Introduction to critical theory*. Berkeley and Los Angeles: University of California Press.

Horkheimer, M. (1972). *Critical theory*. New York: Seabury.

Jacoby, J. (1984). Perspective on information overload. *Journal of Consumer Research,* *10*(March), 432-435.

Jacoby, J., Speller, D. E., & Kohn, C. A. (1974, February). Brand choice behavior as a function of information load. *Journal of Marketing Research, 11,* 63-69.

Jameson, F. (1991). *Postmodernism: Or, the cultural logic of late capitalism.* Durham, NC: Duke University Press.

Jay, M. (1973). *The dialectical imagination.* Boston: Little, Brown.

Kellner, D. (1989). *Jean Baudrillard: From Marxism to postmodernism and beyond.* Stanford, CA: Stanford University Press.

Kincheloe, J. L., & McLaren, P. L. (1994). Rethinking critical theory and qualitative research. In N. K. Denzin & Y. S. Lincoln (Eds.), *Handbook of qualitative research* (pp. 138-157). Thousand Oaks, CA: Sage.

Malhotra, N. K. (1984). Reflections on the information overload paradigm in consumer decision making. *Journal of Consumer Research, 10*(March), 436-440.

McCarthy, T. A. (1978). *The critical theory of Jürgen Habermas.* Cambridge: MIT Press.

Morrow, R. A. (1994). *Critical theory and methodology.* Thousand Oaks, CA: Sage.

Murray, J. B., & Ozanne, J. L. (1991). The critical imagination: Emancipatory interests in consumer research. *Journal of Consumer Research, 18*(September), 129-144.

Murray, J. B., & Ozanne, J. L. (1994). Revitalizing the critical imagination: Unleashing the crouched tiger. *Journal of Consumer Research, 21*(December), 559-565.

Schroyer, T. (1973). *The critique of domination.* New York: Braziller.

Summers, J. O. (1974). Less information is better? *Journal of Marketing Research, 11*(November), 467-468.

Waters, M. (1994). *Modern sociological theory.* Thousand Oaks, CA: Sage.

Wilkie, W. (1974). Analysis of effects of information load. *Journal of Marketing Research, 11*(November), 462-466.

Willis, P. E. (1978). *Profane culture.* London: Routledge & Kegan Paul.

2

Exploring Simultaneous Oppressions

Toward the Development of Consumer Research
in the Interest of Diverse Women

JULIA BRISTOR
EILEEN FISCHER

THE MAJORITY of consumer research to date has been more concerned with enhancing the ability of private sector corporations to make a profit than with advancing the interests of consumers in general or female consumers in particular. Even when topics that could produce findings that would benefit certain female consumers have been studied by consumer researchers, a common tendency has been to focus on "women as women." Although exceptions can be found (e.g., Hill, 1991, who focuses on the particular experiences of homeless women of a variety of races), our own earlier work (Bristor & Fischer, 1993; Fischer & Bristor, 1994) typifies an approach whereby the differences among women are swept aside blithely or ignored altogether.

Although we might expect market-oriented research to focus on privileged segments, it is important for policy-oriented research to recognize multiple segments. In this chapter, we highlight the shortcomings of discussions (our own included) that assume that underneath or beyond the differences among women, there is a shared set of concerns and experiences. We argue that if our work is to inform public policy on consumption-related issues, we must think systematically about the way that sex-based discrimination intersects with (for instance) discrimination based on race, ethnicity, social class, and sexual orientation.

Why Can We Not Speak of "Women's" Experiences as Consumers?

Many feminist theories (e.g., liberal feminism, social feminism) assume commonality of women's characteristics, experiences, or both. Although the assumption that women as a group share a very important part of their identify seems central to the political goals of any movement to better the lot of women, a refusal to take seriously the differences among women "lies at the heart of feminism's politics of domination" (Spelman, 1988, p. 12). This domination means that many women have found little enlightenment about the conditions of their own lives, much less substantive improvements in those conditions, as a result of mainstream feminist thought (Collins, 1991; Glenn, 1991; hooks, 1981; Ortiz, 1994; Zinn & Dill, 1994). Consider the much-used example of Betty Friedan's argument that the solution to women's problems would be for them to get out of the house (Friedan, 1963). Her suggested corrective simply ignored the fact that millions of women have always worked outside their own houses, often as domestic labor for the very women whose concerns Friedan was addressing.

Unwitting neglect of the ways gender intersects with race, class, and sexual orientation in the lives of women has been typical of much feminist thought. This neglect can be traced to an unchallenged assumption that it is possible to consider issues of gender or sex in isolation from issues related to race, class, ethnicity, or sexual orientation. Spelman (1988) has referred to the phrase *as a woman* as the "Trojan horse" of feminist ethnocentrism. It ushers in a presupposition that it is possible to speak about a female's "womanness" in isolation from the other factors that shape her experience. It suggests, misleadingly, that there is a transcendent commonality between the life of a married Asian, middle-class, heterosexual woman living in a metropolitan suburb, the life of a poor, white, lesbian woman living in a rural environment, and the life of a black single mother living in an inner-city ghetto who relies on welfare.

Some feminists have explicitly argued that if we want to understand sexism as distinct from, for instance, classism or racism, we must try to focus only on the oppression visited on women because they are women and we must systematically exclude from focus any oppression stemming from other factors. Richards (1980), for example, states:

> If, for instance, there are men and women in slavery, it is not the business of feminism to start freeing the women. Feminism is not concerned with a group of people it wants to benefit but with a type of injustice it wants to eliminate. (p. 5)

This assertion suggests an assumption (widely observed in practice) that paradigmatic examples of sexism will be found in the lives of those whose oppression is rooted in their womanness and in nothing else. This means that the "norm" or the model for analysis is the experience of the woman who is privileged on all other counts except for her sex. Accepting white middle-class women as the norm preserves their privilege. To ignore race, class, and sexual orientation is to ignore the

> unacknowledged benefits for those who are at the top of these hierarchies—Whites, members of the upper classes, and males. The privileges of those at the top of the hierarchy are dependent on the exploitation of those at the bottom. (Zinn & Dill, 1994, p. 5)

For example, Rollins (1985) has pointed out that privileged women are able to escape some consequences of patriarchy by using the labor of other, less privileged women.

Even feminists who have attempted to "add on" considerations of race, class, and sexual orientation have often unwittingly preserved the status quo. This is because the "reality" to which considerations are "added on" is the experience of white, middle-class, heterosexual women. Yet to "add on" analyses of the race, class, and sexual orientation of women of color, poor women, or lesbians is to ignore the race, class, and sexual orientation of the white, middle-class heterosexual (Harding, 1991; Palmer, 1983). It is to act as though this latter

group's experiences were not a product of their privilege and as
though racism and classism were merely something experienced by
some women rather than something contributed to by other women.
So long as race, class, and sexual orientation are seen to exist in
isolation from gender and can be treated as "special interests," any
proposal to include "different" viewpoints will effectively marginalize
these viewpoints.

An Illustration

The foregoing discussion indicates that we, as consumer researchers,
should be wary of any generalizations concerning women as consumers. In particular, research that is insensitive to these matters will have
limited relevance for public policy purposes. As a means of illustrating
the deep-seated problems we are addressing, we will examine a concept
central to a number of consumer research streams, the household.

THE NONNEUTRALITY OF NOTIONS OF THE HOUSEHOLD

Much of the consumer and marketing research on topics such as
household decision making, durables purchasing, gender roles, the
family life cycle, and the socialization of children as consumers, and
much of the managerial research that assumes the wife is the principal
household purchasing agent often directly or indirectly involves certain assumptions about the household. Sometimes, such research
even aims at improving the lot of the female members of households.
As we shall see, however, the interests of only a limited few are
addressed by research that does not challenge its assumption of what
constitutes a household.

The construct of the household may seem a neutral one. In virtually
all societies, people live in small domestic groups that are amenable
to the label "household." Problems arise, however, when this term is
assumed to be a synonym for the term *family*. A household is a "group
of co-residents, people who live under the same roof and typically
share in common consumption" (Kertzer, 1991, p. 156); these co-
residents may or may not be the kinship relations that define a family.
The problems are compounded when, as is common in consumer

research and elsewhere, the family assumed to constitute a household is a nuclear family composed solely of a married man and woman plus their offspring (DeVault, 1991). Further questionable assumptions are embedded in the common notion that in the typical household composed of such a nuclear family, the husband works outside the home to earn a wage to support his family, whereas his wife stays in the home and is responsible for household management and child care (Collins, 1991). Nevertheless, the image of households as consisting of a wife, children, and a husband who works outside the home is so ubiquitous as to merit the designation "the received view" of the household.

This received view is highly misleading and is under attack from several quarters: Households composed solely of intact nuclear families constitute less than one half of all U.S. households (Roberts & Wortzel, 1984; Schaninger & Danko, 1993). The distortions in the received view are not merely random historical inaccuracies but are rooted in contemporary white, middle-class, heterosexual, and patriarchal ideologies (Collins, 1991; DeVault, 1991). In spite of these inaccuracies, the traditional family norm remains very much intact and serves as the yardstick against which all are measured (Collins, 1991; DeVault, 1991). Thus, alternative family forms—for example, single-parent families, homosexual families, extended economically interdependent families—are still both largely viewed as deviant and ignored by family researchers (DeVault, 1991).

Consider first the assumption that households are inhabited by families with kinship ties. For homosexual couples who choose to cohabit, marriage is prohibited and thus no kinship tie can exist between the principal adult residents of the household. This point is far from a theoretical issue. In Canada, homosexual couples are currently lobbying intensively for the same benefits (e.g., with respect to taxation) enjoyed by heterosexual couples, but they are facing stiff opposition. In the United States, voters in Austin, Texas, overturned an ordinance that granted health insurance to unmarried "domestic partners" of city employees (Farney, 1994). To require heterosexual relationships for family status falsely assumes that gay people do not form lasting relationships, have children, or maintain their blood and adoptive relationships after their orientation is known. Other households lack kinship ties as well. For instance, children may be raised by other adults because their parents are unwilling and/or unable to care for them. Morganthau (1989) has described Miss Nee, a poor black woman who first raised her younger brothers and sisters, then raised five children of her own, and is now raising three kids who are unrelated to her by blood or marriage. In addition, other children frequently stay with her temporarily.

Consider next the assumption that households will be composed of nuclear families—a man, a woman, and their children. This assumption has been shown to be historically inaccurate for many of the European forebears of contemporary North Americans (Hajnal, 1965, 1982). Although it may accurately characterize the patterns in a portion of middle- and upper-class, white, heterosexual, 20th-century households, it certainly does not reflect the experience of many minority households. Historically, enslaved African American families had great difficulty maintaining private family households in a society controlled by white slave-owners. Instead, they developed notions of extended families consisting of their "Black 'brothers' and 'sisters' " (Gutman, 1976, cited by Collins, 1991, p. 49). Thus, "the line separating the Black community from whites served as a more accurate boundary delineating public and private spheres for African-Americans than that separating Black households from the surrounding Black community" (Collins, 1991, p. 49).

Also consider the assumption that within households, women do the "private" (in home) tasks of child care and household maintenance, whereas men participate in the "public" world of work. This assumption has ceased to characterize many white, middle-class households. More important, it has never represented the reality for many poor and/or minority households. In poor families, women have not been limited to the private sphere because they have always needed to earn wages, not for a little something extra but out of economic necessity (Palmer, 1983). For example, poor women of color have always been forced to work, and married black women have especially high labor participation rates because many black men lack sufficient employment opportunities to earn a family wage (Collins, 1991; Davis, 1981; Zinn, 1994). Therefore, whereas many white women have had the "privilege" of remaining in the private sphere and devoting themselves to nurturing and other domestic tasks, poor women, and thus many women of color, have had no choice but to participate in the public sphere. Because many poor women, often from minority racial groups, have never been singularly focused on their homes, neither the perceptions of motherhood and child care as a primary "occupation" nor the valorization of the "cult of motherhood" ever took hold (Collins, 1991; Glenn, 1991).

Consider, finally, the assumption that nuclear family households are economically independent. Poor people often cannot achieve long-term nuclear-family self-sufficiency because of economic insecurity, scarce resources, and economic assault (Glenn, 1991). One result of this is that poor families require various forms of public assistance. Coupled with the fact that many poor women who must work outside their homes earn minimal wages, another result is that they are unable to pay for their own child care. Therefore, poor families frequently develop networks consisting of a broad range of kin and community relations to share the burdens of child care (Glenn, 1991). African American women have a tradition of using communal child care arrangements whereby a few women care for all children and women as a group are accountable for each other's children, giving rise to family terminology such as "othermothers" (Collins, 1991).

Although there is clearly a gap between our ideas about households and the reality faced by many consumers, not all of the limitations of the notion have been subjected to equal challenge. It is disturbing—but not surprising—to note that the deficiencies that have attracted most attention are those relevant to middle-class, white, heterosexual women. As the incidence of divorce, single parenting, and cohabitation without marriage has risen among white, middle-class heterosexuals, consumer researchers have drawn attention to the insupportability of the assumption that households normally include a married adult man and woman. As middle-class, white women have entered the workforce in growing numbers, we have challenged the use of the terms *working* and *nonworking* wives to describe women who are and are not employed outside the home, respectively (Bristor & Fischer, 1993). At the same time, we and others have challenged the assumption that housework and child care are naturally a woman's responsibility, even when she is employed outside the home (e.g., Bristor & Fischer, 1993; Hochschild, 1989).

Tacitly, our critiques have implied that they apply equally to the realities of all women. In fact, they tend to center on the concerns of white, heterosexual, middle-class women to the exclusion of others. For instance, our questioning of the assumption that women will bear primary responsibility for child rearing largely arose from the demographic trend in the latter part of the 20th century in which white, middle-class women began to continue in or reenter the workforce regardless of their childbearing status. For poor women who have always worked outside the home because of economic necessity, this trend is less news than evidence that they are largely invisible in this critique.

The invisibility of other women's experiences is also evidenced by the notion of the double workday, which recognizes that women who are employed actually have two jobs: paid employment and household management. Concerned with exploring ways of alleviating this problem, feminist research has studied the contributions (or lack thereof) of men to household activities (e.g., Chafetz, 1991; Coleman, 1991; Oakley, 1981; Shelton, 1992) and how women who are employed outside the home also cope with their continued household responsibilities by purchasing services such as child care, laundry, housecleaning, and prepared meals (e.g., Hochschild, 1989; Rollins, 1985). Because poor women have always faced a double workday and because it only became a feminist issue when it affected privileged women's experiences, this suggests that the interests of all women are not equally represented in these analyses. For example, much feminist literature is curiously silent about who it is that performs these services that privileged working women are able to purchase. In fact, such reproductive labor has historically been segregated by race and class. Poor minority women have been disproportionately employed as service workers in institutional settings to do "public" reproductive labor because they have been excluded from other jobs and because their male partners have been unable to earn a family wage (Rollins, 1985; Zinn, 1994). Thus, what assists many employed women is the ability to purchase reproductive services from poor women who may not themselves be able to purchase the services they need.

To summarize, assumptions about the household have been shown to lack the neutrality and universality once presumed to exist. Not only are various assumptions blind to gender, but, and more significantly, certain assumptions may be simultaneously blind to gender, race, class, and/or sexual orientation.

IMPLICATIONS FOR CONSUMER RESEARCH

One consequence of employing limiting versions of the household is that other concepts that incorporate the household are also limiting. In marketing and consumer research, in spite of the recognition of the diversity of contemporary households and of the roles and realities of women within them (e.g., see Roberts & Wortzel, 1984), much consumer research knowledge about households has largely come from groups in which women and men have come together in traditional ways. In this section, we illustrate ways in which biased notions of the household affect research in marketing and consumer research.

As one example, one of the authors (Bristor & Qualls, 1984) has critiqued the family life cycle as not being reflective of the variety of U.S. household forms. Although other household forms were introduced (e.g., cohabiting, cooperative) that could incorporate same-sex relationships, heterosexuality was the implied norm. Gilly and Enis's (1981) redefined family life cycle includes same-sex families under the category of married couples. The family life-cycle concept, however, is based on the assumption that families will pass through a number of predictable phases involving childbearing and child rearing. Although sexual orientation does not affect one's ability to have children, many homosexual couples do not have children. Because the family life cycle is an important managerial tool for predicting household consumption (e.g., see Schaninger & Danko, 1993) and because the "gay market" is now recognized as an important market segment (Miller, 1994), the concept may need still further redefinition if it is to incorporate the life cycles of those who do not fit the norm.

As a second example, in a study by Fischer and Arnold (1990), the Christmas shopping behaviors of a random sample of residents of a Northeastern city were posited to be influenced by the sex-role socialization, gender identity, and gender-role attitudes of respondents. Significant positive associations between a person's gender and involvement in Christmas shopping behaviors were taken as evidence that gift shopping is stereotyped as women's work and is part of the "female culture of consumption" that is socially constructed and that heavily influences the work women feel compelled to do. The principal concern was to further an understanding of why women continue to have principal responsibility for one of the labor-intensive categories of consumer work. Although the research was not intended to serve the interests of any group of women more than another and although it makes a passing nod toward the importance of understanding differences among cultures, it selectively distorts the issues faced by women who are too poor to afford gifts, women of religious and ethnic groups for whom Christmas is not a gift-giving occasion, and women who live in same-sex couples. Further, by making generalizations based on the experiences of women who are members of dominant groups, it contributes to the marginalization of those who are members of oppressed minorities.

As a third example, this chapter implies that research on household consumer decision making could be developed in several ways to serve the public interest more fully. Such studies would likely focus not only on different kinds of households but also on different problematics. First, it would be beneficial to conduct research that explicitly attempts to document and explain consumer behaviors in impoverished households in which the decisions to be made may involve trade-offs among subsistence needs rather than among features of major durables; such research could usefully examine how female and male household members interact with the marketing system, and how sex roles constrain or enable various coping strategies. Second, research that explicitly examines the diversity of household forms and the diversity of patterns of decision making within and among types would be useful. Third, further research that, like Webster's (1994), examines the impact of ethnicity, race, or both on decision making would be warranted.

Conclusions and Limitations

This chapter has argued that even the best-intentioned research has not been free from bias, whether the bias is sexism, racism, classism, heterosexism, or some combination of these plus others. It has also argued that as long as these biases remain unchallenged, marketing and consumer research will make limited contributions to the public interest. Sadly, we doubt that it is possible for any individual piece of research to be as comprehensive in the perspectives included as would be ideal from a public policy perspective. Even this chapter has made several generalizations that mask a wide diversity of perspectives. For example, in discussing the double oppression of sexism and racism, we have tended to focus on the case of black women. This selectively ignores the perspectives of Asian, Hispanic, aboriginal, and other minority women. Further, we acknowledge that the term *women of color* encompasses a diverse group of women (Ortiz, 1994). As another example, we are also aware that our discussion selectively ignores other important biases, such as those involving age, religion, and physical ability. Nevertheless, a realistic goal is for researchers to become more aware of, and to articulate, the ways in which the questions asked and the research conducted promote the interests of some and ignore those of others. This would assist our discipline to address the major gaps in our body of knowledge by conducting research that focuses on those perspectives least addressed by current studies.

It is untrue to say that the consumer issues of interest to white, middle-class, heterosexual women have no public policy implications. Yet the very privilege that has led us to focus primarily on the concerns of this empowered group means that many of their concerns that are obviously a matter of public interest (such as overt sexism in advertising) have already been addressed. Until and unless we recognize unwarranted assumptions that sexism can be separated from other biases, such as racism, classism, and heterosexism, even research that notionally addresses women's concerns is actually likely to address the interests of an already privileged few and to reinforce the disenfranchisement of others. The unaddressed concerns of consumers who face simultaneous oppression based on their sex as well their race, class, or sexual orientation are more likely to warrant redress by makers of public policy.

Perhaps our greatest challenge will be not merely to include additional perspectives to the problematics we have already studied within our discipline (such as consumers' reactions to images of beauty in advertising) but to identify issues previously unaddressed by consumer researchers, including major forms of oppression. For instance, one underresearched topic is how single mothers construct the choice between going on welfare versus leaving their children in questionable care-providing situations so that they may work. Although some of our theories of consumer choice may provide a starting point for such research, the topic is likely to provide a unique set of challenges.

One major barrier stems from the fact that researchers, including the present authors, who, although they face some forms of discrimination as women, are members of highly privileged groups, lack the authority to speak for those who are subject to multiple oppressions. Although we may be able to help identify problems, we cannot fully comprehend the solutions that are required. One route to overcoming this barrier is to seek out the input of women who have been marginalized, using a participant observation approach or other interactive qualitative research techniques (e.g., Hill, 1991; Oakley, 1981). Their ideas can be taken into account in shaping the subject matter and the findings of the research. A related idea is to include, whenever possible, a woman who is subject to multiple oppressions as a member of any feminist research team investigating consumer issues.

References

Bristor, J. M., & Fischer, E. (1993). Feminist thought: Implications for consumer research. *Journal of Consumer Research, 19*, 518-537.

Bristor, J. M., & Qualls, W. J. (1984). The household life cycle: Implications for family decisionmaking. In M. L. Roberts & L. H. Wortzel (Eds.), *Marketing to the changing household: Management and research perspectives* (pp. 25-40). Cambridge, MA: Ballinger.

Chafetz, J. S. (1991). The gender division of labor and the reproduction of female disadvantage: Toward an integrated theory. In R. L. Blumberg (Ed.), *Gender, family, and economy: The triple overlap* (pp. 74-94). Newbury Park, CA: Sage.

Coleman, M. T. (1991). The division of household labor: Suggestions for future empirical consideration and theoretical development. In R. L. Blumberg (Ed.), *Gender, family, and economy: The triple overlap* (pp. 245-260). Newbury Park, CA: Sage.

Collins, P. H. (1991). *Black feminist thought: Knowledge, consciousness, and the politics of empowerment.* New York: Routledge & Kegan Paul.

Davis, A. Y. (1981). *Women, race, and class.* New York: Vintage.

DeVault, M. L. (1991). *Feeding the family.* Chicago: University of Chicago Press.

Farney, D. (1994, October 7). Gay rights confront determined resistance from some moderates. *Wall Street Journal,* p. 1.

Fischer, E., & Arnold, S. J. (1990). More than a labor of love: Gender roles and Christmas gift shopping. *Journal of Consumer Research, 17*, 333-345.

Fischer, E., & Bristor, J. M. (1994). A feminist poststructuralist analysis of the rhetoric of marketing relationships. *International Journal of Research in Marketing, 11,* 317-331.

Friedan, B. (1963). *The feminine mystique.* New York: Norton.

Gilly, M., & Enis, B. (1981). Recycling the family life cycle: A proposal for redefinition. In A. Mitchell (Ed.), *Advances in consumer research* (Vol. 9, pp. 271-276). Ann Arbor, MI: Association for Consumer Research.

Glenn, E. N. (1991). Racial ethnic women's labor: The intersection of race, gender, and class oppression. In R. L. Blumberg (Ed.), *Gender, family, and economy: The triple overlap* (pp. 173-201). Newbury Park, CA: Sage.

Gutman, H. (1976). *The black family in slavery and freedom, 1750-1925.* New York: Random House.

Hajnal, J. (1965). European marriage patterns in perspective. In D. Glass & D. Eversley (Eds.), *Population in history* (pp. 101-43). Chicago: Aldine.

Hajnal, J. (1982). Two kinds of preindustrial household formation systems. *Population Development Review, 8,* 449-494.

Harding, S. (1991). *Whose science? Whose knowledge?: Thinking from women's lives.* Ithaca, NY: Cornell University Press.

Hill, R. P. (1991). Homeless women, special possessions, and the meaning of "home": An ethnographic case study. *Journal of Consumer Research, 18,* 298-310.

Hochschild, A. (1989). *The second shift: Working parents and the revolution at home.* New York: Viking.

hooks, b. (1981). *Ain't I a woman: Black women and feminism.* Boston: South End.

Kertzer, D. I. (1991). Household history and sociological theory. *Annual Review of Sociology, 17,* 155-179.

Miller, C. (1994, July 4). Top marketers take bolder approach in targeting gays. *Marketing News,* pp. 1-2.

Morganthau, T. (1989, September 11). Children of the underclass. *Newsweek,* pp. 16-27.

Oakley, A. (1981). Interviewing women: A contradiction in terms. In H. Roberts (Ed.), *Doing feminist research* (pp. 30-61). London: Routledge & Kegan Paul.

Ortiz, V. (1994). Women of color: A demographic overview. In M. B. Zinn & B. T. Dill (Eds.), *Women of color in U.S. society* (pp. 13-40). Philadelphia: Temple University Press.

Palmer, P. M. (1983). White women/black women: The dualism of female identity and experience in the United States. *Feminist Studies, 9,* 151-170.

Richards, J. R. (1980). *The skeptical feminist.* Boston: Routledge & Kegan Paul.

Roberts, M., & Wortzel, L. H. (1984). Introduction. In M. L. Roberts & L. H. Wortzel (Eds.), *Marketing to the changing household: Management and research perspectives* (pp. xv-xxv). Cambridge, MA: Ballinger.

Rollins, J. (1985). *Between women: Domestics and their employers.* Philadelphia: Temple University Press.

Schaninger, C. M., & Danko, W. D. (1993). A conceptual and empirical comparison of alternative household life cycle models. *Journal of Consumer Research, 19,* 580-594.

Shelton, B. A. (1992). *Women, men and time: Gender differences in paid work, housework and leisure.* Westport, CT: Greenwood.

Spelman, E. (1988). *Inessential women: Problems of exclusion in feminist thought.* Boston: Beacon.

Webster, C. (1994). Effects of Hispanic ethnic identification on marital roles in the purchase decision process. *Journal of Consumer Research, 21,* 319-331.

Zinn, M. B. (1994). Feminist rethinking from racial-ethnic families. In M. B. Zinn & B. T. Dill (Eds.), *Women of color in U.S. society* (pp. 303-314). Philadelphia: Temple University Press.

Zinn, M. B., & Dill, B. T. (1994). Difference and domination. In M. B. Zinn & B. T. Dill (Eds.), *Women of color in U.S. society* (pp. 3-12). Philadelphia: Temple University Press.

PART II

THIS SECTION examines aspects of the consumer/marketer interface that have resulted in physical, emotional, and/or financial trauma for members of our society. In the first chapter, Beth Hirschman provides three vantage points from which to understand the devastating impact of addiction on the personal and professional lives of substance abusers. Her telling of this "story" is particularly compelling because it involves the lives of well-known persons whose existences have been transformed due to their addictions. Jim Gentry and Cathy Goodwin investigate how individuals who have just suffered the loss of a loved one cope with immediate as well as long-term consumption decisions that often place them in new roles. Finally, Linda Alwitt provides a thorough look at the marketplace imbalance that favors marketers over poor consumers, and she suggests solutions that propose to remedy this relationship problem.

As noted in the Introduction, a look at the negative side of the marketing system is a rare and mostly recent phenomenon. Social criticisms previously came from other professions like psychology, medicine, communications, and law. Authors such as these scholars have filled the void in our literature that was filled in the past by these "outsiders."

Additional Readings

Alwitt, L. F. (in press). *Marketing and the poor: Adjusting the balance.* Thousand Oaks, CA: Sage.

Gentry, J. W., Kennedy, P. F., Paul, C., & Hill, R. P. (1995). The vulnerability of those grieving the death of a loved one: Implications for public policy. *Journal of Public Policy & Marketing, 14*(1), 128-142.

Hirschman, E. C. (1992). The consciousness of addiction: Toward a general theory of compulsive consumption. *Journal of Consumer Research, 19,* 155-179.

3

Professional, Personal, and Popular Culture Perspectives on Addiction

ELIZABETH C. HIRSCHMAN

THIS CHAPTER weaves together three strands of thought concerning addiction. At the outset, I provide a brief overview of professional theorization regarding addiction. Although there are currently multiple schools of thought concerning this phenomenon, primary focus will be placed on the conceptualization that many favor to win the explanation race—the biopsychosocial model developed by Donovan (1988). In keeping with the observations of many social scientists involved in understanding addictive and excessive behaviors (e.g., see Faber, 1992; Hirschman, 1992a; Jacobs, 1989; Levison, Gerstein, & Maloff, 1983; Marlatt, Baer, Donovan, & Kivlahan, 1988; O'Guinn & Faber, 1989), the biopsychosocial model proposes that these are, in fact, diverse manifestations of obsessive-compulsive disorders that share similar etiologies and origins.

The next portion of the chapter introduces popular culture narratives representative of current cultural understandings of addiction. Similarities and differences among these socially constructed accounts of addiction and those constructed by social scientists will be explored, especially in terms of their ramifications for the cultural identification and treatment of persons who are addicted. The third portion of the chapter develops my personal perspectives regarding the phenomenon of addiction. As both a recovering addict and a practicing social scientist, I will attempt to describe the intermingling of etic and emic perspectives that this dual status has brought to my own life.

Where Does Addiction Come From?

The scientific community's response to the very simple and somewhat simplistic question of where addiction comes from has undergone a radical transformation over the past decade. Prior to the early 1980s, most social science models of addiction emphasized its sociological (Davison & Neale, 1986) and psychological (Orford, 1985; Zuckerman, 1979) precursors. There were treatises on the addictive personality (Mendelson & Mello, 1986), which viewed addiction as essentially a set of problematic personality characteristics. There was also ample discussion of the sociological factors correlated with tendencies toward addiction (e.g., child abuse, school absenteeism, minority racial membership, etc.; Goodwin & Jamison, 1990) and of sociocultural factors observed to direct the type of addiction engaged in (e.g., white middle-class women and eating disorders, young professionals and cocaine, black teenagers and crack, college students and alcohol/marijuana, etc.; Hirschman, 1992b).

Yet at the same time these readily observable social truths were making themselves self-evident, tantalizing evidence of inherited addiction tendencies was emerging. Ever since the 1960s and 1970s, longitudinal studies had provided evidence that alcoholism "ran" in families (Bohman, Sigvardson, & Cloninger, 1981). In particular, studies on identical twins reared apart from their biological parents documented the presence of heritability for this type of addiction (Collins, 1985). The 1980s and 1990s witnessed an outpouring of studies identifying genetic bases for tendencies to develop a variety of illnesses, from heart disease to esophageal cancer to kidney disease ("The Good News," 1994). Similarly, persons suffering from addictive disorders were also found to have families with genetic histories of addictive behavior (Crabbe, McSwigan, & Belknap, 1985).

THE ROLE OF BRAIN CHEMISTRY

In conjunction with this research, recent progress in the understanding of mental illnesses, such as unipolar depression and bipolar disorder (i.e., manic-depression), generalized anxiety disorder, and obsessive-compulsive disorder, has implicated hereditary abnormalities in brain chemistry as contributing causes (e.g., see Goodwin & Jamison, 1990; Jamison, 1993; Kramer, 1993). As with addiction, mental illness runs in families. Perhaps equally significant is the concurrent finding that addictive disorders and mental disorders are highly correlated (Goodwin & Jamison, 1990; Jamison, 1993). That is, many persons who suffer from mental illness also engage in addictive behaviors such as alcoholism, compulsive gambling, and cocaine and heroin addiction; and a significant proportion of persons who are addicts and compulsive consumers also exhibit mental disorders such as manic-depression and generalized anxiety disorder (Goodwin & Jamison, 1990; Jamison, 1993; McElroy, Satlin, Pope, Keck, & Hudson, 1991; Popkin, 1989). One important assumption that will be made in later discussions is that, generally, in persons exhibiting both mental disorders and addictive behaviors, the mental disorder precedes the addiction.

I intend to argue (as have several others, e.g., see Goodwin & Jamison, 1990; Jamison, 1993) that addictive behaviors are often initiated by persons as ways of self-medicating the emotional and mental discomfort they experience as a result of preexisting mental disorders. I believe that mild or moderate levels of mental disorder very commonly go unrecognized, undiagnosed, and, therefore, untreated among large numbers of people in the general population (see also Kramer, 1993; Wallis, 1994). Because these persons believe that nothing is "wrong" with them,[1] they do not seek psychiatric remedies such as antidepressants or antianxiety medications that could successfully treat the underlying chemical imbalances that lead to their emotional disorders. Instead, they will turn to (or stumble onto) "folk remedies" (e.g., alcohol) for emotional symptoms such as anxiety, anger, depression, and manic behavior.

For example, the undiagnosed manic may seek out addictive behaviors and substances that heighten the high of mania—such as cocaine, exercise, promiscuity, gambling, and amphetamines. The

undiagnosed anxious consumer may seek out binge eating, tranquilizers, and alcohol to "calm" the nerves and provide a feeling of
self-control. The undiagnosed depressed and angry consumer may
seek out heroin and alcohol to dull dysphoria, and so forth. Although
my simplistic linking of specific emotional disorders with specific
addictive "medicines" may be inappropriate, I believe the underlying
premise is sound. That is, addiction originates in consumers' rational
efforts to make themselves feel better. Consumers who existentially
experience an intolerable—or even mildly uncomfortable—level of
emotional distress will naturally attempt to treat and cure that distress
with whatever substances or behaviors they are able to discover or
devise that provide relief—at least in the short run.

NATURE AND NURTURE

   To this point, I have argued that the emotional disorders that lead
to addiction are essentially inborn or genetic. That is, one inherits
genetic tendencies toward abnormal brain chemistry. The abnormalities in brain chemistry (e.g., a low level of serotonin) give rise to
emotional disorders, such as manic-depression. There is, however,
additional evidence that early childhood events, such as physical,
psychological, and/or sexual abuse, may permanently alter an individual's brain chemistry, resulting in emotional disorders, such as
manic-depression and generalized anxiety disorder, that are indistin-
guishable from those originating through heredity (e.g., see Goodwin
& Jamison, 1990; Kramer, 1993).
   Children born to parents who exhibit addictive behaviors thus may
be doubly at risk to develop addictive behaviors in their own lives. First,
to the extent that parents' addictive behaviors are hereditarily based
(because of abnormal brain chemistry), the traits may be passed on
to their children. Second, parents whose behavior is erratic because
of addiction and/or underlying, untreated emotional disorders are
likely to abuse their children, thus triggering negative, socially grounded
alterations in their young children's brain chemistry. Furthermore, to
the extent that these children come to model their responses to their
emotional distress after their parents' behavior, they, too, may choose
to self-medicate with alcohol, cigarettes, tranquilizers, food, cocaine,
and so forth, just as their parents do. Hence, the cycle of emotional

disorder and addiction may be passed intergenerationally through both nature (i.e., heredity) and nurture (i.e., abuse, modeling).

Popular Culture Perceptions

One reason why the linkage between undiagnosed mental disorders and addiction has been so long ignored, I believe, lies in our cultural ideology concerning addiction and mental illness. Very often, consumers' addictive behaviors go unrecognized and untreated, just as mild-to-moderate exhibitions of mental disorder go undetected. This is because culturally we reserve the term *addiction* for only certain types of addictive behavior and overlook—or mislabel—other, widespread manifestations of this phenomenon. In my view, only a very small percentage of persons who are addicted to a substance or behavior are actually labeled as addicts.

The second reason is that our culture tends to view addiction and mental illness as either/or dichotomous phenomena. One is either an addict (or mentally ill) or one is not. More properly, both addiction and mental illness should be viewed as continua (e.g., see Kramer, 1993). The behaviors that are manifested in mental disorders and addiction are extensions of behaviors that occur daily within the general population. It is only when one's behavior reaches the apex of these continua, however, that one is likely to be culturally labeled as an addict (or as mentally ill). Furthermore, only a subset of addictive behaviors is likely to be labeled as addictions by the surrounding popular culture; for example, cocaine or heroin dependence would likely now be labeled as an addiction, whereas nicotine or caffeine dependence would not.[2] Similarly, compulsive gambling and sexual promiscuity are clinically viewed as addictions but are seen more as deviant or immoral behaviors within popular culture. Anorexia and bulimia are addictive/compulsive behaviors in a clinical sense but are culturally viewed as illnesses or diseases.

To illustrate popular culture ideology regarding addiction, I chose virtually at random four current magazine articles describing drug abuse by celebrities: a May 30, 1994, article in *Newsweek* (Starr, 1994) and a May 30, 1994, article in *People* (Reed, 1994) on the tennis player Jennifer Capriati; a May 30, 1994, article in *People* (Gliatto, 1994) on the actress Brett Butler; and a June 2, 1994, article in *Rolling Stone* (Strauss, 1994) on the rock singer Kurt Cobain. I will give an account of each article's implicit model of addiction and compare it to the biopsychosocial model described earlier.[3]

JENNIFER CAPRIATI

The two magazine stories concerning Jennifer Capriati, 18, recount her recent arrest for drug possession after police discovered her in the company of a runaway girl and a "drifter" boy at a rundown motel in Coral Gables, Florida. According to both accounts, the trio had in their possession a broad array of drugs, including marijuana, crack cocaine, heroin, pain killers, alcohol, and cigarettes. Other teenagers, unfortunately, also find themselves in the same situation as Capriati, but their troubles do not usually make "news" in major magazines. Capriati did, of course, because she is the youngest women's tennis player ever to rank in the Top 10 and because she was, according to the accounts, earning $6 million annually in endorsements for various corporations.

Despite the celebrity status that catapulted her drug arrest to the forefront of national attention, Capriati is presented in each story as a troubled teenager whose misfortunes may provide a cautionary tale to overly ambitious parents and feed into our popular culture love-hate relationship with fame and commercialism. Both accounts lay some "blame" for Capriati's drug use on the "pressures" to perform in a commercial venue by corporations who used her fame as a tennis star to celebritize their products. The principal of her high school is quoted as saying, "It has to do with how we position young athletes in our society; what we overlook if there is money changing hands" (Reed, 1994, p. 83).[4]

The *Newsweek* article broadens the circle of guilty suspects to include "parents and other adults who bungled their jobs, fans, commentators and writers who operate the myth-making machinery, and, as in the case of other, less celebrated teens, the kid herself" (Starr, 1994, p. 73).[5] The *People* article further indicts Capriati's father, Stephano, who apparently had decided his daughter would be a tennis pro even before she was born and regimented her from infancy onward, pressing successfully to have the Women's Tennis Council exempt her from the rule barring professional play by girls under age 14. This article quotes Stephano as saying, "where I come from we have a proverb: when the apple is ripe, eat it" (Reed, 1994, p. 84). Both articles also note that Capriati was arrested in December 1993 for shoplifting a $34.99 ring from a shopping mall kiosk and that she had been in a drug rehabilitation clinic for "over a week" several months earlier.

Thus, these accounts of Capriati's drug use differ in some respects from the biopsychosocial model presented earlier but are consistent with it in others. The cause of her drug use is primarily identified as sociological: Pressure to perform as an adult by her father, various corporate sponsors, and the media created an acute personal response of rejection and rebellion. Drugs were used to escape the social pressure to perform. Furthermore, Capriati was socially influenced by "bad" teenagers (the runaway, the drifter) to use drugs.

We also see evidence in these accounts of popular culture norms regarding drug use. Popular culture believes it appropriate for white, affluent teenagers to drink alcohol and smoke cigarettes and marijuana, whereas cocaine and heroin are seen as off-limits for this group. For example, the *Newsweek* article reports: "descriptions by the revelers at the Gables Inn range from mild teenage excess involving beer, pot and Valium to a sustained drug orgy allegedly involving crack cocaine and heroin" (Starr, 1994, p. 71). The phrases "mild teenage excess" and "sustained drug orgy" are used to segregate socially acceptable from socially unacceptable drug use.

Notably, neither article makes even subtle allusion to underlying mental and emotional disorders of either Capriati or her parents. Yet reading between the lines, observers cognizant of mild forms of obsessive-compulsive disorder may speculate that telltale symptoms were perhaps present in both the daughter and the father in the Capriati family. Very few fathers declare their as-yet-unborn children to be sports champions and then prop pillows under them as infants to assist their doing sit-ups, as Stephano Capriati is reported to have done (Reed, 1994).

Very few children respond by "bulldozing [at tennis] girls her age and several years older" as Jennifer Capriati did (Reed, 1994, p. 83). In fact, in both father and daughter, we see the single-minded, extraordinary commitment to accomplishing a repetitive task that often marks obsessive-compulsive disorder. When obsessive-compulsive behavior results in outstanding achievement, it is often lauded as self-direction and ambition; when it results in failure and destructiveness, it is condemned as fanaticism.

BRETT BUTLER

Brett Butler, 36, is the star of a successful new sitcom, *Grace Under Fire*, featuring a divorced mother of three with a blue-collar job and an acerbic wit. The *People* magazine story in which she is featured describes correspondences between Butler's character's life (i.e., divorced from an abusive husband) and events in her own life. Butler's mother married and divorced two abusive men, having five children in the process. According to Butler, her mother was "simply unable to cope with life" and did not care properly for her children (Gliatto, 1994, p. 48).

Butler herself repeated the pattern, marrying a violent man whom she later divorced. The article reports that, "their three-year marriage . . . boiled down to her drinking and taking beatings," and a picture is captioned with a quote from Butler that reads, "I wasted a lot of time being an underachiever and drinking and being sad" (Gliatto, 1994, p. 50).[6] In this article, unlike in the Capriati narrative, there is more explicit discussion of the hereditary mental illness and childhood modeling contributing to Butler's experiences with alcohol, consistent with the biopsychosocial model of addiction. The article reports that after divorcing her mother, Butler's father moved back to his mother's home, where he lived as a recluse until his death. His room reportedly contained 500 to 600 books, many filled with his handwritten comments "obsessively scrawled in red ink" (Gliatto, 1994, p. 48). Butler comments in the article that her father "was nuts. . . I feel like I lived through the demons that probably ended up doing him in" (Gliatto, 1994, p. 49).

What is constructive about this article, in my view, is its provision of a life-history context with which to interpret Butler's current circumstances. The intergenerational cycle of physical abuse, mental illness, and alcoholism is presented in a coherent, gestaltlike manner. The article, however, does not tell us what resources—personal, social, institutional—Butler called upon to overcome her early-life difficulties and arrive at her current, successful status as an actress. Providing this kind of information would have made it a more useful text for readers who found themselves in troubled circumstances similar to Butler's early life.

KURT COBAIN

Kurt Cobain, the 27-year-old singer, guitarist, and songwriter for the rock group Nirvana, shot himself in the head on April 5, 1994. Cobain's suicide was reported in a lengthy article in *Rolling Stone.* According to the text, "Cobain's friends, family and associates had been worried about his depression and chronic drug use for years" (Strauss, 1994, p. 35).[7] And several attempts had been made over the weeks prior to Cobain's death to obtain professional treatment for him. Significantly, this article reports that Cobain had exhibited "clinical depression" as early as high school and prior to developing his later dependencies on alcohol and heroin—a high level of which he had consumed just prior to committing suicide.

Descriptions of Cobain's behavior provided by the article suggest that he may have been more accurately diagnosed as manic-depressive with tendencies toward rapid cycling (Goodwin & Jamison, 1990), a clinical condition in which the individual cycles rapidly—and uncontrollably—between feelings of elation, frustration, anger, and depression. For example, the article states that,

> Many who were close to Cobain confess that the musician frequently suffered dramatic mood swings. . . . "Kurt could be very outgoing and funny and charming . . . and a half-hour later he would just go sit in the corner and be totally moody and uncommunicative." "He was a walking time bomb and nobody could do anything about it." (Strauss, 1994, p. 40)

The article details several interventions that were attempted by Cobain's friends and family, the last one undertaken by his wife, rock musician Courtney Love, the week before his death. After being convinced to enter a drug rehabilitation clinic in Los Angeles, Cobain literally "jumped the fence" after 2 days, headed back to his home in Seattle, and shot himself 4 days later. His suicide note indicated that his feelings of depression had overwhelmed his ability to enjoy his music and his life: "I'm too much of an erratic, moody person and I don't have any passion anymore, so remember—it's better to burn out than to fade away" (Strauss, 1994, p. 40).

The tragedy of Cobain's short, highly creative, highly self-destructive life, as the article implicitly communicates, was not that he was a drug addict (although he certainly was) but that the mental disorders he struggled with from childhood were not successfully treated.[8] As band member Krist Novoselic told a newspaper reporter after Cobain's death, "just blaming it on smack [heroin] is stupid. . . . Smack was just a small part of his life" (Strauss, 1994, p. 43). Indeed, it is likely that Cobain used heroin as self-medication to dissociate himself from the depressive episodes that he floundered in. There is no mention in the article of whether Cobain was ever treated with psychiatric medications, such as Lithium and Tegrenol, to alleviate his depression or—as the article seems to suggest—he was simply detoxed several times from his dependence on heroin. It is possible that removing heroin from his life, while simultaneously failing to substitute other, more appropriate mood-stabilizing medications, actually may have deepened his sense of hopelessness and futility.

SOME THOUGHTS

At the conclusion of these popular culture articles, we find the three persons they discuss at very different life statuses. Kurt Cobain is dead; no amount of reanalysis and hashing over what should have been done will resurrect him. Jennifer Capriati is in drug rehab, likely struggling with issues of who she is and where her life is going. Brett Butler is poised for stardom atop a hit TV series and initiating divorce from her second husband. The only one whose future interplay between mental disorders and addiction is known with certainty is Cobain. Many, many paths are possible for Capriati and Butler, but all of them are likely to be influenced to some extent by their past experiences with drug dependence, their internal emotional construction, and their surrounding social milieu.

A Personal Perspective

The life outcomes for Cobain (i.e., death), Capriati (i.e., uncertainty), and Butler (i.e., current success) inform us that emotional disturbance coupled with addiction can be fatally destructive or personally empowering. To the extent that individuals can experience emotional disturbance and addiction and survive, they not only may go on to lead a "normal, healthy" life but also may even develop a deepened soulfulness and empathic knowledge of the human condition not accessible to others. For many others, however, these experiences may—and often do—lead to lives of unhappiness and unfulfilled potential.

I now want to explore in a more directly personal way the issues that persons with emotional disturbances and addictive tendencies and those who are close to them must struggle with over the course of their lives. It is important to understand that these issues are never resolved or finished; they must be grappled with each day of one's existence. And responses to them that may be appropriate for one person during one phase of life may be inappropriate for another person or another phase.

WHO AND WHAT IS THE REAL ME?

Perhaps the most daunting challenge for people who are off-the-norm emotionally and who use some addictive substance or activity to help bring order to their life is developing a firm sense of self-identity. As described in an article on the consciousness of addiction (Hirschman, 1992a, 1992b), most addicts experience a profound sense of personal inauthenticity. Phenomenologically, their lives and sense of self are so bound up in the compulsive behaviors they use to keep themselves together, that they have great difficulty envisioning themselves independent from their compulsions and addictions. Yet they simultaneously recognize that the substance or behavior that they "must have" to survive is not a normal or healthy aspect of human behavior. It permits them to keep body and soul in some tortured form of integration, yet at the same time their awful dependence on the addiction prohibits normal human interaction. It is a terrible dilemma that no doubt contributes to many suicides and homicides among those afflicted.[9]

It is important to acknowledge, however, that this sense of self-inauthenticity may originate even before the individual develops a pattern of addictive dependence. If the model of biopsychosocial addiction presented earlier is correct and addiction does indeed spring from underlying emotional abnormalities, then the roots of the inauthentic self extend to early childhood (and even to conception). Persons who are born with and/or socialized into emotional patterns of depression, manic-depression, obsessive-compulsive disorder, generalized anxiety disorder, and the like undergo mood changes that range from mild to moderate to severe, depending on the depth of their disorder. These mood changes—for example, from buoyancy to anger or from contentment to depression—are usually uncontrollable and may cause the individual to feel continuously decentered and in flux. Without the experience of stable emotionality that normal people possess, these individuals may have great difficulty developing a confident sense of who they are and how they feel about themselves, about others they interact with, and about life events. To have one's own emotional responses become impossible to predict or control can create enormous existential anxiety. Knowing and feeling comfortable with one's self and with others is transformed into a continuous struggle for stability.

Given these conditions, it is very easy to see how such individuals would gravitate quickly toward behaviors or substances that granted some relief—even if it is short-lived and ultimately harmful—from the disintegrated identity they experience. In my view, this is exactly how full-blown addiction and mild-to-moderate dependencies and compulsions are born: The emotionally floundering person—whose mental disorders have not been recognized or properly treated—stumbles across some activity or substance that provides a temporary respite from distress. The activity or substance is quickly latched onto as a lifeline to emotional stability, and soon it becomes an essential ingredient of the self. Over the life course, many such lifelines may be grasped, either concurrently or in a series (Hirschman, 1992a, 1992b).

Thus, emotionally disturbed persons who become addicts are crippled by two existential shortcomings in constructing an identity. First, they are initially unable to achieve sufficient emotional stability to create an accurate sense of who they are and how they feel. Second, emotional stability purchased at the cost of addiction to a substance or activity leaves the individual's sense of autonomy and independent selfhood critically mortgaged to the addiction; one must go through life tethered to the addiction, unable to function fully as a self-sufficient individual.

WHAT IS PERSONAL RESPONSIBILITY AND FREE WILL?

The mental and emotional condition of persons who are disordered and/or addicted makes the issue of assessing personal responsibility and determining free will highly problematic, both for themselves and others. I am certainly not competent to write on this subject from a legal or psychiatric perspective; however, this is an issue that I have confronted as an individual on many levels and across several life events. When most of us—and the popular culture, in general—form judgments of others' behaviors (e.g., whether they are acceptable or unacceptable, right or wrong, moral or immoral), we usually do so based on the presumption that the person about whom we are making the judgment is normal. We assume that the person has a reasonable level of emotional stability, is thinking rationally, and is acting based on conscious, logical motivation.

We therefore feel ourselves justified in getting angry if that person treats us in a hurtful manner if, in our judgment, we have done nothing to merit such treatment. We express shock, amazement, and disbelief if that person acts in ways that seem obviously self-destructive or destructive to others. We feel hurt and betrayed if that person suddenly—and seemingly without cause or provocation—becomes aggressively abusive. We feel shut out and rejected if that person— whom we believed to be caring and committed—turns morose, sullen, and withdrawn. These are "natural," normal responses for people to have when confronted with the behaviors described.

And yet, to invoke Shakespeare, here's the rub. What if a portion, at least, of these people's bad behavior is not an expression of their free will? What if it, in small, medium, or large part, is something that simply erupts in them? What if their moods, feelings, and responses to others are, in part or whole, outside of their purposeful control? What do we do then? How are we to judge them?

In my own recent life, I have been on both sides of this situation—a provider of somewhat out-of-control emotional responses and a receiver of the same. From being on both the giving and the receiving ends of this emotional equation, I have learned that arriving at an appropriate response (to quote a Southern cliché) is a very hard row to hoe. Much of our response to seemingly inappropriate behavior on the part of those who are emotionally disordered and/or addicted turns on our internal assessment of how much free will they are able to exercise over their behavior. This is a very difficult and trying calculus to undertake, but one that is necessary in order for us to formulate moral responses to their behaviors.

If we believe that the individuals are predominately in charge of their behavior and that that behavior is inappropriate, dangerous, or damaging to themselves or others, then we are rightly justified in being upset and in telling them so. We are correct in labeling such individuals as criminals if their actions have broken the law; we are right in holding them responsible for the bad outcomes caused by their actions and in demanding an apology, jail time, financial compensation, or whatever else is culturally accepted recompense.

On the other hand, if we look carefully at these persons and come to the judgment that the balance of their behavior is simply beyond willful control, then we cannot hold them responsible for the consequences of their actions. This "truth" is easy to overlook in judging those who are moderately (as opposed to very severely) disordered or moderately (as opposed to very severely) addicted. It is relatively easy to recognize the crazed actions of a raving lunatic or a collapsed heroin addict as irrational. It is much tougher yet much more frequent to have to assess responsibility for the wrongheaded actions of those around us who are still functioning but are largely overwhelmed by emotional and/or addictive problems.

A practical example may help to clarify (or perhaps muddy) these moral waters. As a hypothetical instance, let us assume that I had a serious, professional conflict with a colleague who, in my view, undertook several actions that were damaging to my career and the careers of others. Although I am aware that this colleague suffers from emotional instability and is substance dependent, I may choose to hold him responsible for the negative consequences of these actions, because I believe they were primarily conducted by his conscious will; that is, he knew what the likely outcomes of his behaviors would be and, although they were in part stimulated by irrational feelings, he chose to undertake them. Although it would have been a struggle, given his mental state, I believe he could have stopped himself if he had wanted to.

As a contrary instance, let us assume that a second colleague has acted in ways that were even more personally damaging to me. Despite the negative consequences and periodic upsurges of anger and frustration I may feel toward him, however, I choose not to hold him responsible for his behavior. On reflection, I realize that the primary reason I arrived at these two very different judgments is based on my knowledge of each of these two hypothetical men's lives. The first colleague, despite periodic irrational episodes, has been able to maintain a very successful career, his marriage, and his social contacts. The second colleague, on the other hand, has passed through a succession of jobs, has a failed marriage, and has alienated all but a few members of his social network. His life is clearly out of control, and so I do not hold him responsible for the harm he has caused me. And indeed, I feel great sadness over the harm he has (and is) causing himself.

I realize also that in forming these two distinct judgments, I have used my own self-knowledge as the barometer. In my estimation, I have been about as strung-out as the first colleague. Because of my own emotional disorders and substance dependence that largely mirror his hypothetical maladies, I, too, have been irrationally angry, selfish, paranoid, anxious, manic, suspicious, and demanding. Yet I also know that during these difficult times, I possessed sufficient self-control and self-awareness to censor and edit my behaviors. I did not always want to, I did not always do so, but I could have if I had tried.[10]

The second hypothetical colleague, given our present purposes, can be viewed as having passed over that amorphous line that separates free will from free fall. Although portions of his life remain functional, the larger share of his existence has gone haywire. His own suffering is so much worse than any he has caused me or others that it would be cruel to attempt to add to it through reprisals.

When confronted with such persons, the moral challenge to the rest of the community becomes not so much one of withholding condemnation but rather of accepting our social responsibility to intervene in some humane way. Yet very disturbingly, we are normatively proscripted from taking action to influence other adults' lives unless and until they flagrantly become "a danger to themselves or to others." Ironically, with both mental illness and drug addiction, help usually arrives too late or not at all rather than too early. More ironically, if we saw a friend or even a stranger about to step in front of an oncoming car or floundering in a river, we would not hesitate to take forceful action to save them. Yet if that same friend, or stranger, is cramming cocaine up the nose or behaving like a lunatic, we turn away, fearful of overstepping some social boundary in pulling them back from the abyss.

If Kurt Cobain had been forced by his friends and family to enter a psychiatric hospital where not only his heroin addiction but also his depression could have been treated, he might not have blown off his highly talented head at the age of 27. If we could figure out a way and summon the will to induce the second colleague to enter psychiatric care, he might be able to rehabilitate what once was a brilliant career. Will we? Probably not. And that is why a lot of good people end up destroyed, because we do not yet have the means as a culture or as individuals to arrive at comfortable judgments of free will. We err, I believe, too far on the side of granting the assumption of rationality to disturbed, addicted persons who would much more surely benefit from caring, thoughtful intervention to save their lives.

TAKING THE BAD WITH THE GOOD

Despite the sadness of the foregoing discussion, life is not always unrelentingly bad for emotionally disturbed addicts, especially if they are operating at the mild-to-moderate end of the continuum. Sometimes—even frequently, if one is fortunate—life can be extraordinary. The term *extraordinary* means beyond the bounds of normal experience, and this is the realm in which I and persons like me—that is, the moderately wacko and compulsive—spend most of our waking hours (and probably many of our unconscious ones). In talking with several people who are emotionally disturbed and/or addicted, it is striking that we all seem to share a common trait of feeling different from other people, of existing in a mental realm unlike the psychic spaces that most persons inhabit. Perhaps this feeling of being different—set apart—is why many of us seek out the company of others like ourselves as friends and mates.[11] We have thoughts and feelings and patterns of behavior that are confusing and unsettling to normal folk but that make sense within our tribe of offbeat souls.

This tribe knows the constant tug of obsessive thoughts and images. It feels the relentless pressure to perform tasks perfectly again and again. It knows the ecstatic beauty of seeing huge arcs of images and ideas unfolding effortlessly in its mind's eye. It feels the intense, unreasonable, exhausting frustration of having a mental motor that revs too high for days on end and then falls into numb stasis without warning. It has collectively glimpsed the edges of madness into which some of its members pass, never to return. It has felt the happiest joy and the saddest sorrow—sometimes within the space of a day or an hour.

And if psychiatric accounts of this tribe are correct (e.g., see Jamison, 1993), this little band of troubled addicts has produced much of the Western world's most beautiful poetry, influential social science, profound philosophy, and moving literature.[12] When they are bad, they are likely to be horrid; but when they are good, they are brilliant.

The apocryphal story was told to me that a very famous and gifted film director takes himself off medication for manic-depression each time he makes a motion picture. He has to be his "crazy self," he says, to make the film as he wants it to be. As frustrating and befuddling as it may seem to ordinary folk, there is a lot that we—the addicted and disturbed—do not want to get well from. We do not necessarily want to be like everyone else. In fact, at times I believe we wantonly revel and grovel in our excesses. But there are portions of ourselves that we would like to tame.

I recently went to a psychiatrist and asked her to put me on Prozac, a drug that I had witnessed work miracles on others. I was careful to explain to her that I did not want to really alter my personality; it just needed a little "trim around the edges." During the spring, my old demons of hyperactivity, anxiety, and compulsiveness were starting to gnaw at me. I wanted something that would keep them at bay but still permit me to be "me"—erratic, vivid, spontaneous.

Should Prozac (or something akin to it) not exist, however, and I be forced to live with myself as I am or use some treatment that would resign me to complete normalcy, I would probably choose to remain me—even with all the demons—than to give up the ability to fly out to the far reaches of consciousness, which is the most essential, basic part of myself. But this is a personal choice and not one I would deign to impose on others. In a letter I wrote to one troubled colleague, I talked to him about the emotional burden we both share: The kind of heads we have are such a wonderful gift, but for them we have to pay a very terrible price. For many of our kind—the Kurt Cobains, the Ernest Hemingways, and all the other troubled souls, both great and small—the price overwhelms and destroys the gift. And for centuries, self-medication in the form of addiction was the only respite available. Fortunately, recent advances in understanding the chemistry in which these addled brains percolate may help many of the most troubled of us hang on to whatever talents we may possess, at a lower price in emotional pain and turmoil.

Some Closing Thoughts

Mental illness and addiction are closely interwoven phenomena. For many persons, they are inseparable entities that can affect the quality (and quantity) of life from childhood through old age. They are amazingly powerful phenomena as well. Like Superman ("able to leap tall buildings in a single bound"), mental illness and addiction are able to leap across generations, affecting entire lineages with their disruption and disfunctionality (e.g., see Collins, 1985; Jamison, 1993).

They exist widely among us, frequently disguised as personal eccentricities, eating disorders, violent tempers, and chronic indebtedness. As a culture, we need to recognize better their existence and their meaning. We need to understand better how it is that people go crazy and become addicts. Perhaps most profoundly, we need to feel compassion rather than revulsion or condemnation for those afflicted.

In a letter to *Rolling Stone* shortly after the article on Kurt Cobain's death appeared, one reader angrily condemned Cobain as a "coward" who did not "fight hard enough" against his depression and addiction. This writer truly did not understand (and doubtless had never personally experienced) the kind of utterly overwhelming compulsions to which Cobain was in tow. Why *would* someone with so much talent, money, success, a loving wife, and a new baby kill himself? Why, indeed do thousands of similar souls take the same course every year? Why do people gamble themselves into bankruptcy, force themselves to vomit food until they die, shoot heroin into their arms, or shoot each other over 5 dollars' worth of crack? Obviously, these actions are not those of persons in normal states of existence. They are the acts of people whose lives and minds are clearly out of control. The greatest good we can do for them is to avoid the twin errors of condemnation and rejection and instead seek, through research and personal contact, to help them find a better way to construct their lives.

Notes

1. Although they may view themselves and be viewed by others as nervous, moody, anxious, shy, irritable, "neurotic," or hot-tempered, these are seen as merely manifestations of normal variations in personality and not as symptoms of underlying emotional disorders.

2. This is changing, however. Cultural perceptions of tobacco and cigarettes appear to be in flux, and soon they may be socially labeled as drugs (Levy, 1994a, 1994b).

3. These accounts are provided not to challenge the veracity of the foregoing social science model but rather to illustrate that it exists alongside other, socially constructed discourses regarding addiction.

4. Used by permission from *People* magazine.

5. From NEWSWEEK © 1994, Newsweek, Inc. All rights reserved. Reprinted by permission.

6. Used by permission from *People* magazine.

7. From Rolling Stone © 1994, Straight Arrow Publishers, Inc. All rights reserved. Reprinted by permission.

8. In keeping with the biopsychosocial model, other articles in the same issue of *Rolling Stone* provided accounts of Cobain's troubled childhood.

9. At the time this chapter was being written, O. J. Simpson had been indicted on charges of murdering his former wife and her friend, purportedly as a result of obsessional love (Schindehette, 1994). Also, rock singer Axl Rose, a drug user and manic-depressive, was being sued by two women for abusive behavior during their relationships with him (Dougherty, Johnson, & Benet, 1994).

10. It is part and parcel of being emotionally distressed and addicted that sometimes you really *want* to be awful to other people.

11. Jamison (1993) notes that there is a very strong tendency for persons with manic-depression and similar mental disorders to marry one another—a phenomenon called associative mating.

12. Much of Freud's theory, Hemingway's novels, Byron's poetry, and Williams's plays (to mention only a few) were written under the influence.

References

Bohman, M., Sigvardson, S., & Cloninger, C. R. (1981). Maternal inheritance of alcohol abuse. *Archives of General Psychiatry, 38,* 965-969.

Collins, A. C. (1985). Inheriting addictions: A genetic perspective with emphasis on alcohol and nicotine. In H. B. Milkman & H. J. Shaffer (Eds.), *The addictions: Multidisciplinary perspectives and treatment* (pp. 3-10). Lexington, MA: D. C. Heath.

Crabbe, J. C., McSwigan, J. D., & Belknap, J. K. (1985). The role of genetics in substance abuse. In M. Galizio & S. A. Maisto (Eds.), *Determinants of substance abuse treatment* (pp. 45-63). New York: Plenum.

Davison, G. C., & Neale, J. M. (1986). *Abnormal psychology.* New York: John Wiley.

Donovan, D. M. (1988). Assessment of addictive behaviors: Implications of an emerging biopsychosocial model. In D. M. Donovan & G. A. Marlatt (Eds.), *Assessment of addiction behaviors.* New York: Guilford.

Dougherty, S., Johnson, K., & Benet, L. (1994, July 18). Bye, bye, love. *People,* pp. 48-53.

Faber, R. J. (1992). Money changes everything: Compulsive buying from a biopsychosocial perspective. *American Behavioral Scientist, 35,* 809-819.

Gliatto, T. (1994, May 30). No pain, no fame. *People,* pp. 47-50.

The good news. (1994, June 27). *Time,* p. 26.

Goodwin, F. K., & Jamison, K. R. (1990). *Manic-depressive illness.* New York: Oxford University Press.

Hirschman, E. C. (1992a). The consciousness of addiction: Toward a general theory of compulsive consumption. *Journal of Consumer Research, 19*(3), 155-179.

Hirschman, E. C. (1992b). Recovering from drug addiction: A phenomenological account. In J. F. Sherry & B. Sternthal (Eds.), *Advances in consumer research* (pp. 541-549). Provo, UT: Association for Consumer Research.

Jacobs, D. F. (1989). A general theory of addictions: Rationale for and evidence supporting a new approach for understanding and treating addictive behaviors. In H. J. Shaffer, S. A. Stein, B. Gambino, & T. N. Cummings (Eds.), *Compulsive gambling: Theory, research and practice.* Lexington, MA: D. C. Heath.

Jamison, K. R. (1993). *Touched with fire: Manic depressive illness and the artistic temperament.* New York: Free Press.

Kramer, P. D. (1993). *Listening to Prozac.* New York: Viking.

Levison, P. K., Gerstein, D. R., & Maloff, D. R. (1983). *Commonalities in substance abuse and habitual behavior.* Lexington, MA: Lexington Books.

Levy, D. (1994a, June 22). FDA: Y-1 boosts nicotine. *U.S.A. Today,* p. A1.

Levy, D. (1994b, June 21). When smoke gets in their lives. *U.S.A. Today,* p. D1.

Marlatt, G. A., Baer, J. S., Donovan, D. M., & Kivlahan, D. R. (1988). Addictive behaviors: Etiology and treatment. *Annual Review of Psychology, 39,* 223-252.

McElroy, S. L., Satlin, A., Pope, H. P., Jr., Keck, P. E., Jr., & Hudson, J. I. (1991). Treatment of compulsive shopping with antidepressants: A report of three cases. *Annals of Clinical Psychiatry, 3,* 199-204.

Mendelson, J., & Mello, N. (1986). *The addictive personality.* New York: Chelsea House.

O'Guinn, T. C., & Faber, R. J. (1989). Compulsive buying: A phenomenological exploration. *Journal of Consumer Research, 16,* 147-157.

Orford, J. (1985). *Excessive appetites: A psychological view of addictions.* Chichester, UK: John Wiley.

Popkin, M. K. (1989). Impulse control disorders not elsewhere classified. In H. I. Kaplan & B. J. Sadock (Eds.), *Comprehensive textbook of psychiatry* (pp. 1145-1155). Baltimore, MD: Williams & Wilkins.

Reed, S. (1994, May 30). Losing her grip. *People,* pp. 80-84.

Schindehette, S. (1994, June 27). Shadow of suspicion. *People,* pp. 95-102.

Starr, M. (1994, May 30). Fault, Miss Capriati. *Newsweek,* pp. 70-73.

Strauss, N. (1994, June 2). The downward spiral. *Rolling Stone,* pp. 35-42.

Wallis, C. (1994, July 11). Medicine for the soul. *Time,* p. 64.

Zuckerman, M. (1979). *Sensation seeking: Beyond the optimal level of arousal.* Hillsdale, NJ: Lawrence Erlbaum.

4

Social Support for Decision Making During Grief Due to Death

JAMES W. GENTRY
CATHY GOODWIN

PSYCHOLOGICAL VULNERABILITY has been described as "special risk for negative outcomes from stressful experiences" (Thompson & Spacapan, 1991, p. 2), such as a disease or crime. Those who lose a loved one are particularly vulnerable as consumers for at least two reasons. First, grief is stigmatized in many Western cultures. "Too evident sorrow," Aries (1974) has written, "is the sign of mental instability or of bad manners" (p. 90). The isolation of mourning creates additional stress, "leav[ing] many people uncertain, socially unsupported and vulnerable when it comes to dealing with death" (Shilling, 1993, p. 189). In general, people are not well socialized to meet adult life crises such as bereavement. Second, the active role of consumers includes the ability to make informed choices (Maynes, 1976). Among the bereaved, (a) decision-making processes are disrupted and (b) taboos surround critical decisions.

Decision Processes. When a family member dies, routine interactions are replaced by problematic situations that require repeated decision making: "During stressful events, families lose their repertoire of background understandings, assumptions, traditions, secrets and rituals that previously made it possible to function implicitly" (Sillars & Kalbflesch, 1988, p. 202). The emergence of more explicit decision making, however, reminds survivors of the deceased member's expertise in specific household domains, such as car repair or meal preparation. At the same time, the bereaved often wish to avoid making decisions at all, because no decision can allow them to return to the time when the deceased was alive and the family was functioning happily.

Taboos. Simmons (1975, p. 9) has noted that comparison shopping for funerals is taboo, that service trial is not possible, that postpurchase evaluation is avoided, that word-of-mouth communication about funerals is rare, and that people display selective perception and tune out information about funerals. Because these taboos deny the consumer advice and information, and because the consumer's motivation to search is sharply reduced, the bereaved often turn to the funeral director for guidance. The funeral director is viewed as a friend and advisor rather than a seller of products and services: "The family . . . hires and wants a normal mind to guide and advise its abnormal minds in every manner that it may show proper respect to its deceased according to customs and caste" (Bowman, 1959, p. 32).

The use of a commercial service provider as a source of social support has been explored by services researchers (Adelman, Ahuvia, & Goodwin, 1994). Those who lack social networks, such as those who face life transitions, are especially likely to turn to retailers or services for support (Stone, 1954). In seeking support from service providers at a time of weakened consumer effectiveness, the bereaved increase their risk for adverse marketplace interactions. Although the Federal Trade Commission (FTC) has developed guidelines on funeral-related purchases, consumers are at risk as they seek support from other services. Marketers and policy makers, like most North Americans, often lack understanding of bereavement and are inhibited from learning more because of the stigmatized nature of the subject. Therefore, business practices can inadvertently serve to isolate and increase the discomfort of the bereaved.

This chapter suggests the importance of services as social support for the bereaved. First, through experiential accounts, we identify social, psychological, and material needs that contribute to the stress of bereavement. Second, we suggest that traditional sources of social support, such as family and friends, have been supplemented by consumer interactions with commercial service providers. Finally, we develop public policy implications.

Methodology

Phenomenological inquiry is a qualitative approach that has gained recent acceptance by consumer researchers (McAlexander, Schouten, & Roberts, 1993; Thompson, Locander, & Pollio, 1989). This approach uses the individuals' testimony to describe their lived experiences and the meanings that emerge from them. The fragile nature of many of our informants required a flexible interview agenda as well as guidance from the director of the local Grief Center. We developed a series of grand-tour questions designed to deal with consumption activities prior to the death of the loved one, near the time of the death, and several months afterward. Prompts were used to uncover areas of interest to the researchers.

Following the Grief Center's five-session training, three interviewers became volunteers. Most of the early interviews were arranged through the center's staff and volunteers. Because most of these informants had already reconciled their grief, attempts were made to interview others who had suffered more recent losses. Thus, 50 letters were sent to survivors identified from 3-month-old published obituaries. A total of 12 responses yielded 9 completed interviews. In all, 38 interviews were completed.

Stressors Associated With Bereavement

The bereaved experience not only the pain of grief but also forced identity change and socialization into new roles. These stressors present unique coping difficulties because they reduce access to existing social support sources.

Mental Confusion and Pain. The pain of grief affected physical and mental functioning. Informants discussed drinking problems, medical problems, panic disorders, and periods of withdrawal and immobility. (More elaborate descriptions of these processes can be found in Gentry, Kennedy, Paul, & Hill, in press, 1995).

Identity Loss. Death causes the loss of relationship, of status, of a way of being, and of mundane assistance (Lofland, 1982). Informants spoke of the need to establish a new reality and a new personal identity; such statements as "life is never the same" were heard often. The bereaved need to negotiate a new self- and social identity. For example, as a widow learns roles previously performed by her spouse, she must also deal with her own and others' perceptions of herself as an unmarried person. The new identity emerges from a combination of changes in responsibilities and social relationships (Rodgers & Cowles, 1991, p. 450).

Ball (1976-1977) has written of a widow who said she "felt she had no name or label now. She was not a 'wife' or 'housewife' and with no job, it gave her no concept of who she was" (p. 329). In this study, two informants associated the loss of their last parent with the loss of their roots:

> As we were driving home from the funeral, I was crying, closing a part of my life, leaving the history, the people, closing the door on my childhood. I can never go back to my childhood. (Lynn H.)

> What upsets me the most is that there is no future [for the family]. My mother, father and brother are all dead. In addition, the past is gone. There is no one alive who remembers me as a child, no one to reminisce with. (Nadia R.)

New Consumer Roles. New roles often require new consumer knowledge. Widows may be forced to assume responsibility for home and car repairs, whereas widowers may have to learn new parenting and housekeeping roles (see Gentry et al., in press, for several descriptions of the difficult adjustment to new consumer roles). Two factors hinder the learning process. First, survivors report lower self-esteem and self-efficacy. For instance, Brent N., who lost a son to sudden infant death syndrome (SIDS), reported, "Prior to the death, I was invincible. I could do it. When the baby died, I was a worm." Second, financial distress frequently results from the combination of lost income and large medical and funeral expenses. Survivors often need material forms of social support, whereas the lack of funds may deny them access to resources ranging from housekeeping services to private mental health care. In summary, the stressors associated with identity change and role learning make it more difficult for the bereaved to obtain social support.

The Role of Social Support in Grief

Social support has been conceptualized as a network of relationships that (a) provides continuous support regardless of stress in a person's life, (b) comes into existence during times of stress, or (c) creates perceptions of support that can be activated during times of stress (Wethington & Kessler, 1986). The loss of a loved one disrupts existing social networks and perceptions of potential support, and taboos often inhibit interaction with those networks and creation of new ones. These stressors change the way individuals relate to others and therefore cut off potential support.

MEANINGFUL SOCIAL SUPPORT

The most effective support tends to come from those who share a context of meaning (Albrecht & Adelman, 1987) rather than those with special training; for example, job-related support relieves work stress more effectively than more generalized forms of support (LaRocco, House, & French, 1980). Silver and Wortman (1980, p. 314) have summarized research suggesting that well-intentioned statements can be seen as intrusive, especially when one person tries to help another find meaning in a loss.

Some informants instinctively understood this point. John R. was displeased with his minister's efforts but noted that "you have to have had a similar experience in order to understand." George and Sharon S., who had lost a young son to SIDS, were asked to visit another couple who had also experienced a SIDS death: "We walked into the house, which was full of people we did not know. The couple seemed to sense who we were, and they got up and took us to another room where the four of us talked."

Support groups allow people to seek social support proactively from those who have this shared experience—to create the experiences of George and Sharon S. in a more systematic fashion. Although most of the informants found support groups to be positive, others reported mixed experiences. Susan S., whose daughter was stillborn, gained comfort from contrasting her situation—her health, financial standing, and four remaining children—with support group members who were blind, poor, or childless. In contrast, Greg H. described Ray of Hope, a support group for those grieving suicides, as "just a rehashing of events. . . . It seemed that it was one person trying to outdo another with their own tragedy."

TRADITIONAL NONFAMILY SUPPORT:
CHURCH AND FRIENDS

Traditional forms of nonfamily support had mixed effects. Ann T. reported support from multiple sources: her husband's teaching colleagues "called a lot"; the pastor visited daily; "ladies" from the church brought meals; and both church and employer joined to provide the funeral lunch. At the other extreme, some informants reported gaps in these sources.

Church Support. Church was viewed both as a source of social interaction and as a means of finding meaning in the death. Daniel A., a minister, talked at length about the support from his congregation and the importance of his faith to the reconciliation of his wife's death. Stephanie and Carl W. were attending Mass daily when interviewed 3 months after their son's accidental death; they appreciated both the priest and the church. Janeen N., whose son committed suicide, sees a Christian therapist regularly and finds comfort from reading the Bible and praying.

Other informants expressed disappointment about the support from religious sources. For example, Greg H., whose daughter committed suicide, noted that a visiting pastor from Germany "did a nice job on the service and the message to the young people. The other pastors were too busy. Here's the church and where was the support?"

Friendships. In the past, the bulk of support came from family and friends:

> Neighbors and friends customarily prepared food for the widow and her children. In addition, they temporarily, and for fairly specified periods, take over other daily functions, such as shopping and children. . . . These rituals symbolize that the society is involved in the individual's crisis, and thus convey to the individual that he or she is not alone in this trying period. (Lipman-Blumen, 1976, pp. 248-249)

Similarly, Jim D., a university counselor, recalled that, "Years ago, neighbors would come into the home while the family was at the funeral and clean up the room of the departed." Yet the norms of friendship appear to be changing. John S., a professor of death and dying, said, "We have friends, but they seem to come and go, and therefore, when we need a good friend we may not have one to rely on."

Other writers have noted this increasing alienation associated with mobility and displacement from extended families (Lofland, 1973). Arnould, Price, and Walker (1994) have noted that in postmodern society, the absence of authority and continuity provided by tradition creates a need to search for a sense of cohesion and integration. Community is no longer a viable source of identity. Even when family and friends come for the funeral, they return home after a few days. Yet the larger community lacks effective available resources that can replace the family. To some extent, the workplace fills the gap. Cathleen R., recovering from a grandson's SIDS death, felt "lucky, as I have excellent co-workers who have been through death and dying courses." Other employers offered support by supplying professional services. Greg H. appreciated the one-on-one counseling available through his Employee Assistance Program (EAP). Bonnie W. said her husband's company was wonderful; an attorney from the company helped her understand and invest money from a profit-sharing plan. The trend of recommending professionals is reflected in the individual choices of the bereaved, who often look for support among commercial providers rather than among personal sources.

Commercial Service Providers

Service providers can find themselves in caregiving roles simply because they are accessible:

Urban agents include those nonprofessionals who are involved in less formal helping relationships. . . . Their roles within the community put them in key positions to offer direct help to troubled people or at least to serve a liaison function to appropriate professional agencies. Potential urban agents are such people as shopkeepers, foremen, taxicab drivers, bartenders and beauticians. (Gershon & Biller, 1977, p. 80)

Just as the workplace offers ritualized interactions and activities with familiar people, the marketplace offers opportunities for people to enact familiar social roles and experience self-efficacy (Mehrabian, 1976).

When the consumer turns to services as substitute friends, the relationship becomes problematic (Goodwin, 1994). Despite a resemblance to family and friendship, the core service ultimately represents a commercial transaction for which immediate monetary payment is expected. Thus, not surprisingly, the response of providers has been reported as both supportive and dysfunctional. As noted elsewhere in the literature, the type of support was generally related to the service provider's business. For instance, McAlexander et al. (1993) have reported the experience of a divorced woman who asked for a scalp massage to experience touch. Bartenders and hairdressers provide supportive interaction in a relaxed environment (Cowen et al., 1979; Cowen, McKim, & Weissberg, 1981).

Implications for Public Policy

As service providers assume support functions traditionally performed by friends and family, the problematic aspects of the relationship can create further distress for the bereaved consumer. There is a need both to protect the emotionally impaired from commercial sources of stress and to provide resources to enhance the consumer's well-being. Our research offers direction to policymakers who seek to achieve these goals.

1. Understand the grief process. There is a need to educate the general population about the realities of grief and mourning, particularly because the bereaved interact with strangers in commercial settings as they attempt to resolve their grief. The increasing use of support groups suggests the need for lay people to obtain knowledge so they will not dismiss the lingering pain of the bereaved and encourage them to "get on with it." Those who make policy need to be aware of the unique needs of the bereaved.

First, vulnerability is temporary but it is incapacitating. The pain is real and takes many forms. Second, people withdraw and seem unresponsive to others. Therefore, what appears to be insensitivity or lack of gratitude can be an expression of deep pain. Loss of sensitivity to others may be a frequent aftereffect of stress (Cohen, 1980). Third, recovery time varies widely. The definition of adjustment is especially difficult in the absence of normative data. Silver and Wortman (1980) have found that women were often viewed as maladjusted when they reported coping difficulties 6 months after a rape, but in fact 25% of rape victims do not feel recovered for as long as 4 to 6 years later.

It is important to question the myth that time heals all wounds; some people struggle with events for years, especially when the event has significance or they have trouble finding meaning in the event (Tait & Silver, 1989). The experiences reported here suggest that people will have trouble being reconciled: "When a meaningful and acceptable interpretation is not forthcoming, the search may persist for extended time periods, contributing to ongoing cognitive and emotional involvement in the event" (Tait & Silver, 1989, p. 355).

2. Recognize the needs of the bereaved and the lack of institutional support. People may be advised to "get some help" when in fact sources of help are unavailable, expensive, and/or stigmatized. Our study supports previous reports identifying the substantial material and psychological needs of the bereaved. When the community fails to provide resources to meet those needs, bereaved consumers will turn to commercial service providers who may lack training or ethics. Cowen et al. (1979, 1981) have found that considerably more people sought help from hairdressers and bartenders than from professional counselors; similar stigma-free (Albrecht & Adelman, 1987) sources also were chosen by the bereaved in this study. Support groups, an employee's EAP, and a Christian therapist were the only professionalized support services mentioned. Therefore, we suggest that policy groups recognize the importance of commercial sources as a supplement to professionals.

3. Recognize the mental health implications of services as sources of support.
There is evidence that firms and industries explicitly recognize their
role as support for the bereaved. Levine (1992) noted that funeral
directors are expanding their roles to become grief specialists, by
providing comforting calls to bereaved family members after the
burial and on holidays. Sales representatives for an insurance firm are
taught to contact the bereaved immediately, encourage them to avoid
quick decisions, and wait at least 2 weeks before presenting new
investment options (Jason N., a vice president of marketing at an
insurance firm). A county sheriff reported informal policies for dealing with parents of SIDS death infants:

> People are in a state of shock and very little is recalled. We try to provide
> information to them of a helpful nature. We offer an opportunity to
> have us come back and fill in the missing pieces at some later point in
> time. (Tim C.)

Some mental health professionals advocate even more explicit
attention to the emotional needs of the bereaved. Gold (1983) has
suggested that lawyers need to learn to tolerate emotional expression,
that providers need to be sensitized to distressed clients who "at times
will transfer their resentment to the lawyer, and lawyers should accept
this as part of their jobs" (p. 141). Gramlich (1974) has made almost
identical recommendations for doctors; we suggest that all service
personnel need such training.

Other mental health professionals have expressed concerns about
the ability to provide this support. Bissonette (1977) has noted that
bartenders often function as mental health "gatekeepers" who provide referrals to more conventional sources. Yet he cautions, "It is
evidently risky to employ an individual for crisis intervention or
similarly delicate kinds of activities who has not been thoroughly
socialized in such things as professional ethics and confidentiality" (p.
98). Barbieri (1981) quotes a skeptical psychotherapist who claims
that the concern of service providers arises from a desire for larger
tips.

There is evidence that service providers recognize the seriousness
of their roles. Barbieri (1981) has described a bartender who is careful

to refer troubled customers to a pastor or rabbi, and a massage therapist who expressed uncertainty as to how to handle a client crying on her table following the suicidal death of her daughter. The massage therapist discussed plans to study psychology to help her clients more effectively. Training programs and guidelines have been established to assist bartenders (Bissonette, 1977; Hunt, 1972; Miller, 1973) and hairdressers (Wiesenfeld & Weis, 1979).

In summary, distressed consumers will turn to service providers for support, regardless of the attitudes of mental health professionals. Cowen et al. (1979) have emphasized the importance of understanding the way these "de facto help-giving mechanisms" enhance "society's total help-giving effort" (p. 647). Rather than repudiate these consumer choices, Cowen et al. (1981) have urged professionals to "strengthen the frontline contribution of support systems and informal caregivers" (p. 728).

At the same time, the informality of these service interactions makes them difficult to regulate. Therefore, we suggest that policy makers continue to develop and support voluntary educational programs that will sensitize providers to the needs of consumers, particularly stressed consumers such as the bereaved. There seems to be greater harm from dysfunctional interactions than from well-meaning providers who offer support.

We observed that, in some cases, service providers added to the pain faced by the bereaved. As she returned from the funeral, newly widowed Joy Y. was served by a sheriff's deputy with a judgment of $18,000 for charges from a local medical institution. Stephanie and Carl W. mentioned that the insurance policy on their son's life was paid promptly, but the representative who delivered the payment tried to sell them an annuity. Adding to their pain, their son's workplace insurance firm questioned the verdict of accidental death; a representative approached the couple at the grave site immediately after the funeral to discuss the situation. Writing in the *New York Times,* Ginsburg (1990) poignantly described her experience as a newly widowed consumer. As a solo consumer, she was offered inferior accommodations and treatment, as providers considered her half of an incomplete couple rather than an individual in her own right.

Conclusion

When a death occurs, those in grief need social support. Yet increasingly, such support is difficult to obtain in our society, in which families and friends are separated by distance and divorce. Professional mental health services are often expensive, difficult to find, and stigmatized. It is likely that commercial service providers will play an increasing role in helping people deal with the psychological aspects of bereavement, just as they help with other psychological problems. We argue that the marketing system must expand its ethical and legal awareness to incorporate these new realities and responsibilities.

References

Adelman, M., Ahuvia, A., & Goodwin, C. (1994). Beyond smiling: Social support and service quality. In R. Roland & R. Oliver (Eds.), *Service quality: New directions in theory and practice*. Thousand Oaks, CA: Sage.

Albrecht, T., & Adelman, M. B. (1987). Communicating social support: A theoretical perspective. In T. Albrecht, M. B. Adelman, & Associates (Eds.), *Communicating social support* (pp. 18-39). Newbury Park, CA: Sage.

Aries, P. (1974). *Western attitudes toward death: From the middle ages to the present* (P. M. Ranum, Trans.). Baltimore, MD: Johns Hopkins University Press.

Arnould, E. J., Price, L. L., & Walker, B. (1994, August). *Questing for self and community in postmodernity through consumption*. Paper presented at the MacroMarketing Conference, Boulder, CO.

Ball, J. F. (1976-1977). Widow's grief: The impact of age and mode of death. *Omega: The Journal of Death and Dying, 7,* 307-333.

Barbieri, S. M. (1981, December 8). Shrinks who work for tips. *Chicago Tribune,* Section 5, p. 12.

Bissonette, R. (1977). The bartender as a mental health service gatekeeper: A role analysis. *Community Mental Health Journal, 13*(Spring), 92-99.

Bowman, L. (1959). *The American funeral: A study in guilt, extravagance and subliminality*. Washington, DC: Public Affairs Press.

Cohen, S. (1980). Aftereffects of stress on human performance and social behavior: A review of research and theory. *Psychological Bulletin, 88,* 82-108.

Cowen, E. L., Gesten, E. L., Boike, M., Norton, P., Wilson, A. B., & DeStefano, M. A. (1979). Hairdressers as caregivers: A descriptive profile of interpersonal help-giving involvements. *American Journal of Community Psychology, 7,* 633-648.

Cowen, E. L., McKim, B. J., & Weissberg, R. P. (1981). Bartenders as informal, interpersonal help agents. *American Journal of Community Psychology, 9,* 715-729.

Gentry, J. W., Kennedy, P. F., Paul, C., & Hill, R. P. (in press). Family transitions during grief: Discontinuities in household consumption. *Journal of Business Research*.

Gentry, J. W., Kennedy, P. F., Paul, C., & Hill, R. P. (1995). The vulnerability of those grieving the death of a loved one: Implications for public policy. *Journal of Public Policy & Marketing, 14*(1), 128-142.

Gershon, M., & Biller, H. B. (1977). The urban agents. In *The other helpers: Paraprofessionals and nonprofessionals in mental health* (pp. 79-84). Lexington, MA: Lexington Books/D. C. Heath.

Ginsburg, G. D. (1990, December 2). Hers: Life after death. *New York Times Magazine*, p. 34.

Gold, G. M. (1983). True counselors: Helping clients deal with loss. *ABA Journal, 69*(February), 141.

Goodwin, C. (1994, May). *Private roles in public encounters: Communal relationships in service exchanges.* Paper presented at the Third International Research Seminar in Services Management, Institut d'Adminstration des Entreprise, University d'Aix-Marseille, France.

Gramlich, E. P. (1974). Recognition and management of grief in elderly patients. In J. Ellard, V. D. Volkan, & N. L. Paul (Eds.), *Normal and pathological responses to bereavement* (pp. 186-202). New York: MSS Information Corporation.

Hunt, W. J. (1972). *Training program for bartenders as mental health referral agents: Preliminary report.* Milwaukee, WI: Milwaukee County Mental Health Assn.

LaRocco, J., House, J., & French, J., Jr. (1980). Social support, occupational stress and health. *Journal of Health and Social Behavior, 21*, 202-219.

Levine, J. (1992, May 11)). Cash and bury. *Forbes*, pp. 162-166.

Lipman-Blumen, J. (1976). A crisis perspective on divorce and role change. In J. R. Chapman & M. Gates (Eds.), *Women into wives: The legal and economic impact of marriage* (Sage Yearbook in Women's Policy Studies, Vol. 2). Beverly Hills, CA: Sage.

Lofland, L. H. (1973). *A world of strangers: Order and action in urban public space.* New York: Basic Books.

Lofland, L. H. (1982). Loss and human connection: An exploration into the nature of the social bond. In W. Ickes & E. S. Knowles (Eds.), *Personality, roles, and social behavior* (pp. 219-242). New York: Springer.

Maynes, E. S. (1976). *Decision making for consumers: An introduction to consumer economics.* New York: Macmillan.

McAlexander, J. H., Schouten, J. W., & Roberts, S. D. (1993). Consumer behavior and divorce. *Research in Consumer Behavior, 6*, 231-260.

Mehrabian, A. (1976). *Public places and private spaces.* New York: Basic Books.

Miller, H. (1973). *A mental health education program for North Dakota's beverage handlers.* Bismarck: North Dakota Mental Health Association.

Rodgers, B. L., & Cowles, K. V. (1991). The concept of grief: An analysis of classical and contemporary thought. *Death Studies, 15*, 443-458.

Shilling, C. (1993). *The body and social theory.* London: Sage.

Sillars, A. L., & Kalbflesch, P. J. (1988). Implicit and explicit decision-making styles in couples. In D. Brinberg & J. Jaccard (Eds.), *Dyadic decision making* (pp. 179-214). New York: Springer.

Silver, R. L., & Wortman, C. B. (1980). Coping with undesirable life events. In J. Garber & M. E. P. Seligman (Eds.), *Human helplessness: Theory and applications* (pp. 279-340). New York: Academic Press.

Simmons, M. G. (1975). Funeral practices and public awareness. *Human Ecology Forum, 5*(Winter), 9-13.

Stone, G. P. (1954). City shoppers and urban identification: Observations on the social psychology of city life. *American Journal of Sociology, 60*(July), 36-45.

Tait, R., & Silver, R. C. (1989). Coming to terms with major negative life events. In J. S. Uleman & J. A. Bargh (Eds.), *Unintended thought* (pp. 351-381). London: Guilford.

Thompson, C. J., Locander, W. B., & Pollio, H. R. (1989). Putting consumer experience back into consumer research: The philosophy and method of existential-phenomenology. *Journal of Consumer Research, 16,* 133-146.

Thompson, S. C., & Spacapan, S. (1991). Perceptions of control in vulnerable populations. *Journal of Social Issues, 47*(4), 1-21.

Wethington, E., & Kessler, R. C. (1986). Perceived support, received support, and adjustment to stressful life events. *Journal of Health and Social Behavior, 27*(March), 78-89.

Wiesenfeld, A. R., & Weis, H. M. (1979). Hairdressers and helping: Influencing the behavior of informal caregivers. *Professional Psychology, 10,* 786-792.

5

Marketing and the Poor

LINDA F. ALWITT

EXCHANGE IS a basic concept of marketing. When each party to an exchange has something the other party or parties value, they can carry out a transaction that satisfies their needs and wants (Kotler, 1994). In marketing, the concept of exchange is useful in describing exchanges between businesses and consumers or other businesses, and between nonprofit organizations and their constituencies (Kotler, 1982). Some people, however, want to be a party to marketing exchanges but consistently lack things of value to exchange. I am referring to poor people. For poor people, the marketing exchange is generally unbalanced in favor of the marketer. One of the results of this imbalance in marketing exchanges for many products and services is that poor people pay more for goods and services (Hudson, 1993; Troutt, 1993) and are not offered the variety available to more affluent members of society. Another result is that they are not part of the mainstream community and are often treated as "strangers" who are outside society. Their status as strangers causes them to suffer

AUTHOR'S NOTE: A grant from the Kellstadt Center for Marketing Planning and Analysis of DePaul University to support some of this work is gratefully acknowledged.

disadvantages both in their market dealings and in their other relationships to society. Hence, the imbalance in the marketing exchange
increases the alienation and separation of poor people from the
mainstream society.

> I see them walk by every day. I like the pretty white stockings and the
> gym shoes and the purse and umbrella. The downtown people—they
> got money and self-esteem. Sometimes they look tired. They probably
> feel good about themselves. They're working and getting paid. They
> don't have to wait on no aid check or no man. (Recent high school
> graduate, one of 150 from a starting class of 500, quoted in Wilkerson,
> 1994, p. A9.)[1]

At the same time, for-profit marketers face ethical conflicts when
they carry out transactions with poor consumers. For-profit marketers
face demands from diverse sectors: their firms, including the corporate culture, philosophy, economic status, and demands of supervisors
and stockholders; their personal situations, ranging from personal
ambitions to personal economic situations and values; and societal
expectations about the behavior of for-profit firms and the individual
members of society. These demands are not always consistent in
guiding actions, which results in ethical conflicts for the marketer to
poor consumers.

This chapter presents some of the evidence that there is an imbalance of exchange between poor consumers and for-profit marketers,
describes marketer conflicts, and offers both a general and a specific
approach to more equitably balancing this exchange. Specifically, this
chapter presents two examples of the extent of the inequitable balance of marketing exchange between for-profit marketers and poor
consumers; discusses ethical conflicts faced by for-profit marketers
when they enter into transactions with poor consumers; presents a
marketing exchange model that includes poor consumers and for-
profit marketers; uses ethical foundations for exchange and the marketing exchange model to develop ways to more equitably balance the
exchange with poor consumers; and explores one implication in
detail as an example of how ethical foundations of exchange can be
used to more equitably balance the marketing exchange between
for-profit marketers and poor consumers.

Perspective From the Past

Although marketers have maintained interest in social marketing in the past 20 years (e.g., Fine, 1990; Kotler, 1982), there has been much less interest in marketing issues that concern low-income households. The social consciousness of the 1960s and 1970s was the last major stimulus for a focus on marketing and poor people. It produced excellent books and articles, including Goodman's "Do the Poor Pay More?" (1968), Sturdivant's *The Ghetto Marketplace* (1969), and the superb review of the conceptual and empirical work of that time by Alan Andreasen, *The Disadvantaged Consumer* (1975).

However, numerous changes in the demographic profile of the United States, and in social mores, governmental policies, and the economic environment since the 1970s, have influenced the composition and motivations of poor people. The number of people who become and remain poor has been influenced by changes in federal laws during the Reagan and Bush administrations (Day, 1989); by decreases in government and military jobs, once a popular path out of poverty (Madigan, 1992); by the changed role of women at home and in the workplace; and by the increasing trend of children being born to unmarried women (Day, 1989; DeParle, 1993; Holmes, 1994; Northrup, 1990). In addition, abandonment of urban ghettos by middle-class/ -income households (Raspberry, 1991; Wilson, 1987) has exacerbated urban poverty and the development of that subset called the "underclass." Abandonment of urban centers by manufacturers who use low-skilled labor (Day, 1989; Wilson, 1987) has increased the number of young unemployed urban males. Decreased influence by labor unions (Day, 1989) has contributed to the increased number of low-wage jobs. Changes in banking laws have influenced the way poor people must manage their financial transactions. Among the results of these changes are, for example, that fewer low-income households are headed by an older person and more are headed by single mothers. As a consequence, 38% of children are raised in poverty during some period of their lives ("Many Children," 1992).

The 39.3 million poor people today are 15.1% of the population, the largest number since 1964 (Pear, 1992; "U.S. Loses," 1994). Of those below the government poverty line in 1990, 66% were white,

40% had less than a high school education, and 70% were younger
than 44 years. In about half the households, a householder worked
during the previous year (U.S. Bureau of the Census, 1992).

Evidence of the Imbalance of Exchange
Between Poor Consumers and For-Profit Marketers

Although overall expenditures are obviously lower for poor households than for more affluent ones, poor people consume many of the
same products and services as everyone else. For all households,
expenditures are greatest for housing, food, and transportation, all of
which are nondiscretionary items. For the lowest-income quintile of
households, however, 69% of total expenditures are spent on these
items, whereas for all consumer units, only 57% of the budget is spent
for these items (U.S. Bureau of the Census, 1992, pp. 442-443).

Although numerous examples could be offered in evidence of an
imbalance of exchange between poor consumers and for-profit marketers, there is room for only two in this chapter; they are considered
in detail. The examples are housing and financial management.

HOUSING

Housing needs make up 37% of expenditures for low-income
households and are their largest single expenditure (Ambry, 1993).
Low-income households are more likely to rent than to own homes.
For many people, a sign of financial security is paying 30% or less of
one's income for rent, the average paid in the United States (Ambry,
1993). In 1987, however, 21% of the 32.7 million renter households
paid more than 50% of their income for rental housing, and 12.3%
paid more than 70% (Braus, 1991).

Low-income households that try to own their dwellings often have
more difficulty than more affluent households in financing this investment. This is particularly true for members of minority groups (Thomas,
1992). Mortgage lenders are required by the federal Community
Investment Act regulations to get input from the community in which
they are located and to support community needs (Hixon, 1991), but
they naturally try to reduce their risks. Several factors work against

making loans to low-income mortgage borrowers. First, if the down payment is large (e.g., 20% or more), the lender is more likely to overlook negative credit indicators on the theory that a person with an investment in the property is more likely to keep up the mortgage payments. Many low-income households cannot make large down payments, however, so they do not benefit from a lender's judgment in their favor. Second, even a small loan does not work in favor of a minority or low-income borrower. The lender finds the effort is equal but the profit is lower in making a small versus a large loan, and is therefore biased against making small loans. Third, low-income borrowers may have income that is not easy to verify, such as several jobs or income from boarders. Because these borrowers are atypical, lenders are not willing to take the risk of making a loan. Fourth, Federal Housing Administration (FHA) loans have flexible down payments and are government insured, but they involve so much paperwork that lenders tend to avoid them (Thomas, 1992). Nevertheless, a recent study found that, in Chicago, more African American borrowers for housing mortgages are sent to FHA than to alternative loan sources (Caine, 1993; Stangenes, 1993a). Fifth, low-income households that do not have a relationship with a bank use currency exchanges; lenders look askance at this way of dealing with money. Sixth, the most frequent reason for denial of a mortgage loan is credit history (Stangenes, 1993a). Unpaid debts are more common in low-income households, and when they are paid, it is not uncommon that they may be incorrectly recorded on credit records, which is yet another mark against the borrower.

It has been argued that federal intervention in housing has exacerbated the decline of neighborhoods rather than diminished that decline (Bradford & Cincotta, 1992, p. 233; Caine, 1993). Specifically, when the FHA forecloses on a house bought with its loan, it often abandons the house, lets it decay and be vandalized, and thereby devalues the neighborhood (Caine, 1993). In addition, fair housing laws have not been aggressively applied to banks. The growth of secondary mortgage markets (Federal National Mortgage Association [FNMA or Fannie Mae] and Federal Home Loan Mortgage Corporation [FHLMC or Freddie Mac]), which rely on standardized mortgages, exclude lower income people (Bradford & Cincotta, 1992).

Poor people thus pay more for rental housing and face formidable barriers when they seek other forms of housing. Marketers of housing for low-income households, however, face ethical conflicts. On the one hand, they perceive the financial risks of non-payment of rents or mortgage loans, so they charge high rates or erect other barriers to compensate for these risks. At the same time, there is a limited amount of low-cost housing (Harvey, 1987), so the ratio of supply to demand determines the cost of this housing, which may result in inflated costs. On the other hand, housing suppliers do offer this needed resource to poor consumers, rather than limiting their offerings to higher profit-margin and less risky affluent consumers.

FINANCIAL MANAGEMENT

Financial management includes use of checking and savings accounts, automatic teller machines (ATMs), credit cards, loans, and other ways in which people manage money. Deregulation of financial services in the 1980s made banking too expensive or inconvenient for many people from low-income households. For example, bank fees were raised, minimum balances were often required, and unprofitable branches, many of which were located in low-income neighborhoods, were closed ("They Will Gladly," 1992). There is also evidence that consolidation of banks through mergers has resulted in higher costs to the banking customer (Bradford & Cincotta, 1992). The result of these changes is that 44% of those with annual incomes of less than $15,000 do not use banks (Belew, 1989). Compare that percentage with the 19% of the general population that is "unbanked." To consider it another way, 82% of households without savings or checking accounts earned less than $20,000 (Joyal, 1992). Poor people offer various reasons for being unbanked, ranging from insufficient funds to save to paying high monthly fees to insufficient financial management skills in managing a checkbook (Belew, 1989).

Low-income households have a few other options for financial management. One is to use credit unions, which offer an advantage for low-income people because they require only a low balance and offer high-risk loans. About 21% of low-income households use a credit union. Many low-income householders, however, are simply not aware of credit unions as an alternative financial resource (Joyal, 1992).

A second option is to pay utility bills through a bill collection system such as Easy Pay or National Payments Network Inc. (NPN), both owned by Western Union. These collection systems arrange to collect payments made at neighborhood stores or convenience stores ("Customers Bank on Drugstores," 1991; "The Emerging Entrepreneur," 1990). The utility pays a fee for each utility payment, and the retailer is paid a transaction fee. All parties benefit: For the retailer, customers who pay a bill at the retail store may spend on other goods; customers pay bills conveniently and without a bank account; NPN or Easy Pay makes a profit.

The main financial management option open to poor people, however, is the currency exchange, or check-cashing outlet. These firms offer services for fees—such as cashing checks; issuing money orders; selling postage stamps, food stamps, and lottery tickets; advancing loans on income tax refunds; or doing electronic money transfers. The industry's 1990 fee income was $790 million ("They Will Gladly," 1992). The fees are typically unregulated and vary widely, however: A check cashing fee can be as high as 20%. In Chicago, African Americans and Latinos are more likely to use currency exchanges and less likely to use banks than are other consumers, and 20% of Chicago residents use currency exchanges to pay their bills (Stangenes, 1993b).

The banking industry is under governmental pressure to provide services to the unbanked, but finds it less profitable and more risky than targeting more affluent customers. Efforts to educate low-income consumers about financial management tactics have been somewhat successful in creating responsible use of, for example, a credit card (Bowers & Crosby, 1980). Several banks have successfully offered "limited checking accounts" in branches in low-income neighborhoods (Lunt, 1992).

From a marketer's point of view there are several ethical conflicts. For financial institutions there is a conflict between running a profitable, efficient organization and price discrimination against the poorest portion of the population. For currency exchanges, there is a conflict between the marketing concept of providing a needed service and exploiting the consumers of those services.

Ethical Conflicts for Marketers

In the previous section, some specific ethical conflicts for marketers were described. In this section, I consider how marketing ethics might guide marketers' conflicts in their transactions with poor consumers. For-profit marketers need to be guided by ethical principles because they have responsibilities to multiple sectors: themselves, the corporation for which they work, and society. Demands from these sectors often conflict. Marketers may call upon the two classical bases for ethical behavior, *deontology*, the idea that universal ideals direct our ethical behavior, and *utilitarianism*, the idea that ethical behavior is based on a social cost-benefit analysis that results, for example, in the greatest good for the greatest number (e.g., Robin & Reidenbach, 1987). Rules derived from these bases still offer conflicting guidelines, however, when demands from several sectors of society are considered. An ideal—although probably unrealistic—solution is for marketers to consider a "meta"-ethical principle: "one of the principal justifications of ethical standards in any society is protection against the misuse of power by others" (Robin & Reidenbach, 1993, p. 100).

Gundlach and Murphy (1993) have proposed four ethical foundations for marketing exchanges. They are: *trust* that the parties to an exchange will fulfill their obligations; *equity* of the perceived inputs and outputs by parties to the exchange; *responsibility*, or the obligation of each party to the transaction; *commitment* to the exchange, which implies a willingness to compromise and to amortise the benefits derived from the exchange over more than a single transaction.

All four of these foundations are unbalanced in exchanges between marketers and poor consumers. Marketers do not trust that poor consumers have sufficient resources to pay for goods or services, whereas poor consumers do not trust that they will receive the quality of goods or services for which they exchange their limited funds. This may be part of the reason that in the Los Angeles riots, retail stores owned by people perceived to have offered unfair exchanges with the residents were destroyed but other stores were spared (e.g., Boyer & Ford, 1992; Chua, 1994). Sellers do not value what poor consumers offer for exchange, so they sometimes extract other, nonmonetary, input to obtain what they perceive to be an equitable exchange. For example, poor blood donors were treated less courteously than were more affluent blood donors. This was probably because the staff perceived middle-class donors as engaging in a voluntary charitable act, whereas they perceived the low-income donors as pursuing a personal necessity—payment. As a result, the staff of blood donation centers demean poor blood donors, demanding passivity and compliance and requiring long periods of waiting as though poor people's time is not valuable (Kretzmann, 1992). A societal motivation has more "exchange value" in this context than does a personal motivation, so extra "value," in the form of psychologically demeaning poor donors, is extracted.

Because poor people are not part of the "real" society, marketers may not feel obligated to carry out their part of the exchange. For example, when a food stamp user noted that supermarket cashiers replenish their supply of change when they discover he is using food stamps, another customer noted that this is the way they exact an additional exchange value (Rank, 1994). Finally, marketers to poor consumers do not seem to have a commitment to maintaining the poor consumer as a long-term customer. They often act as though they are unaware that most poor people are only temporarily in poverty. In fact, it is cost-effective for marketers to encourage them to be brand-loyal.

The point of discussing marketing ethics is to indicate that marketers are not villains in their marketing exchanges with poor consumers. Rather, they often must select, and sometimes compromise, among demands that create ethical conflicts. These conflicts must be resolved by compromising between short- and long-term benefits and losses, and between direct personal and indirect societal benefits and losses. It is here proposed that a revised marketing exchange model, together with consideration of ethical bases of exchange, can lead to actions that strengthen the exchange balance more in favor of poor consumers.

Marketing Exchange Model and Revision
When Poor Consumers Are a Party to an Exchange

Marketing exchange requires that each party has something different to exchange and that the exchange will result in adding value or "potency" to the resources of each of the parties (Alderson, 1965, cited in Houston, Gassenheimer, & Maskulka, 1992, p. 10). That is, all parties must benefit from the exchange. In addition, potency is not only derived from the goods or services exchanged, but also from the act of exchanging. That is, there are psychological consequences to an exchange act (Bagozzi, 1979), such as feeling good about having made a good bargain. Further, the potency of the outcome of an exchange may extend beyond the immediate exchange transaction and offer benefits over time (Houston et al., 1992), as in relationship marketing (Gundlach & Murphy, 1993). Exchange is an ethical ele-ment in our lives because it is a necessary, though not a sufficient, condition for community (Koehn, 1992). This point, made by Aris-totle, holds because no person in a society is self-sufficient, so we obtain the things we do not have by exchange with others. The act of exchange requires relationships with other people, and relationships lead to community, the precondition for society (Koehn, 1992). Most important, people who do not participate in an exchange because they have nothing to exchange that is of value to others are isolated from the community and treated like strangers. This is the condition of poor people. The imbalance in exchanges between poor consumers and other parties not only affects their economic situations, but also their social relationships with the rest of society.

The traditional and simplest view of exchange is of that between two parties, most often a buyer and a seller. As Bagozzi (1975) has noted, however, social marketing exchange transactions often include more than one party. Even though Bagozzi's model of the social marketing exchange applies to social rather than economic relation-ships, such as between a social worker and a poor person, it includes the key components. It is here revised to include exchanges with for-profit marketers.

Figure 5.1 shows a revised marketing exchange model that includes poor consumers and for-profit marketers. Society pays taxes to gov-ernment and donations to social service agencies, government pro-vides welfare, and social agencies provide services to poor people. As Bagozzi has pointed out, by providing welfare and services to poor people, government and social services give the rest of society protec-tion against other means by which poor people could obtain what they need (such as taking it), carry out the social obligation individuals have toward the society in which they live, and offer reassurance that,

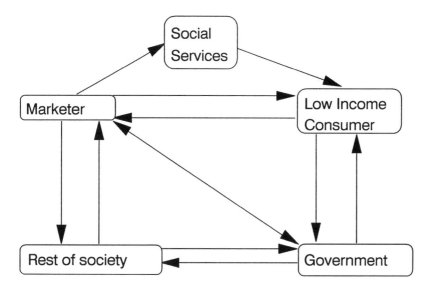

Figure 5.1. Revised Model of Marketing Exchange With Poor Consumers and For-Profit Marketers

if it is needed in the future (or has been needed in the past), a safety net is available for people without the means to enter the exchange alone. In addition, government can regulate marketers and reduce marketer risks in transactions with poor consumers. The more affluent sectors of society can, by their purchases, enable marketers to carry out social marketing that can be used to benefit the poor directly. Nevertheless, the exchange between marketer and poor consumer may be unbalanced unless the paths among the components of the model are used to find ways to make this exchange more equitable.

Public and Social Policy Implications: General

One goal pursued in this chapter is that of finding ways to enhance the ethical foundations of exchange for parties to marketing exchanges that include poor consumers. Table 5.1 shows five approaches to reducing the imbalance in exchanges that involve marketers and poor consumers, and the ethical foundation of exchange they are likely to increase.

TABLE 5.1 Five Public and Social Policy Implications to Equalize the
Balance in Marketing Exchanges With Poor Consumers

Implication	Ethical Foundation
1. Increase what poor consumers have to exchange	Equity
2. Increase the exchange power of poor consumers	Commitment, equity
3. Decrease the exchange power of marketers	Equity
4. Alter what marketers have to exchange	Equity
5. Reduce the risk perceived by marketers	Responsibility, trust

One approach is for regulators to *increase what poor consumers have
to exchange*. This approach has been used primarily by government
entitlement programs for poor people that were mainly initiated
during President Johnson's War on Poverty in the late 1960s (Mead,
1992). Some poor consumers may exchange food stamps for consu-
mables; single mothers may obtain WIC foods for their children under
age 5; Aid to Families with Dependent Children (AFDC) can be used
to obtain housing, transportation, clothing, and other necessities of
life; housing subsidies can be exchanged for shelter and Medicaid for
health care. It has been argued that this method of balancing the
exchange between poor consumers and marketers may lead to disin-
centives for poor people to find other means of obtaining objects to
exchange, such as working to earn money (Mead, 1992; Murphy,
1994). It has also been demonstrated that welfare benefits the poor.
One example is that nutritional needs of eligible nonrecipients of
food stamps are not as well met as are those of recipients (Bishop,
Formby, & Zeager, 1992).

A second approach is for government regulators or social service
agencies to *increase the exchange power* of poor consumers. One way to
increase the exchange power of poor consumers is to allow and
encourage the poor to take more responsibility for how, when, and
what they exchange. For example, some states are experimenting with
"cashing out" food stamp programs. They allow purchases by food
stamps to be determined by the recipient ("Debate Stirs," 1994).
Other experimental programs substitute electronic entitlement transfers similar to a debit card to poor people who are eligible for food
stamps. This program has the potential to reduce poor peoples' need
for more costly currency exchanges. This approach also can increase

the exchange power of poor consumers by requiring that they take greater responsibility for budgeting their resources. Another way for poor consumers to increase their power in exchanges with marketers is to take advantage of an approach long used by businesses—saving by buying in quantity (discussed in the final section).

A third approach is to *decrease the exchange power of the marketer.* The marketer's advantage in exchange situations can be controlled by implicit societal mores, explicit governmental regulation, or explicit societal pressure. For example, outright violations of the laws of exchange, such as not delivering goods that have been paid for, are clearly unacceptable to society and are illegal. Unethical practices in advertising and in marketing of goods and services are controlled by numerous regulations at the federal, state, and local levels. An example of social pressure to decrease the exchange power of marketers is the removal from the market of Uptown cigarettes, a brand targeted to low-income African Americans, by R. J. Reynolds after vociferous complaints from the community (Ramirez, 1990).

A fourth approach is to *alter what marketers have to exchange.* As markets mature, competition for market share frequently demands that products and services offer added value to the consumer (Park, Jaworski, & MacInnis, 1986). As a result, products or services that initially offered just functional value are subsequently marketed in a range of varieties, but the enhancements may diminish in their *incremental* value to the consumer. These enhancements often raise the cost of the product or service. Many product categories in the United States are in the mature stage, and it is often difficult to find models that offer the basic functional value. Marketers who offer functional, no-frills products or services at a fair price would be welcomed by low-income consumers as well as by more affluent consumers. This is an underexplored marketing opportunity.

A fifth approach is for regulators to *reduce the risk perceived by marketers* when they enter into exchanges with poor consumers. This approach includes establishing enterprise zones to reduce taxes for businesses that locate in low-income neighborhoods or waive regulations like zoning laws to encourage marketing exchanges with poor consumers. For example, baby food manufacturers vie for contracts with states to provide WIC brands to mothers of young infants and children. The reduced risk to the firms is that their sales are guaranteed for a specified time period. In addition, they gain profit and they have an opportunity to create brand-loyal consumers (Gibson, 1993). That is, although most people receive welfare for a very short time (e.g., Rank, 1994), once exposed to a brand, they are more likely to buy that familiar brand in the future when they are no longer WIC recipients.

Public and Social Policy Implication:
Small Buying Groups as an Example

One approach to a more equitable balance of the exchange between poor consumers and for-profit marketers is to increase the power of poor consumers. A way to accomplish this is by buying in quantity. Poor consumers, with their limited funds, are usually unable to stockpile products and, indeed, there is evidence that they purchase smaller quantities than do more affluent consumers (Kalyanam & Putler, 1994). If poor consumers were organized into small buying groups, however, they would be able to buy larger quantities, which are generally offered at a lower cost. Further, they would have more power in a marketing exchange. As an entity that purchases large quantities on a regular basis, they would be more profitable, and offer less risk and lower transaction costs to the marketer. There are also advantages to the members of a small buying group: cost savings for each member of the group; enhanced bargaining power; social and emotional support; learning from each other; and practicing interpersonal and decision-making skills. Small buying groups can be formed by poor consumers on their own, or they can be facilitated by regulators or social service agencies. The benefit of these groups for society is lower costs of goods and services to the poor. In addition, because this system demands that each individual take responsibility for the group's actions, it allows responsible societal habits to be learned or practiced. Finally, because the group reinforces the responsibility practiced by its members by group pressure, risk of failure is reduced for the sponsors. Success not only increases the self-esteem of individual members of a group, it also offers them a place within the community, and reduces the burden of support from the government. Small buying groups can be modeled on the "borrowing circles" introduced in Bangladesh by economist Mohammad Yunus, who founded the Grameen Bank (Kamaludden, 1993; Montemayor, 1993). This bank offers funds to groups of five women for business projects. Every member of the borrowing circle is responsible for repayment of the loan. If it is not repaid, none of the five can apply for another loan. The amount of the first loan is small, but if it is paid back, subsequent loans can be larger. This model has been adopted by organizations in several other nations including the United States, such as the Good Faith Fund in Arkansas and the Full Circle Fund of the Women's Self-Employment Project in Chicago (Welles, 1994; Zehr, 1992).

One of the key features of this model in all countries is that it has been limited to women because women are considered more financially responsible. Indeed, it has been reported (Carrington, 1994; Montemayor, 1993) that the loan repayment rate is exceptionally high in the United States and other nations. One reason it may work well for women may be that women's ethical behavior differs from men's (Gilligan, 1977; Gilligan & Attanucci, 1988). Because women tend to have a more interpersonal and caring perspective than do men, they tend to focus more on moral and ethical conflicts in terms of their effects on other people. For this reason, women who take responsibility as members of a group are likely to be particularly sensitive to the effects of ethical actions on the other members of the group (Eagly & Wood, 1991).

Because households headed by women constitute a disproportionately large segment of poor households, the small buying group approach to increasing the exchange power of poor consumers should have a high potential for success. It may also be readily adopted by poor women: It has been reported that group buying has been self-organized by borrowing circles in Chicago (Women's Self Employment Project, personal communication, June 13, 1994).

Note

1. Copyright © 1994 by The New York Times Company. Reprinted by permission.

References

Alderson, W. (1965). *Dynamic marketing behavior.* Homewood, IL: Richard D. Irwin.

Ambry, M. (1993). *The official guide to household spending* (2nd ed.). Ithaca, NY: New Strategist.

Andreasen, A. R. (1975). *The disadvantaged consumer.* New York: Free Press.

Bagozzi, R. P. (1975). Marketing as exchange. *Journal of Marketing, 39*(October), 32-39.

Bagozzi, R. P. (1979). Toward a formal theory of marketing exchanges. In O. C. Ferrel, S. W. Brown, & C. W. Lamb, Jr. (Eds.), *Conceptual and theoretical developments in marketing* (pp. 431-447). Chicago: American Marketing Association.

Belew, J. (1989). The unbanked. *Journal of Retail Banking, 6*(4), 55-56.

Bishop, J. A, Formby, J. P., & Zeager, L. A. (1992). Nutrition and nonparticipation in the U.S. food stamp program. *Applied Economics, 24,* 945-949.

Bowers, J. S., & Crosby, K. (1980). Changes in the credit repayment performance of low income consumers: An exploratory study. *The Journal of Consumer Affairs, 14*(1), 96-108.

Boyer, E. J., & Ford, A. (1992, May 8). Black-owned businesses pay a heavy price. *Los Angeles Times,* pp. A1, A5.

Bradford, C., & Cincotta, G. (1992). The legacy, the promise, and the unfinished agenda. In G. D. Squires (Ed.), *From redlining to reinvestment* (pp. 228-286). Philadelphia: Temple University Press.

Braus, P. (1991, November). One paycheck from the poorhouse. *American Demographics, 13*(11), p. 4.

Caine, P. (1993, January). The dream that died. *Chicago Reporter,* pp. 3-7, 13.

Carrington, T. (1994, June 22). In developing world, international lenders are targeting women. *Wall Street Journal,* p. A1.

Chua, L. (1994, April 25). Opening up for business. *Los Angeles Times,* pp. D1, D2.

Customers bank on drugstores when paying utility bills. (1991, May 6). *Drug Topics,* p. 86.

Day, P. J. (1989, May). The new poor in America: Isolationism in an international political economy. *Social Work,* pp. 227-233.

Debate stirs as states "cash out" food stamps. (1994, March 8). *Chicago Tribune,* Section 1, p. 3.

DeParle, J. (1993, March 2). Food stamp users up sharply in sign of weak recovery. *New York Times,* pp. A1, A18.

Eagly, A. H., & Wood, W. (1991). Explaining sex differences in social behavior: A meta-analytic perspective. *Personality and Social Psychology Bulletin, 17,* 306-315.

The emerging entrepreneur. (1990, January). *Inc.,* pp. 59-62.

Fine, S. H. (1990). *Social marketing: Promoting the causes of public and nonprofit agencies.* Boston: Allyn & Bacon.

Gibson, R. (1993, March 29). U.S. aid plan for poor helps big food firms. *Wall Street Journal,* pp. B1, B6.

Gilligan, C. (1977, November). In a different voice: Women's conceptions of self and of morality. *Harvard Educational Review, 47*(4), 481-517.

Gilligan, C., & Attanucci, J. (1988). Two moral orientations. In C. Gilligan, J. V. Ward, J. M. Taylor, & B. Bardige (Eds.), *Mapping the moral domain* (pp. 73-86). Cambridge, MA: Harvard University Press.

Goodman, C. (1968). Do the poor pay more?. *Journal of Marketing, 32*(January), 18-24.

Gundlach, G. T., & Murphy, P. E. (1993). Ethical and legal foundations of relational marketing exchanges. *Journal of Marketing, 57*(October), 35-46.

Harvey, F. B., III. (1987). The Enterprise Foundation approach to financing housing for poverty-level families. *The Real Estate Finance Journal*, pp. 44-48.

Hixon, R. M. (1991, May). Building business. *Mortgage Banking*, pp. 5, 35-39.

Holmes, S. A. (1994, July 20). Birthrate for unwed women up 70% since '83, study says. *New York Times*, p. A1.

Houston, F. S., Gassenheimer, J. B., & Maskulka, J. M. (1992). *Marketing exchange transactions and relationships*. Westport, CT: Quorum.

Hudson, M. (1993). How the poor pay more: Big premiums on big ticket items. *Business and Society Review, 85*, 43-46.

Joyal, V. (1992). The low-income household. *Credit Union Executive, 32*(2), 37-43.

Kalyanam, K., & Putler, D. S. (1994). *A consistent framework for incorporating demographic variables in brand choice models*. Unpublished manuscript. (Available from Kirthi Kalyanam, Department of Marketing, Santa Clara University, Santa Clara, CA)

Kamaludden, S. (1993, March 18). Lender with a mission. *Far Eastern Economic Review, 156*(11), 38-40.

Koehn, D. (1992). Toward an ethic of exchange. *Business Ethics Quarterly, 2*(3), 341-355.

Kotler, P. (1982). *Marketing for nonprofit organizations*. Englewood Cliffs, NJ: Prentice Hall .

Kotler, P. (1994). *Marketing management* (8th ed.). Englewood Cliffs, NJ: Prentice Hall.

Kretzmann, M. J. (1992). Bad blood: The moral stigmatization of paid plasma donors. *Journal of Contemporary Ethnography, 4*(January), 416-441.

Lunt, P. (1992, September). How seven banks serve low income markets. *ABA Banking Journal*, pp. 57-66.

Madigan, C. M. (1992, May 13). Racial stereotyping: An old, virulent virus. *Chicago Tribune*, Section 1, pp. 1, 4-6.

Many children are poor, but few chronically so. (1992, July 29). *Wall Street Journal*, p. B1.

Mead, L. M. (1992). *The new politics of poverty*. New York: Basic Books.

Miller, C. (1994, January 17). Rediscovering the inner city. *Marketing News, 28*, p. 1.

Montemayor, B. T. (1993, March). Banking on the poor. *Far Eastern Economic Review, 156*(10), p. 29.

Murphy, D. J. (1994, July 18). The jaws of the welfare trap. *Investor's Business Daily, 69*, pp. 1-2.

Northrup, E. M. (1990, March). The feminization of poverty: The demographic factor and the composition of economic growth. *Journal of Economic Issues, 24*(1), 145-160.

Park, C. W., Jaworski, B. J., & MacInnis, D. J. (1986). Strategic brand concept-image management. *Journal of Marketing, 50*(October), 135-145.

Pear, R. (1992, September 4). Ranks of U.S. poor reach 35.7 million, the most since '64. *New York Times*, p. A1.

Ramirez, A. (1990, January 12). A cigarette campaign under fire. *New York Times*, p. D1.

Rank, M. R. (1994). *Living on the edge: The realities of welfare in America*. New York: Columbia University Press.

Raspberry, W. (1991, August 5). The black underclass—Two strategies. *Washington Post*, pp. A9, A13.

Robin, D. P., & Reidenbach, R. E. (1987). Social responsibility, ethics, and marketing strategy: Closing the gap between concept and application. *Journal of Marketing, 51*(January), 44-58.

Robin, D. P., & Reidenbach, R. E. (1993). Searching for a place to stand: Toward a workable ethical philosophy for marketing. *Journal of Public Policy and Marketing, 12*(Spring), 97-105.

Stangenes, S. (1993a, May 26). FHA lending uneven by race, study says. *Chicago Tribune,* Business section, pp. 1, 2.

Stangenes, S. (1993b, May 20). Study: Disparity in bank use by whites, minorities. *Chicago Tribune,* Business section, pp. 1, 2.

Sturdivant, F. (1969). *The ghetto marketplace.* New York: Free Press.

They will gladly take a check. (1992, December 1). *New York Times,* pp. D1, D22.

Thomas, P. (1992, November 30). Persistent gap: Blacks can face a host of trying conditions in getting mortgages. *Wall Street Journal,* pp. A1, A4-A5.

Troutt, D. D. (1993). *The thin red line.* San Francisco: Consumers Union of US, Inc., West Coast Regional Office.

U.S. loses more ground to poverty. (1994, October 7). *Chicago Tribune,* pp. 1, 25.

U.S. Bureau of the Census. (1992). *Statistical abstract of the United States: 1992* (112th ed.). Washington, DC: Government Printing Office.

Welles, E. O. (1994, May). It's not the same America. *Inc.,* pp. 82-98.

Wilkerson, I. (1994, June 13). Graduation: Where 500 began, 150 remain. *New York Times,* pp. A1, A9.

Wilson, W. J. (1987). *The truly disadvantaged: The inner city, the underclass, and public policy.* Chicago: University of Chicago Press.

Zehr, M. A. (1992, November/December). Imported from Bangladesh. *Foundation News, 33*(6), 28-32.

PART III

THE PERVASIVE exposure of advertising to all citizens is undeniable. We are literally bombarded with brand images that may cause us to question our sense of self as well as others. In this section, several different perspectives are presented on the role the media plays or should play in the marketplace. Debra Ringold goes against popular opinion and posits a model of *all* consumers that suggests we are capable of making informed and appropriate consumption decisions regardless of gender and race. Marsha Richins, on the other hand, believes that idealized advertising images of material affluence raise consumers' expectations and may negatively influence perceptions of our existences. Ray Taylor, Ju Lee, and Barbara Stern take the middle ground and demonstrate that images of minorities in advertisements have improved over the years, but still remain stereotyped enough to warrant concern.

Of course, the debate over the nature of the influence of advertising on our lives is not answered completely by these articles. Nonetheless, the current parameters of the debate are well articulated, and important research agendas are clear.

Additional Readings

Calfee, J. E., & Ringold, D. J. (1994). The seventy percent majority: Enduring consumer beliefs about advertising. *Journal of Public Policy & Marketing, 13,* 228-238.

Richins, M. L. (1991). Social comparison and the idealized images of advertising. *Journal of Consumer Research, 18,* 71-83.

Taylor, C. R., & Lee, J. Y. (1994). Not in *Vogue:* Portrayals of Asian Americans in magazine advertising. *Journal of Public Policy & Marketing, 13*(2), 239-245.

6

Social Criticisms of Target Marketing

Process or Product?

DEBRA JONES RINGOLD

IN THE CONTEXT of controversies associated with Camel, Dakota, and Uptown cigarettes, Cisco fortified wine, and Black Sunday and Power-Master malt liquors, the targeting of specific demographic groups has been roundly criticized. In so doing, religious leaders, consumer groups, and health activists have called into question the very foundation of modern marketing practice, and marketers have worried that these criticisms will permanently erode consumer goodwill.

Meanwhile, demographers predict that early in the next century, one third of all Americans will belong to a minority racial or ethnic group (Fisher, 1991; Jones, 1992). By the year 2000, nonwhites, women, and immigrants will make up more than five sixths of the American workforce (Novak, 1992). Predictably, manufacturers, re-tailers, and service providers have redoubled their efforts to market more effectively to women and to ethnic and racial minorities (Yarrow, 1991; Zuckoff, 1992). To many, target marketing *is* corporate Amer-ica's response to living in the age of diversity (Berman, 1991), and it has been praised in conjunction with the development and marketing of clothing, education programs, food, health care, mortgages, personal care products, and toys for women and minorities.

To what, then, can one attribute the simultaneous praise and criticism of target marketing to women and minorities? This chapter presents a review of literature germane to target marketing, particularly in the cigarette and alcoholic beverage markets. It summarizes criticisms of target marketing, suggests a definition and several operationalizations of target marketing, and examines assumptions about consumers implicit in evaluations of targeted strategies.

This literature suggests that the social acceptability of targeting is largely a function of individual commentators' judgments about particular consumers and specific products. Targeting that involves consumers who are viewed as essentially "equal participants" in transactions is typically regarded as acceptable. Transactions involving "acceptable" or "socially desirable" products are generally evaluated as beneficial. On the other hand, objections are almost certain if targeting entails "disadvantaged" or "vulnerable" consumers participating in transactions involving products such as alcohol and cigarettes. The implications of this conclusion for public policy are offered last.

Criticisms of Target Marketing

Commentators assert that manufacturers of cigarettes and alcohol are intentionally directing marketing efforts (i.e., advertising) to specific demographic groups: young people, racial and ethnic minorities, and women (Amos, 1990; Brown, 1992; Johnson, 1992; Pollay, 1993; Pollay, Lee, & Carter-Whitney, 1992; Scott, Denniston, & Magruder, 1992; Strickland, Finn, & Lambert, 1982; Taylor, 1990). These commentators contend that these groups are at risk—that is, more prone than others in society to marketers' influence. Some in Congress have engaged in efforts to ban or restrict advertising aimed at particular groups, and investigations of alcohol and cigarette manufacturers by the Bureau of Alcohol Tobacco and Firearms (BATF) and the Federal Trade Commission (FTC) have been interpreted as responses to target marketing activities. Former Department of Health and Human Services Secretary Louis W. Sullivan has criticized tobacco marketers for targeting minorities and women, and has described young, blue-collar, white women as particularly vulnerable and blacks as already bearing more than their share of smoking-related illness and mortality ("DC Hearings," 1990; Hilts, 1990; Ramirez, 1990). Former Surgeon General Antonia Novello cited Cisco fortified wine as an example of irresponsible targeting of minorities ("Editor's Note," 1991) and stated that much of alcohol advertising "misleads, misinforms, and unabashedly targets American youth" (Novello, 1991, p. 3). During hearings on the Protect Our Children From Advertising Act, Representative Thomas Luken (D-OH) charged that tobacco marketers target young people, minorities, and women ("DC Hearings," 1990; Schlossberg, 1990). The BATF rescinded its approval of PowerMaster on the basis of its inner-city promotions (Blalock, 1992), and the FTC investigation of R. J. Reynolds Tobacco Company was motivated by Joe Camel's potential appeal to young people (Federal Trade Commission [FTC], 1994). And although targeting gender, racial, or age groups encompasses more than advertising (e.g., pricing, distribution), it has become part and parcel of the cigarette and alcoholic beverage advertising debate.

Unfortunately, like much of the debate in this area, "moral bias rather than scientific rigor" often dominates discussions of target marketing (Strickland, 1984, p. 87). To evaluate the social consequences of targeting, it must be defined, operationalized, and measured. In the advertising context, it has been suggested that researchers examine (a) differences in advertising messages directed to various groups, (b) differences by group in the intensity and media of exposure, and (c) the relative "susceptibility" of groups to marketing influence (Strickland, 1983). Only then can the linkages between targeted advertising efforts and consumption be explored.

Definition, Operationalizations, and Examples

The following general definition of *target marketing* is offered:

> Targeting is the intentional pursuit of exchange with a specific group through advertising or other marketing activities. Targeted marketing activities are designed and executed to be more appealing to the target market than to people in other segments.

In the advertising context, this definition has been operationalized in essentially three ways. Note that the first and second focus on the nature of advertising stimuli and that the third focuses on advertising effects. Targeting may be operationalized as customized advertising content and can be measured via comparative content analyses. Alternatively, targeting can be operationalized as differential intensity of ad placement in media with different readers or viewers and can be assessed by comparative intensity measures.[1] In the third approach, targeting is operationalized as the achievement of differential advertising effects and can be assessed in laboratory settings. From a policy perspective, this third operationalization has the advantage of assessing the effects, rather than the efforts, of advertising. The following two studies,[2] which used all three of these operationalizations of target marketing in the cigarette context, provide detailed illustrations.

Cigarette advertisements are often criticized for featuring young models, and this is offered as proof that cigarette manufacturers are targeting youth (*Advertising of Tobacco Products,* 1986; McCarthy & Gritz, 1988). The belief that cigarette manufacturers are targeting youth through the use of younger models appears to be predicated on the assumption that younger models are relatively more attractive to younger viewers. A study by Mazis, Ringold, Perry, and Denman (1992) sought to determine (a) whether cigarette models are perceived by consumers as young and (b) whether younger models are perceived as more attractive by younger viewers than by older viewers.

Participants ($N = 561$) were recruited in a racially and economically diverse shopping mall located in a suburban area of a large east-coast city. Participants were remarkably similar to the U.S. population as a whole and ranged in age from 13 to 82 years. They were asked to volunteer their time for an advertising study sponsored by a local university. The cigarette advertising models they evaluated were featured in advertisements found in virtually every October 1987 issue of the 97 magazines appearing on the Simmons Market Research Bureau, Inc. (1986) list. A total of 393 cigarette advertisements were located; 119 of these were unique executions. Models with clearly visible faces appeared in 30% of the 393 advertisements. Fifty of the 119 unique executions met this criterion, were featured in 65 publications, and were at least a full page in size.

The advertisements were randomly split into two groups of 25, professionally photographed, and developed as slides. Using a standard age and attractiveness measurement procedure, each respondent was asked how old and, on a scale of 1 to 10, how attractive each model appeared to be. The first research question was, "How old are cigarette models perceived to be?" The findings are quite interesting. Of 65 models, 11 were perceived on average to be significantly below 25 years of age. Two out of 65 models were perceived on average to be less than 21 years of age. Not one of the models was on average perceived to be less than 18 years of age. One can reasonably conclude, then, that consumers do not see these models as being under 18 years of age.

On to the second question: "Do younger people find younger models more attractive than older people do?" Consistent with other studies, Mazis et al. (1992) found that regardless of the viewer's age, younger models were preferred to older models. Older and younger viewers equally found younger models to be attractive. Not surprisingly, youth is universally attractive. One could very reasonably make the case that if cigarette advertisers wanted to target particular markets, they would not use younger models who are universally appealing but would rely on the use of older models who are differentially attractive to older audiences. This would be targeting with model age. Using younger models in advertising is not targeting; younger models are attractive to everyone.

A related issue is advertising themes and frequency of placement as target marketing tactics. If cigarette marketers were targeting youth, differentially appealing advertising themes would be developed for this segment. In addition, one would expect cigarette advertisements to be placed with greater frequency in magazines read by younger rather than older audiences.

A study by King, Reid, Moon, and Ringold (1991) addressed these issues. Cigarette advertisements in eight popular consumer magazines published continuously between 1954 and 1986 were analyzed with respect to themes and frequency of placement. The magazines represented five distinct audience orientations (the median audience ages in parentheses are from Simmons Market Research Bureau, 1987). The eight publications were a general interest magazine, *Time* (37.3); two older women's magazines, *Ladies Home Journal* (41.9) and *Redbook* (37.4); a younger women's magazine, *Vogue* (32.0); two older men's magazines, *Popular Mechanics* (37.5) and *Esquire* (38.0); and two younger men's magazines, *Sports Illustrated* (32.8) and *Playboy* (31.3). One issue of each magazine was selected for each year; every advertisement in each issue was collected. The months of the year were blocked by season to ensure that advertisements would be drawn from different times of the year. This procedure resulted in a sample of 1,100 cigarette advertisements.

Standard content analytic procedures were employed to record the activities featured in the advertisements. The activity categories were adventure (e.g., operating a speedboat); recreation (e.g., playing softball); erotic/romantic relationship between two people (e.g., two people embracing); social activities (e.g., people at a party); work activities (e.g., construction); and individualistic/solitary behavior (e.g., reading a book). The overall inter-rater reliability was 0.89.

The findings are again quite interesting. Critics have charged that the tobacco industry has attempted to allay the fears of youth by de-emphasizing the product itself in favor of healthy images such as adventure, recreation, and romance. They have asserted that such portrayals have become more prevalent in cigarette advertisements over time and that these images appear with greatest frequency in youth and women's magazines (Albright, Altman, Slater, & Maccoby, 1988; Altman, Slater, Albright, & Maccoby, 1987; Warner, 1985). Over the 33-year period examined in this study, only portrayals of adventure have increased; models engaged in recreational activities did not vary, and romantic/erotic portrayals actually decreased over time.

Cigarette advertisements placed in younger men's and younger women's magazines were no more likely to portray models engaged in recreational activities than advertisements placed in other magazines. Similarly, erotic/romantic portrayals were no more common in advertisements placed in women's or youth magazines than magazines appealing to other audiences. Only cigarette advertisements placed in older men's magazines were more likely to portray models as adventurous. In summary, this study found a striking universality of theme regardless of magazine orientation. Individualistic/solitary and recreational themes were most frequently portrayed in virtually all magazine types.

The results contradict as well critics who assert that in an effort to target youth, more cigarette advertisements are placed in youth-oriented magazines than in magazines that target other segments of the population. This inverse relationship between age of readership and frequency of advertisements was not found. In fact, no significant differences were found across magazine types.

These two studies, when taken together, offer empirical evidence that contradicts several aspects of the commonly asserted "youth targeting" justification for further regulation of cigarette advertising. Critics have charged that the tobacco industry uses younger models to appeal to youth. In fact, not one of the models found in these cigarette advertisements was judged on average to be less than 18 years of age. More important, younger models were found (in this and other studies) to have universal appeal. This is the embodiment of mass, not target, marketing. This work also indicates that images of adventure, recreation, and romance are no more likely in magazines with younger audiences than in those that appeal to older segments of the population. Although critics have asserted that youths are targeted through the heavier placement of cigarette advertisements per issue, no such relationship was found.

The lack of definitive evidence of youth targeting notwithstanding,[3] targeting cigarettes or alcoholic beverages to underaged people is an indefensible position. Not so with women and minorities. Given that women and minorities represent increasingly important market segments, manufacturers of a variety of products and services can be expected to target these groups.

Minorities, Women, and Target Marketing

Minorities are now the majority in 51 of the nation's 200 largest cities, including New York, Los Angeles, and Chicago (Zuckoff, 1992). The 1990 census figures show that as a percentage of the total U.S. population, the African American, Asian American, and Hispanic American populations will continue to grow dramatically (Novak, 1992). As the 20th century closes, white men are already less than half of the labor force (Waldrop, 1990). By the year 2000, nonwhites, women, and immigrants will make up more than five sixths of the American workforce (Novak, 1992). Demographers have suggested that in the 21st century everyone will belong to a minority group (Waldrop, 1990).

As their consumer power increases, minorities no longer wait patiently for companies to discover them but actively demand marketers' attention (Zuckoff, 1992). Repeatedly, African American, Asian, and Hispanic business leaders state that these consumers, like other segments of the population, respond best to targeted offerings (Astor, 1982; Campanelli, 1991; Fost, 1990; Livingston, 1992; Santoro, 1991; Shao, Power, & Zinn, 1991). "As the rapid growth of the African-American market continues," Legette (1993) has written, "enterprising companies that target this market will have a competitive advantage, particularly in those categories in which black consumer spending is significant" (p. 7). Spurred by the market imperatives illustrated by the 1990 census, banks, cosmetic companies, insurance companies, retail chains, and toy manufacturers have followed the lead of other industries in examining how they can market more effectively to ethnic and racial groups (Zuckoff, 1992).

Apparently, these proponents of target marketing subscribe to a competent consumer model (Bauer, 1964; Calfee & Ringold, 1992, 1994). This model suggests that consumers are generally skeptical of commercial information, recognizing its limitations and usefulness. That is, consumers are simultaneously skeptical of marketing communications in general yet willing to use commercial information when it provides valuable information. They are aware of sellers' incentives to exploit consumer ignorance, and both consumers and sellers take these incentives into account when devising their marketplace strategies. Competent consumers demand products and services that meet their needs; inferior products tend to succumb quickly to superior alternatives. Marketers have responded with targeted offerings designed to serve consumers effectively and efficiently. Thus, proponents of target marketing see it as corporate America's response to living in the age of diversity (Berman, 1991), as a responsibility of corporate America (Zuckoff, 1992), and as a transactional process that maximizes market efficiency (Calfee, 1991; Levitt, 1986).

Conversely, critics of target marketing subscribe to the vulnerable consumer model (Bauer, 1964; Calfee & Ringold, 1992). This model characterizes consumers as limited in their ability to process information relevant to their own welfare. Thus, advertising is a powerful influence that consumers are ill prepared to resist. In this view, sellers routinely deceive consumers. Leventhal (1964) observed that, it is only a mild exaggeration to say that most people view mass-media audiences, excepting perhaps themselves, as a large group of relatively helpless, isolated individuals, each urged by the hypnotic force of his TV set, radio, or magazine into a course of action which he would otherwise never undertake. Much as Pavlov's dogs salivated at the ringing of a bell, the listener obeys the demands of mass communication. (pp. 270-271)

Consistent with this view, some see target marketing as inherently manipulative—a practice that capitalizes on the vulnerability of particular population segments (Hacker, Collins, & Jacobson, 1987).

Although a definition of vulnerability is somewhat illusive, the notion of consumer capacity has figured prominently in past and current formulations (Andreasen, Cooper-Martin, & Smith, 1994). Vulnerability, at least in the context of commercial information, implies that targeted groups exhibit a diminished capacity to understand the role of advertising, product effects, or both. Thus, two propositions underpin the criticisms of target marketing of cigarettes and alcohol:

1. Young people, women, and racial and ethnic groups are inherently less skeptical of advertising and less capable of extracting useful information from it.
2. Young people, women, and racial and ethnic groups are inherently less knowledgeable about product effects.

Skepticism

A review of the literature and relevant poll data suggests, however, that consumers are neither naive with respect to advertising nor ignorant with regard to the health effects of smoking and alcoholic beverage consumption. A large share of consumer information is distributed by sellers in the form of advertising. Some have said that it is "information needed to make a free choice" (*Central Hudson Gas & Electric Corp. v. Public Service Commission,* 1980, p. 568). Although advertising reduces buyers' search costs, it is obviously biased because the seller is using the message both to provide information and to persuade. For this reason, proponents of the economic theory of information have long held that consumers are skeptical of advertising (Akerlof, 1970; Darby & Karni, 1973; Nelson, 1970, 1974, 1978; for a review, see Calfee & Ford, 1988). Moreover, these researchers have asserted that consumers do more than simply distrust advertisers. It has been suggested that consumers speculate about the motives and practices of advertisers, that consumers appreciate when advertisers have the incentive to speak truthfully because the market will inflict penalties on untruthful behavior, and that consumers believe that sellers take consumer perceptions of advertising behavior into account (Wright, 1986). Given this skepticism, at its most potent, advertising teases our appetites but does not change our basic tastes, values, or preferences (Etzioni, 1972).

That adult consumers are, in reality, sophisticated with respect to advertising can be demonstrated through examining public opinion on advertising (Calfee & Ringold, 1994). This research suggests that the majority of consumers view advertising as an essential source of useful product information and simultaneously appreciate advertising's role as persuader. Thus, consistent with the skepticism predictions of the economic theory of information, polls demonstrate that a relatively small minority of consumers believe that advertising is completely truthful. This is not to say that consumers find little merit in advertising overall. In fact, the majority of consumers seem to feel that the benefits of advertising outweigh the costs. What the literature does show, however, is a baseline skepticism against which individual sellers must contend in seeking to inform and persuade. Moreover, "there is no evidence to suggest that . . . vulnerability [to persuasive communications] is associated with race, ethnicity, or gender" (Stewart & Rice, 1992, p. 26).

The literature also suggests that children and adolescents may not in reality be the often-portrayed "hapless victims" of advertising (Ward, 1971, p. 464). Ward (1972) found that whereas kindergartners show no understanding of the purpose of advertising, second graders understand that the purpose is to sell goods, and fourth and sixth graders comment on the techniques employed toward this end. Furthermore, Ward concluded that there is a general distrust of advertising among children and that this distrust of advertising increases with age.

The perceptions of advertising by first, third, and fifth graders were examined by Robertson and Rossiter (1974). Their results show clear developmental trends toward increasingly sophisticated cognitions about, and less positive attitudes toward, advertising. For example, whereas just over 50% of first graders recognized the persuasive intent of advertising, 99% of all fifth graders did so. Of all the first graders, 65% indicated that they trusted all commercials, whereas less than 8% of fifth graders provided this response. Overall, Robertson and Rossiter's (1974) results suggest that as children age they increasingly attribute persuasive intent to commercials, believe commercials less, like commercials less, and are less likely to want the products advertised. Not surprisingly, these findings are quite consistent with the developmental sequence of children's understanding of economic concepts found by Berti and Bombi (1988).

Linn, de Benedictis, and Delucchi (1982) addressed some of these issues with a somewhat older cohort of children. Their results indicate that seventh and eighth graders display substantial skepticism of advertisers and of product tests conducted by advertisers. They concluded that more than 95% of adolescents are skeptical of advertisers and can name potentially misleading aspects of product tests. The majority appear not to accept the veracity of flawed product test advertisements. Consistent with these findings, Moore and Moschis (1978) concluded that adolescents have generally negative attitudes toward advertising. In particular, advertising was found to have low credibility. Interestingly, these results were not related to the amount of television viewing or communication with family and peers, and led Stewart and Rice (1992) to the following conclusion:

> It appears that this negative attitude toward advertising is already developed by adolescence. . . . This general dislike and skepticism for advertising may result in adolescents tuning out most advertising they are exposed to, and may result in increased vigilance of advertising claims. (pp. 29-30)

When asked to consider cigarette advertising specifically, Fisher and Magnus (1981) reported that as many as 80% of children aged 10 and 11 asserted that the purpose of cigarette advertising is to induce people to smoke. This study "leaves little doubt as to the opinion of this group of Australian 10 and 11 year olds: Cigarette advertisements are intended to lead people to take up smoking and they have this effect on children" (p. 24). A still larger percentage agreed with the notion that cigarette advertising is concerned with trying to get people who are already smoking to change from one brand to another. A large majority also believed that cigarette advertisements try to make smoking look healthy. According to the authors,

> The cynicism of the children toward tobacco company sponsorship of sport was unexpected: More than 65 per cent of children disagreed with the view that "tobacco companies give money to sport because they are generous" and agreed that "sponsorship of sport is really just another way of advertising." (p. 25)

A study of children between the ages of 6 and 16 by Aitken, Leathar, and O'Hagan (1985) demonstrates much the same thing. Some children as young as 6, and all older groups, were able to incorporate a selling component into their definitions of advertising. Primary school children mentioned the health effects of smoking (e.g., cancer), whereas the secondary school children mentioned health consequences and the persuasive techniques used by advertisers to minimize the consideration of these. Secondary school children spontaneously asserted that advertisers are dishonest. There were no discernable differences in these responses by gender.

Wallack, Cassady, and Grube (1990) suggested that children are skeptical of beer advertising as well. Eight groups of fifth and sixth graders participated in numerous focus group discussions designed to understand better how children interpret beer commercials. The authors conclude that,

> All children were aware that the intent of each commercial was to sell beer. . . . There was considerable skepticism about the promises that beer commercials make about the popularity, fun and good times to be had if you buy their brand of beer. . . . In addition, children are aware of the health consequences of drinking and driving and other high risk activities. . . . Most children felt that drinking was morally wrong. (Appendix 3, pp. 6, 3)

Knowledge of Tobacco, Alcoholic Beverages, and Health

Since the mid-1940s, Americans have increasingly come to appreciate the harmful effects of smoking cigarettes (Erskine, 1966; Viscusi,

1992). A report from the federal Office of Smoking and Health confirms this observation, concluding that "in general . . . the 1990 objectives concerning the population's knowledge of the health consequences of cigarette smoking have been met" (Shopland & Brown, 1987). These benchmarks include awareness among 85% of consumers that smoking is a factor in chronic obstructive lung disease, among 90% that it is a factor in lung and certain other cancers, and among 85% that it is a factor in heart disease. Moreover, blacks and women do not differ materially from the population at large with regard to knowledge of the health effects of smoking (Shopland & Brown, 1987; U.S. Department of Health and Human Services, 1990).

Levitt (1971) published the results of a study that considered children's reasons for not smoking. The response most frequently given was "health reasons." A total of 69% of 11,545 boys and 75% of 12,877 girls in Grades 5 through 8 were seemingly aware of the health consequences of smoking as early as 1971. Schneider and Vanmastrig (1974) reported that more than 99% of children aged 7 to 8 years believe that smoking can cause cancer; approximately 97% believe that smoking shortens a person's life; and two thirds believe that it is very hard to stop smoking. More recently, researchers have estimated that 90% of adolescents are aware that smoking is a health hazard (Silvis & Perry, 1987). Younger adults have greater awareness of the health effects of smoking than does the population at large (Shopland & Brown, 1987). Viscusi (1992) reported that in a national probability sample, young people between the ages of 16 and 21 exhibited a higher level of risk perceptions than their older counterparts did. He concludes, "There is certainly no evidence of greater neglect of smoking risks by the very young. Indeed, the opposite is the case" (p. 128). Moreover, gender differences in adolescents' assessments of health risks associated with smoking have not been noted (U.S. Department of Health and Human Services, 1985).

When asked to assess the probability of becoming an alcoholic, adolescents show no more illusion of invulnerability than do adults (Fischhoff & Quadrel, 1991; Quadrel, Fischhoff, & Davis, 1993). As Quadrel et al. (1993) have written, "The most straightforward account of these results is that adults and teens rely on similar, moderately biased psychological processes in estimating these risks" (p. 112). Knowledge of the general risks associated with alcohol is high for junior and senior high school students (Finn & Brown, 1981; U.S. Department of Health and Human Services, 1991), undergraduates (Haemmerlie, Merz, & Nelson, 1992; Kalsher, Clarke, & Wogalter, 1993; Smith & McCauley, 1991), and adults (Kaskutas & Greenfield, 1992). The Department of Health and Human Services (1991) reported that 98% of junior and senior high students know that, "Mothers who drink alcohol during pregnancy have a higher risk of having babies with birth defects" and that 87% of them know that, "A person can die from an overdose of alcohol" (p. 10). A total of 96% reject the statement, "A teenager cannot become an alcoholic"; 93% reject the statement, "Alcohol improves coordination and reflexes." A total of 96% know that, "Alcohol slows the activity of the brain."

Conclusion

As Sowell (1981) has pointed out, reformers have often been offended and disturbed by the choices made by members of racial and ethnic minorities. Rather than recognize the right of others to make choices that reflect economic and social preferences fundamentally at odds with their own, critics have sought to curtail these choices via government intervention. Although such criticism is offered as evidence of elitism (Kirkpatrick, 1986), more important is the conclusion that such prohibitions are unlikely to enlarge the set of options available to female and minority consumers. Government interventions have typically eliminated options for minorities without creating new ones, with concomitant reductions in consumer welfare (Sowell, 1975, 1981).

Civil rights means that all individuals are treated the same under the law, regardless of their race, religion, gender, other social category, or preferences in the marketplace. Thus, a legal framework within which transactors are hindered in making their own economic (and other) decisions in deference to the preferences of others has been assailed as paternalism (Calfee, 1991; Rothenberg, 1990; Sowell, 1981, 1984). More important, inasmuch as target marketing contributes to allocative efficiency by pursuing the best fit between products and consumers, one would expect it to be of particular value to groups traditionally characterized as having fewer choices (Andreasen et al.,

1994). Consistent with this view, target marketing of socially acceptable products (e.g., toys, health care, financial services) has been
praised as maximizing choices and enhancing consumer welfare.
Apparently, the practice has drawn fire only when the product being
marketed is controversial. As Pollay et al. (1992) have written, "Market
segmentation is commonplace among large consumer goods firms
and has incurred criticism only when the product itself is problematic.
. . . Selective targeting can be benign or even beneficial, but only if
the product is" (p. 46). One might conclude, therefore, that recent
critics of target marketing are not motivated by concerns associated
with the process itself but rather by individual product contexts such
as cigarettes and alcohol.

Although some members of all groups are less well equipped to
navigate the marketplace, there is no empirical basis on which to
characterize women and members of racial or ethnic minorities as
vulnerable consumers. On the contrary, consumers, regardless of
gender and race, appreciate the various roles played by advertising
and the health consequences of controversial behaviors. Choices at
variance with those prescribed by critics of tobacco or alcohol do not
constitute a reasonable definition of vulnerability or a justification for
additional regulation. The consumer's right to information and to the
freedom of choice it ensures is not well served by proposals to curtail
target marketing activities. Those who suggest that government shall
decide what speech certain segments of citizens should hear and what
products they should be allowed to buy decline to consider the
sophistication and knowledge of the American public, and more
important, their civil rights.

Notes

1. For a review of studies that use these two operationalizations and related meth-
odologies, see Rifon, Vanden Bergh, and Katrak (1994).
2. For a review of related studies and an alternative interpretation of these, see U.S.
Department of Health and Human Services (1994, chap. 5).
3. Consistent with this, the FTC recently closed its investigation of the Joe Camel
advertising campaign. The majority concluded that there was insufficient evidence to
conclude that the campaign influenced smoking initiation among those under the age
of 18 (FTC, 1994).

References

Advertising of tobacco products: Hearings before the Subcommittee of Health and the Environment of the Committee on Energy and Commerce, House of Representatives, 99th Cong., 2d Sess. 166 (1986) (testimony of W. J. McCarthy).

Aitken, P. P., Leathar, D. S., & O'Hagan, F. J. (1985). Children's perceptions of advertisements for cigarettes. *Social Science and Medicine, 21,* 785-797.

Akerlof, G. (1970). The market for "lemons": Quality uncertainty and the market mechanism. *Quarterly Journal of Economics, 84,* 488-500.

Albright, C. L., Altman, D. G., Slater, M. D., & Maccoby, N. (1988). Cigarette advertisements in magazines: Evidence for a differential focus on women's and youth magazines. *Health Education Quarterly, 15*(2), 225-233.

Altman, D. G., Slater, M. D., Albright, C. L., & Maccoby, N. (1987). How an unhealthy product is sold: Cigarette advertising in magazines, 1960-1985. *Journal of Communication, 37*(4), 95-106.

Amos, A. (1990). How women are targeted by the tobacco industry. *World Health Forum, 11,* 416-422.

Andreasen, A. R., Cooper-Martin, E., & Smith, N. C. (1994). *Who is the vulnerable consumer? The implications for marketing and public policy of objective and subjective consumer vulnerability.* Working paper, Georgetown University, Washington, DC.

Astor, D. (1982, July). Black spending power: $140 billion and growing. *Marketing Communications, 7*(7), 13-16, 18.

Bauer, R. A. (1964). The obstinate audience: The influence process from the point of view of social communication. *American Psychologist, 19*(5), 319-328.

Berman, G. L. (1991, October). The Hispanic market: Getting down to cases. *Sales & Marketing Management,* pp. 65-74.

Berti, A. E., & Bombi, A. S. (1988). *The child's construction of economics.* Cambridge, UK: Cambridge University Press.

Blalock, C. (1992, January). Malt liquors: Worth the black eye? *Beverage Industry,* p. 1.

Brown, J. W., Jr. (1992). Marketing exploitation. *Business and Society Review, 83*(4), 17.

Calfee, J. E. (1991, July 22). "Targeting" the problem: It isn't exploitation, it's efficient marketing. *Advertising Age,* p. 18.

Calfee, J. E., & Ford, G. T. (1988). Economics, information and consumer behavior. *Advances in Consumer Research, 15,* 234-238.

Calfee, J. E., & Ringold, D. J. (1992). The cigarette advertising controversy: Assumptions about consumers, regulation, and scientific debate. *Advances in Consumer Research, 19,* 557-562.

Calfee, J. E., & Ringold, D. J. (1994). The seventy percent majority: Enduring consumer beliefs about advertising. *Journal of Public Policy & Marketing, 13,* 228-238.

Campanelli, M. (1991, May). The African-American market: Community, growth, and change. *Sales & Marketing Management, 143,* 75-81.

Central Hudson Gas & Electric Corp. v. Public Service Commission, 447 U.S. 557, 566 (1980).

Darby, M. R., & Karni, E. (1973). Free competition and the optimal amount of fraud. *Journal of Law and Economics, 16,* 67-88.

DC hearings: Civility up in smoke. (1990, March 5). *Adweek Eastern Edition,* pp. 1, 4.

Editor's note: PowerMaster trips ANA's Dewitt Helm. (1991, July 8). *Adweek's Marketing Week,* p. 12.

Erskine, H. G. (1966). The polls: Smoking. *Public Opinion Quarterly, 30*(1), 140-152.

Etzioni, A. (1972, June 3). Human beings are not very easy to change after all. *The Society Saturday Review*, pp. 45-47.

Federal Trade Commission. (1994). *FTC closes investigation of R. J. Reynolds Tobacco Company* (FTC File No. 932 3162). Washington, DC: Author.

Finn, P., & Brown, J. (1981). Risks entailed in teenage intoxication as perceived by junior and senior high school students. *Journal of Youth and Adolescence, 10*, 61-76.

Fischhoff, B., & Quadrel, M. J. (1991). Adolescent alcohol decisions. *Alcohol Health & Research World, 15*(1), 43-51.

Fisher, C. (1991, August 5). Ethnics gain market clout. *Advertising Age*, p. 3.

Fisher, D. A., & Magnus, P. (1981). "Out of the mouths of babes . . . ": The opinions of 10 and 11 year old children regarding the advertising of cigarettes. *Community Health Studies, 5*(1), 22-26.

Fost, D. (1990). California's Asian market. *American Demographics, 12*(10), 34-37.

Hacker, G. A., Collins, R., & Jacobson, M. (1987). *Marketing booze to blacks*. Washington, DC: Center for Science in the Public Interest.

Haemmerlie, F. M., Merz, C. J., & Nelson, S. B. (1992). College vs junior high school students' knowledge of alcohol as a teratogen. *Psychological Reports, 71*(3, Pt. 1), 809-810.

Hilts, P. J. (1990, January 19). Health chief assails a tobacco producer for aiming at blacks. *New York Times*, pp. A1, A20.

Johnson, E. M. (1992). Harmful targeting. *Business and Society Review, 83*(4), 16-17.

Jones, C. (1992). A nation of "minorities." *Life Association News, 87*(7), 59-62.

Kalsher, M. J., Clarke, S. W., & Wogalter, M. S. (1993). Communication of alcohol facts and hazards by a warning poster. *Journal of Public Policy & Marketing, 12*(1), 78-90.

Kaskutas, L. A., & Greenfield, T. K. (1992). First effects of warning labels on alcoholic beverage containers. *Drug and Alcohol Dependence, 31*(1), 1-14.

King, K. W., Reid, L. N., Moon, Y. S., & Ringold, D. J. (1991). Changes in the visual imagery of cigarette ads, 1954-1986. *Journal of Public Policy & Marketing, 10*, 63-80.

Kirkpatrick, J. (1986). A philosophic defense of advertising. *Journal of Advertising, 15*(2), 42-64.

Legette, C. (1993). Marketing to African Americans. *Business and Economic Review, 39*(3), 3-7.

Leventhal, H. (1964). An analysis of the influence of alcoholic beverage advertising on drinking customs. In R. D. McCarthy (Ed.), *Alcohol education for classroom and community* (pp. 267-297). New York: McGraw-Hill.

Levitt, E. E. (1971). Reasons for smoking and not smoking given by school children. *Journal of School Health, 41*, 101-105.

Levitt, T. (1986). Marketing and its discontents. In *The marketing imagination* (pp. 215-227). New York: Free Press.

Linn, M. C., de Benedictis, T., & Delucchi, K. (1982). Adolescent reasoning about advertisements: Preliminary investigations. *Child Development, 53*, 1599-1613.

Livingston, S. (1992). Marketing to the Hispanic-American community. *Journal of Business Strategy, 13*(2), 54-57.

Mazis, M. B., Ringold, D. J., Perry, E. S., & Denman, D. W. (1992). Perceived age and attractiveness of models in cigarette advertising. *Journal of Marketing, 56*(1), 22-37.

McCarthy, W. J., & Gritz, E. R. (1988). *Teenagers' responses to cigarette advertising*. Working paper. (Available from W. J. McCarthy, University of California, Los Angeles)

Moore, R. L., & Moschis, G. P. (1978). Teenagers' reactions to advertising. *Journal of Advertising, 7,* 24-30.

Nelson, P. (1970). Information and consumer behavior. *Journal of Political Economy, 78,* 311-329.

Nelson, P. (1974). Advertising as information. *Journal of Political Economy, 82,* 729-754.

Nelson, P. (1978). Advertising as information once more. In D. Tuerck (Ed.), *Issues in advertising: The economics of persuasion.* Washington, DC: American Enterprise Institute.

Novak, C. A. (1992, March). Profiting from diversity. *Best's Review, 92*(11), 18-22, 99-101.

Novello, A. C. (1991, November 4). *Youth and alcohol—Advertising that appeals to youth* [Press conference statement]. Washington, DC: U.S. Department of Health & Human Services.

Pollay, R. W. (1993). Targeting the young is an old story: A history of cigarette advertising to the young. In J. B. Schmidt, S. C. Hollander, T. Nevett, & J. N. Sheth (Eds.), *Contemporary marketing history: Proceedings of the sixth conference on Historical Research in Marketing and Marketing Thought* (pp. 263-282). Atlanta, GA: Emory University, Graduate School of Business.

Pollay, R. W., Lee, J. S., & Carter-Whitney, D. (1992). Separate, but not equal: Racial segmentation in cigarette advertising. *Journal of Advertising, 21*(1), 45-57.

Quadrel, M. J., Fischhoff, B., & Davis, W. (1993). Adolescent (in)vulnerability. *American Psychologist, 48*(2), 102-116.

Ramirez, A. (1990, February 18). New cigarette raising issue of target marketing. *New York Times,* p. C28.

Rifon, N. J., Vanden Bergh, B. G., & Katrak, P. (1994). *The gender partitioning and targeting of the cigarette market: A longitudinal analysis of advertising expenditures in consumer magazines from 1959 to 1990.* Unpublished manuscript, Department of Advertising, Michigan State University at East Lansing.

Robertson, T. S., & Rossiter, J. R. (1974). Children and commercial persuasion: An attribution theory analysis. *Journal of Consumer Research, 1,* 13-20.

Rothenberg, R. (1990, March 9). The stresses of marketing to minorities. *New York Times,* p. D17.

Santoro, E. (1991, October). Hispanics are hot. *Direct Marketing, 54*(6), 28-32.

Schlossberg, H. (1990, April). Segmenting becomes constitutional issue. *Marketing News, 24*(8), 1-2.

Schneider, F. W., & Vanmastrig, L. A. (1974). Adolescent preadolescent differences in beliefs and attitudes about cigarette smoking. *Journal of Psychology, 87,* 71-81.

Scott, B. M., Denniston, R. W., & Magruder, K. M. (1992). Alcohol advertising in the African-American community. *Journal of Drug Issues, 22*(2), 455-469.

Shao, M., Power, C., & Zinn, L. (1991, June 17). Suddenly, Asian-Americans are a marketer's dream. *Business Week,* pp. 54-55.

Shopland, D. R., & Brown, C. (1987). Toward the 1990 objectives for smoking: Measuring the progress with 1985 NHIS data. *Public Health Reports, 102*(1), 68-73.

Silvis, G. L., & Perry, C. L. (1987). Understanding and deterring tobacco use among adolescents. *Chemical Dependency, 34*(2), 363-379.

Simmons Market Research Bureau, Inc. (1986). *Simmons 1986 study of media and markets.* New York: Author.

Simmons Market Research Bureau, Inc. (1987). *Simmons 1987 study of media and markets.* New York: Author.

Smith, R. H., & McCauley, C. R. (1991). Predictions of alcohol abuse behaviors of undergraduates. *Journal of Drug Education, 21*(2), 159-166.

Sowell, T. (1975). *Race and economics.* New York: David McKay.

Sowell, T. (1981). *Markets and minorities.* New York: Basic Books.

Sowell, T. (1984). *Civil rights: Rhetoric or reality?* New York: William Morrow.

Stewart, D. W., & Rice, R. (1992). *Integrated marketing: New technologies, non-traditional media, and nonmedia promotion in the marketing of alcoholic beverages.* Working paper, National Institute on Alcohol Abuse and Alcoholism Working Group on the Effects of the Mass Media on the Use and Abuse of Alcohol, Washington, DC.

Strickland, D. E. (1983). Advertising exposure, alcohol consumption and misuse of alcohol. In A. Williams, M. Plant, & M. Grant (Eds.), *Economics and alcohol: Consumption and controls* (pp. 201-222). London: Croom Helm.

Strickland, D. E. (1984). Content and effects of alcohol advertising: Comment on NTIS Pub. No. PB82-123142. *Journal of Studies on Alcohol, 45,* 87-93.

Strickland, D. E., Finn, T. A., & Lambert, M. D. (1982). A content analysis of beverage alcohol advertising: I. Magazine advertising. *Journal of Studies on Alcohol, 43,* 655-682.

Taylor, P. (1990). Testimony on alcohol advertising, U.S. House of Representatives Subcommittee on Transportation and Hazardous Materials, March 1, 1990. *Journal of Public Health Policy, 11*(3), 370-381.

U.S. Department of Health and Human Services. (1985). *The health consequences of smoking for women: A report of the Surgeon General* (GPO Publication No. 1985 O-470-822). Washington, DC: U.S. Department of Health and Human Services, Public Health Service, Office of the Assistant Secretary for Health and Office of Smoking and Health.

U.S. Department of Health and Human Services. (1990). *Smoking, tobacco, and cancer program: 1985-1989 status report* (NIH Publication No. 90-3107). Washington, DC: U.S. Department of Health and Human Services, Public Health Service, National Institutes of Health, National Cancer Institute.

U.S. Department of Health and Human Services. (1991). *Youth and alcohol: A national survey: Drinking habits, access, attitudes, and knowledge* (OEI-09-91-00652). Washington, DC: U.S. Department of Health and Human Services, Office of Inspector General.

U.S. Department of Health and Human Services. (1994). *Preventing tobacco use among young people: A report of the Surgeon General* (S/N 017-001-00491-0). Atlanta, GA: Department of Prevention, National Center for Chronic Disease Prevention and Health Promotion, Office on Smoking and Health.

Viscusi, W. K. (1992). *Smoking: Making the risky decision.* New York: Oxford University Press.

Waldrop, J. (1990). You'll know it's the 21st century when . . . *American Demographics, 12*(12), 22-27.

Wallack, L., Cassady, D., & Grube, J. (1990). *TV beer commercials and children: Exposure, attention, beliefs, and expectations about drinking as an adult.* Washington, DC: AAA Foundation for Traffic Safety.

Ward, S. (1971). Television advertising and the adolescent. *Clinical Pediatrics, 10,* 462-464.

Ward, S. (1972). Children's reactions to commercials. *Journal of Advertising Research, 12*(2), 37-45.

Warner, K. E. (1985). Tobacco industry response to public health concern: A content analysis of cigarette ads. *Health Education Quarterly, 12*, 115-127.

Wright, P. (1986). Schemer schema: Consumers' intuitive theories about marketers' influence tactics. *Advances in Consumer Research, 13*, 1-3.

Yarrow, R. (1991, October 11). Bank of America enhances affirmative lending guidelines. *Business Wire*, p. 1.

Zuckoff, M. (1992, June 6). Reaching out to minority consumers. *Boston Globe*, p. 73.

7

Materialism, Desire, and Discontent

Contributions of Idealized Advertising Images and Social Comparison

MARSHA L. RICHINS

FOR GENERATIONS, Americans have been showing a persistent desire to increase their wealth and obtain more goods (Bredemeier & Toby, 1960; Fox & Lears, 1983; Wachtel, 1983), and the stereotype of "materialistic" has been readily applied to American society (Karlins, Coffman, & Walters, 1969). One manifestation of this materialism is the extent to which Americans view money (and the possessions it provides) as an important instrument in the pursuit of happiness. In one national survey (Roper Starch Worldwide, 1994), 69% of respondents said that having more money would make them happier. The desire for more is also illustrated by the extent to which Americans are willing to go into debt to acquire goods. In 1992, nearly 30% of after-tax household income went to debt payments other than household mortgages, and the total of short- and long-term indebtedness approached 80% of income (Eugeni, 1993).

Although American materialism was recognized more than a century ago (de Tocqueville, 1835/1954), the desire for goods seems to be increasing. Between 1976 and 1986, the percentage of high school seniors who said it would be important for them to have at least two cars increased from 40% to 63%. Similarly, increasing emphasis was placed on having such goods as a high quality stereo, the latest style in clothes, and a vacation house (Easterlin & Crimmins, 1988). The increase in materialism is also evident among adults. In 1975, 38% of American adults questioned said that "a lot of money" was one of the things they want out of life; by 1988 this had increased to 62% (Easterlin & Crimmins, 1991).

Although the desire for more has been credited with raising Americans' standard of living, it also has generated some social, economic, and environmental consequences that are less positive. For instance, it is associated with envy and discontent (Richins & Dawson, 1992), and religious leaders have repeatedly warned of the spiritual hazards of wanting more (see Belk, 1983; Rudmin & Kilbourne, in press). Others have described the harm to interpersonal relationships it may cause (e.g., Fromm, 1976). More recently, the excessive desire for goods has been criticized for its negative impact on the earth's resources. Unbridled materialism uses natural resources at an unnecessarily high rate and contributes to pollution and the destruction of habitat and species (Durning, 1992; Meadows, Meadows, Randers, & Behrens, 1972; Worster, 1993).

Concerns have also been raised about the ability of the present economic system to support individuals' material desires. In the United States and Western Europe, there is growing recognition that economic resources are more strained than previously thought. Lower rates of job growth have combined with increasing demands on those resources due to political reorganization, demographic changes, immigration, rising health costs, and increased social welfare demands. The result is that many societies are no longer economically capable of sustaining a materialistic ideal. Standards of living are not likely to rise as they have in the past; for many, they have declined. It has been suggested that the inability of individuals to achieve their materialistic ideal contributes (in part) to disturbances in social systems. These disturbances may include excessive personal debt and increasing personal bankruptcy rates, dissatisfaction and resentment among ordinary citizens, increases in property crimes, and intolerance of immigrants and other out-group members.

Consumers' desires for more have shaped the marketing institutions of the 20th century and have been the engine of their success. In turn, marketing institutions have themselves contributed to consumers' desire for more and to the social problems associated with this desire. This chapter explores one way in which one of these marketing institutions—advertising—augments dissatisfaction with individuals' personal circumstances and in so doing influences the desire for more. Specifically, it examines the impact of idealized advertising images on consumer desire.

Idealized Images in Advertising

Consumers are exposed to countless media images in the form of billboards, magazine images, and television programs. Some of these images are actively sought, as when consumers read a newspaper or rent a videotaped movie; others, such as the magazine covers at the grocery checkout stand or advertising on buses, infringe on their senses unsought. It has been observed that taken collectively, these media images present a rather idealized version of life in the United States. Individual media images, as well, may be idealized. This is particularly true of advertising.

Of course, not all advertising depictions are idealized. Some advertising is relatively straightforward and factual, and television commercials often show ordinary characters using products in mundane situations like those faced by all consumers. But many advertisements contain idealized images; and these advertisements are the focus of this chapter.

Several characteristics of an image itself or of the techniques used in its production can result in idealization. Three such characteristics are described below.

One characteristic of many idealized media images is the depiction of highly desirable circumstances that can be achieved by only a few members of society. For instance, Belk and Pollay (1985) found that the level of wealth or material comfort displayed in many advertisements is well beyond that available to middle-class households. Similarly, the level of beauty and physical attractiveness possessed by nearly all actors and models (especially female) is characteristic of an extremely small segment of the population. Collectively, media images present a biased, undemocratic view of life in that they do not represent a cross-section of American life as it truly exists. Jordan and Bryant (1979), for example, analyzed the portrayals of couples in magazine advertisements and found no old, poor, sick, or unattractive couples in the 500 ads sampled.

Second, media images are idealized in that they almost necessarily present an edited version of life. One appealing commercial for United Airlines showed an attractive business person who is also a mother. She drops her daughter off at day care, flies to a business meeting, and returns at the end of the day in time to pick up her smiling, delighted daughter. The boring things are omitted. Viewers do not see this woman brushing her teeth or standing in line to buy a newspaper. Unpleasant things are also omitted. As far as we know, this woman never has a run in her pantyhose, never has to wait in the rain for a cab, and her daughter never whines. In media, time and space are costly. Including boring or unpleasant aspects of life in a television commercial or program is expensive and in most cases detrimental to the advertiser's or director's goal, so these elements are excluded. But the resulting image depicts an idealized version of life that is not achieved even by the most fortunate members of society.

Third, technology and special effects are often used to make media images appear more perfect or ideal than they otherwise are. Air-brushing, cropping, and editing techniques make the imperfect more perfect, and lighting effects or camera angles can make the ordinary seem special. Music or sound tracks are particularly effective for the latter purpose. Walking a few blocks on a city street or driving to work becomes an exciting adventure when accompanied by a John Williams score. Even the mundane task of doing the laundry can seem special when the appropriate sound track is used.

The idealized media images of most interest in the study of materialism are those that represent idealized levels of wealth and consumption. It is argued here that continued exposure to images idealized in these ways increases the desire for more, at least among some consumers. Many authors and social critics have complained that media images create materialism and are a cause of excessive concern with consumption in contemporary culture (see Pollay, 1986, for a review). This chapter uses social comparison theory to place such concerns in a theoretical framework and uses this framework to examine some of the mechanisms by which idealized media images might influence materialism, consumer desire, and discontent.

It is proposed that idealized images can stimulate the desire for more through at least two mechanisms. First, the ubiquitous presence of idealized images in advertising leads to self-comparisons with those images. In these comparisons, the consumer inevitably falls short, leading to dissatisfaction and, for some consumers, increased striving to achieve the idealized state. The second mechanism involves an upward shifting of consumers' expectations or reference point (Hoch & Loewenstein, 1991) for the standard of living they believe they should achieve.

Each of these mechanisms is described below as it relates to advertising images. Although idealized images are presented in nearly all media forms, this chapter focuses particularly on advertising images and their impact on consumers' perceptions and feelings about themselves. The effects described, however, apply to other forms of media as well. Further, these effects are described in the context of U.S. media, although they probably apply to media images in other industrialized economies as well.

Idealized Images, Satisfaction, and Striving

Idealized images affect satisfaction with the one's circumstances through social comparison (Richins, 1991). People desire to know about themselves, and one way to know one's self is to compare with others. After reviewing the extensive literatures on comparison, Pettigrew (1967) concluded that, "there appears to exist a pervasive motive to evaluate, particularly self-evaluate," and these evaluations "furnish forceful motivation for a variety of specific behaviors" (p. 243). Evidence of social comparison appears early in life. Every parent has heard the complaint, "Billy's piece of cake is bigger than mine" or overheard a child claim to a playmate that her mom/dad/sibling is stronger/smarter/better than the playmate's. Social comparison theory (Festinger, 1954; Goethals & Darley, 1977; Wood, 1989) addresses how people develop self-knowledge and make social choices based on their comparisons with others.

THE MOTIVES FOR SOCIAL COMPARISON

At least two types of information can result from social comparison. First, people use comparison to determine whether they are "correct" or "normal." Among adolescents, for instance, there is quite a bit of overt and covert locker room examination of peers' sexual characteristics. This helps teenagers assess whether their own development is "normal." During political campaigns, many voters discuss candidates and political views. One of the purposes of these discussions is to determine the correctness or acceptability of one's own views.

The other type of information resulting from social comparison concerns relative standing. This information is most likely to result from comparisons of abilities or circumstances. Through social comparison, individuals determine whether they are smarter or not as smart, richer or poorer, better off or worse off than others.

The information on correctness and relative standing obtained through social evaluation leads to positive, neutral, or negative self-ratings that are relative to the individual's standards employed for comparison (Pettigrew, 1967). This notion of a comparison standard and the fact that one's relative standing depends on the comparison standards used are important ideas to which we will return.

THE DOMAINS OF SOCIAL COMPARISON

People can compare themselves with others on any visible criterion, from eye color to driving skill to the attractiveness of their spouse (Kruglanski & Mayseless, 1990). Some comparison criteria are more important than others, however, and what is important to one individual may be unimportant to another. Hence, for some people academic accomplishments matter, while for others it may be the difficulty of mountain ascents, the breadth of travel experiences, or the number or quality of one's sexual conquests. The most important comparisons are on those criteria that most importantly define a person's identity and that constitute the core elements of the self.

For many members of the consumer culture, material possessions are particularly important in defining the self (Belk, 1988a; Dittmar, 1992; McCracken, 1986). In addition, members of consumer societies tend to judge themselves and others in terms of their consumption lifestyles (Rassuli & Hollander, 1986), and social comparison is an important mechanism for making these status evaluations. For these reasons, material possessions and consumption experiences are important comparison domains for many consumers, and these consumers can be expected to engage in frequent social comparison on these criteria.

THE COMPARISON STANDARD AND COMPARISON OUTCOMES

According to the original formulation of social comparison theory (Festinger, 1954), individuals prefer objective sources of information over subjective sources. Thus, to evaluate their economic status people would be expected to prefer comparison with government statistics on income distribution, for instance, over their subjective impression of other people's income level. For most comparison criteria, however, objective standards are not available and comparisons must be based on subjective evaluations of other people who are either known personally (e.g., friends and co-workers) or are known about from media descriptions or other sources.

People often control or choose with whom they compare (see Buunk, Collins, Taylor, & Van Yperen, 1990, for a review). Particularly, they often decide (perhaps unconsciously) whether to make a downward or an upward comparison. In downward comparison, a person compares with a worse-off other. This is particularly useful when one's feeling of self-worth is threatened. For instance, a student who gets a D on an exam can partially restore feelings of self-worth by comparing with a student who got an F. Downward comparison can also result in increased satisfaction with one's circumstances. Many people feel a surge of thankfulness and satisfaction with their own lives when they encounter a severely handicapped person and for a moment, at least, find their own dissatisfactions easier to bear.

People may also engage in upward comparison; that is, with a better-off other. In some circumstances this can provide hope and motivation, as when a poverty-stricken medical student looks at better-off practicing physicians as a motivator to endure the hardships of medical training (Taylor & Lobel, 1989). Perhaps more frequently, however, upward comparison results in feelings of inferiority, dissatisfaction, and impaired self-worth. The med student expects eventually to achieve the lifestyle and circumstances of the practicing physician, but the physician's gardener does not. To the extent that the gardener compares his or her circumstances with the physician's, negative feelings are likely to result.

Although social comparison theory originally recognized only sought comparisons, more recently it has been recognized that people cannot always control with whom they compare (e.g., Wood, 1989). Goethals (1986), for instance, noted that,

> It can be hard to hear an extremely intelligent person on the radio, or see an extremely handsome one in the grocery store, or participate on a panel with an expert without engaging in social comparison no matter how much we would like not to. (p. 272)

Perhaps the most frequent social comparison in our culture, often unsought, is with media images (Richins, 1991). Advertising and entertainment media images are pervasive, providing many opportunities to compare with respect to material possessions, level of attractiveness, and other criteria. Also, because most of these images are idealized, the comparison is an upward one and the comparer finds him- or herself deficient with respect to the comparison standard. (Colin Campbell, 1987, has argued that comparisons are made not with media images per se but with illusions and daydreams stimulated by a variety of sources, including advertising and other marketing stimuli. It is likely that these fantasy images are even more idealized than the "best" images provided by advertising, creating an even greater sense of deficiency on the part of the comparer.)

If the comparison domain (e.g., wealth, attractiveness) is important to the individual, the deficiency resulting from comparison with an idealized image leads to negative self-feelings (Salovey & Rodin, 1984; Smith, Diener, & Garonzik, 1990). These negative self-feelings are motivating (Higgins, 1987; James, 1890), and people strive to eliminate the negative feelings and repair their sense of self-worth. At least three ways of dealing with these unpleasant feelings are available.

Perhaps the strongest response to the negative feelings associated with a comparison discrepancy, and one frequently posited by theorists (e.g., Carver & Scheier, 1981; Duval & Wicklund, 1972), is to increase efforts to reduce the discrepancy between oneself and the comparison standard. For consumers viewing media images of "the good life," this means acquiring more possessions in an attempt to approximate the ideal more closely. Thus, idealized media images of wealth reinforce and exacerbate the drive to acquire more of the desired goods, at least among those who perceive that increased effort will in fact move them closer to the desired goal (Duval, Duval, & Mulilis, 1992).

Second, one may reduce or prevent the negative self-feelings that result from comparison with an ideal by reducing the importance of the criterion on which the comparison was made. When persons low in materialism see idealized images of wealth, negative self-feelings are unlikely to result even if their own possessions are relatively modest; material possessions simply are not important to their feelings of self-worth. Research indicates that consumers low in materialism are considerably more satisfied with their standard of living than are those who place a higher value on material things (Richins, 1987; Richins & Dawson, 1992), suggesting indirectly that those low in materialism either do less comparing with idealized images or are less concerned about the outcomes of such comparisons.

Finally, individuals can avoid negative self-feelings by simply refusing to compare themselves with idealized media images. Because many comparisons are unconscious and unsought, however, and because the domain compared upon (in this case, possessions and lifestyle) is important to members of a consumer society, this option is more appealing in the abstract than in practice.

The above discussion describes how idealized media images of wealth and the good life can affect consumers by increasing their motivation to acquire more of the possessions they desire. The following analysis demonstrates how these idealized images may affect consumers by influencing their expectations about life, or "what ought to be."

Idealized Images and "What Ought to Be"

All people have vague, generally unarticulated notions of "what ought to be" in their lives. These include notions of how they should be treated by friends and co-workers; how much fun they should have on vacations; and the standard of living they should have, given their personal talents, occupation, and work effort expended. These notions develop over time and in response to a variety of social stimuli. The following analysis examines one dimension of what ought to be—people's expectations concerning the number and quality of their material possessions. (This analysis could also be extended to consumers' expectations concerning the degree of pleasure or hedonic stimulation they believe they ought to receive from their possessions; see also Campbell, 1987, for a discussion of the role of pleasure in forming consumption desires.)

Early in their lives, children look about them to determine what ought to be. Parents often hear such tearful pleas as, "Linda has a Barbie doll—I want one too," or "Stevie gets to stay up late—how come I can't?" The fact that another child has or is allowed to do something is prima facie evidence of what ought to be.

Among adults we can identify at least three sources of information about what ought to be. Adults, like children, gain such information from their peers. As suggested by relative deprivation theory (Crosby, 1976; Olson & Hazlewood, 1986), most adults view themselves as entitled to approximately the same benefits and quality of life possessed by peers of the same age and with the same general education and skill levels. If my neighbor who happens to be similar to me in those characteristics has the same sort of possessions as I do, my belief in what ought to be is unchallenged. If, however, this same neighbor installs an in-ground swimming pool, acquires a matched set of BMWs, and spends 4 weeks in Europe every summer, I may view this consumption set much like a child views Linda's Barbie doll and eventually see this standard of living as what ought to be.

Aspiration groups provide another source of information about what ought to be. In adolescence and early adulthood (and perhaps to a lesser extent in later years) people look beyond the present to what life will be like when they have "arrived," to the time after graduation, after marriage, or after some other important goal has been reached. This imagining is assisted by identifying others who have already reached that desired state: one's parents, perhaps, or friends of one's parents; or fellow employees who have been working longer and have advanced farther in their careers. The lifestyles of these individuals provide useful information about what ought to be and the standard of living one can expect when one reaches that particular stage of career or life cycle.

The firsthand, immediate access to information about lifestyles and consumption possibilities provided by peers and aspiration groups is necessarily limited by the range of one's acquaintances. Because people tend to know others who are similar to themselves, these firsthand sources of information tend to be appropriate and realistic. This is not necessarily the case for media images, however, the third source of information about what ought to be. Media images such as television shows, movies, and advertising expose us to images and possibilities that are not available through immediate observation or personal experience. Through the power of television we can see how Ted Turner and Jane Fonda live, can see inside the homes of rich celebrities who would never invite us in should we knock on their doors. More frequently, however, the media introduce us to consumption styles of people who do not even exist. We see the homes of Dr. and Mrs. Huxtable, of Roseanne, of people who use Tide to wash their laundry or serve Folgers instant coffee at fancy-dress dinner parties.

These sources, plus a variety of socializing agents such as religion, parental admonition, and the like, create an unconscious expectation of what ought to be with respect to one's assortment of possessions, lifestyle, and standard of living. The processing of information from these sources is automatic and often below the level of consciousness (Lewicki, 1986; Lewicki & Hill, 1987), but has impact nonetheless. Information integration and related theories (Anderson, 1981) provide insight into how information from media and other social stimuli may be integrated to influence people's expectations of what life ought to be.

When new information or social stimuli are symmetrically distributed about a person's expectation level, the expectation level is not changed. Thus, if people see media images of individuals better off and worse off than what they expect in about equal proportions, their expectations remain unchanged. Exposure to stimuli consistently above or below the expectation level, however, will cause it to be raised or lowered, respectively (Anderson, 1975; Helson, 1947; Thibaut & Kelley, 1959; see also Parducci, 1968). Because advertising images tend to be idealized—that is, they usually show people who are well off in terms of possessions—exposure to large amounts of advertising will raise people's expectations of what ought to be. The process by which this information is assimilated is largely unconscious and generally unsought.

This prediction about the effects of idealized images derived from information integration theories is akin to notions advanced by cultivation theorists in the communications field. According to these researchers, individuals exposed to heavy doses of television tend to adopt the "reality" of the television world (Gerbner, Gross, Signorielli, & Morgan, 1980; Hawkins & Pingree, 1981). Because television programming overrepresents middle- and upper-income families (Gerbner & Signorielli, 1982), cultivation theory predicts that heavy television viewers are more likely than others to view American families as more affluent than they actually are. Although empirical support for this prediction is mixed, it has been supported among some demographic subgroups (Carlson, 1993; Fox & Philliber, 1978; Shrum, O'Guinn, Semenik, & Faber, 1991).

Information integration theories were developed to explain judgments of the properties of physical stimuli, such as the weight or length of objects. For such judgments, stimuli are often treated more or less equally in the integration process. When integrating information contained in more complex psychological stimuli such as advertisements, however, some stimuli are more carefully attended to than others, and the stimuli differ in the degree to which they may affect perceptions and expectations. Social and media stimuli that are vivid (Kisielius & Sternthal, 1986; Nisbett & Ross, 1980; Richardson, 1980), realistic (Potter, 1986), and relevant are more likely to affect perceptions of what ought to be than are stimuli that do not possess these characteristics. The particular qualities of advertising images that make them especially potent in affecting perceptions of what ought to be are discussed below.

VIVIDNESS OF ADVERTISING IMAGES

Perhaps the most important goal for an advertisement is to stand out from the media clutter, to be noticed. Vividness is one of the ways to accomplish this. The use of special effects, color, music, and high-quality photography in the hands of highly talented production staff results in advertisements that captivate the viewer and can be beautiful, memorable, and emotionally potent.

REALISM IN ADVERTISING

Even though some advertising uses surreal images or is clearly designed to appeal to consumers' more extravagant fantasies (as when a swimming pool and gorgeous women magically appear when a bottle of beer is opened in the desert), most advertising is designed to be perceived as real and credible. Advertising is to be *believed;* if it is not, the advertiser's money has not been well spent. Furthermore, many advertisements can be viewed as artistic or (in the case of commercials) dramatic creations. An important goal in artistic creation, including advertising, is to cause a suspension of disbelief, to cause the viewer to enter emotionally into the artistic creation as if it were real (Englis, 1992; Gardner, 1983). Recently, advertisers have used technology to blur further the distinction between television commercials and reality. MCI, as part of its "Gramercy Press" serial advertising campaign, made it possible for consumers to send Internet messages to their favorite Gramercy Press characters, who in turn are said to answer each one (Miller & Nayyar, 1994). Even advertisements that employ surrealistic executions can be perceived as real to the extent that their creators are successful in engaging the viewer's willing suspension of disbelief. Such factors, and the large pool of talent in the advertising industry that devote its efforts to effective advertising, ensure that the important elements of most advertising seem very real (or at least plausible) to viewers.

Another factor that makes advertising seem real is the use of photographic images (Ewen, 1988). Photographs seem real, truthful, and objective, and their use in advertising makes the advertisement seem real. As one photographer noted, "If you see all these wonderful, thin, muscular, tall, blonde, white, rich, healthy, young people buy this car, or this hamburger, or whatever it is, *you know that's the truth because you see it right in front of you"* (quoted in Englis, 1992, p. 206). These photographic images, sometimes with special effects, may depict situations or places with which most viewers have no firsthand experience. This hinders the ability of even the more cynical viewer to judge the accuracy of the image presented and encourages the acceptance of that image as truth (see Moog, 1990, pp. 109-139, and Schudson, 1984, pp. 210-222, for additional discussions of realism in advertising).

RELEVANCE OF ADVERTISING IMAGES

In determining what ought to be, some images are more relevant than others. Consumers can observe on television Prince Charles's circumstances when he vacations in the Mediterranean and automatically realize that their vacations will not be like that, nor should they be. A prince's lifestyle and circumstances simply are not relevant in determining what ought to be in an ordinary person's life. When middle-class Americans see newsclips of poverty-stricken Filipinos foraging for food in a garbage dump, they may feel revulsion or concern, but these images have no relevance for what ought to be in their own lives.

Which images, then, are most relevant to viewers? Social judgment theory (Sherif & Hovland, 1961; Sherif, Sherif, & Nebergall, 1965), developed to explain attitude change resulting from persuasive messages, may apply to attitude change that results from images. It is proposed that persuasive images, like persuasive messages, can be divided into zones or latitudes of acceptance, rejection, and noncommitment (a neutral zone). In the case at hand, images of circumstances similar to the viewer's own or that are likely to be achieved by viewers are within the latitude of acceptance (referred to here as the zone of probability); positive images of circumstances viewers can never hope to attain and images of negative or unpleasant circumstances fall in the latitude of rejection (zone of improbability). Images that fall between these two zones are in the zone of possibility.

The attitude change literature shows that the most influential persuasive messages are those that lie in the latitude of noncommitment (e.g., Freedman, 1964; Siero & Doosje, 1993). Likewise, the images that may be most effective in changing perceptions of what ought to be may be those that fall within the zone of possibility. Advertisers, in presenting their products in the most favorable light, choose images that are on the favorable end of the zone of possibility; these images depict circumstances that are more desirable than the circumstances of most consumers' lives.

It is in the marketer's interest to make advertisements seem relevant to viewers. Advertisements in the zone of possibility are more likely than other ads to seem relevant because they depict circumstances that are desirable and that seem to be achievable. Another way to make advertisements seem relevant is to make the *characters* portrayed in them seem relevant. If viewers see the characters as relevant or similar to themselves, they are more likely also to see the featured products as relevant. For advertisers, it is desirable to make the characters seem relevant to the largest number of viewers possible. Decontextualization is an effective mechanism for accomplishing this.

Most characters or models in advertising are decontextualized or are contextualized only loosely. Aside from gross cues such as gender and age, there is little objective information about the characteristics or nature of a person being portrayed in an advertisement and this person's similarity to us, the viewers. Advertising is purposely vague concerning such cues as occupation and income level so that we will be more likely to identify with the model, more apt to imagine that we could be like (as attractive, as popular, as wealthy as) this "person" if we only used the same product. Thus, cues that might indicate the model is *not* like the viewer are removed or minimized.

Through the advertising production process, the model becomes an imaginary, composite person who is somehow real, or possibly real, whom any of us might become, and whose circumstances we might share. In an advertisement for Sheraton hotels showing an attractive man and woman in evening dress dining out in Hong Kong, there is nothing to suggest that we should not be able to have the same. An advertisement showing a beautiful woman giving a man a large diamond includes nothing to suggest that she is a neurosurgeon with an income unobtainable by most consumers. In "real life," a couple entertaining friends at their lakeside cabin and enjoying a Michelob may have worked weekends for 4 years and postponed having children so they could buy the cabin, but there is nothing in an advertisement depicting such a scene that would communicate this kind of information to viewers.

This lack of context serves to obscure the potential irrelevance of idealized advertising images to many consumers, increases the likelihood that these images will be judged in the zone of possibility, and increases the chances that they will be integrated into perceptions of what ought to be, thus raising expectations about the level of material circumstances one deserves and might expect to obtain.

The lack of context, along with visually arresting execution of the advertising images, also facilitates fantasy or daydreaming by the viewer in which the viewer and the featured products play a part. Campbell (1987) has described the important part such fantasies play in modern consumer societies and notes that,

> we [consumers] recognize our "day-dreaming" and fantasizing for what they are (or rather what they are not—that is, "real"). Such "realism," however, merely has the effect of making us dissatisfied with a life which provides actual pleasures so far short of those which illusion can supply; somewhere, we are convinced, it must be possible to experience the latter in reality. (p. 90)

AVAILABILITY OF ADVERTISING IMAGES

In addition to the characteristics of idealized advertising images that result in their disproportionate influence on consumers' expectations of what ought to be, these images can influence perceptions by the sheer weight of their number. This expectation follows from the availability heuristic described by Tversky and Kahneman (1973). In calling to mind what ought to be, events or images that are more readily accessible in memory have a greater impact on perceptions of what ought to be than do less available images. The typical consumer is exposed to thousands of advertising images, and many of these images are idealized. The pervasiveness of these idealized images makes them more cognitively available than other, perhaps more realistic, images of what is or what might be that are stored in memory.

BIASED PROCESSING OF MEDIA IMAGES

Finally, it is proposed that media images are processed in a biased fashion; specifically, that positive and negative images are not equally likely to be integrated into expectations of what ought to be. When people see images or circumstances below their expectation level, perceptual defenses are activated. If, for instance, we see a news program interview of a low-income family in their modest home, we unconsciously put ourselves into a different category of persons and dismiss the information about that family's circumstances as irrelevant to us, or at least irrelevant to our belief in what ought to be. That mother's or father's circumstances simply do not apply to us because we are a different kind of person (more intelligent/motivated/skilled); as a result, this irrelevant information is not integrated into our perception of what ought to be.

On the other hand, when we see an interview with a successful attorney in her well-appointed home or an advertisement with someone driving a Mercedes 500 SL up the drive to his country estate, we are not so quick to dismiss these individuals as dissimilar or irrelevant. In this instance, putting ourselves in a different category from such people would make us seem inferior. Instead, we unconsciously see ourselves to be as good or as worthy as they are and perhaps wonder why we too don't have a country estate. We ask ourselves what these "people" have done to merit such circumstances and wonder how we can get them, too. The information about their possessions and status are thus relevant and integrated into our expectation of what ought to be, raising it somewhat.

Because media, especially advertising, are filled with idealized images of better-off others, consumers' expectations of what ought to be are gradually raised to a level that is unrealistic for most individuals. The frequent exposure to wealthy, beautiful, and happy people generates a false reality in which the uncommon and ideal become mundane and attainable. In our daily unconscious assessments of our lives, we continually fall short. For some, the result is a continual striving and a desire for more accompanied by a feeling of missing out, of having less than what ought to be.

Idealized Images and Discontent

Striving for more may or may not be inherent in the human character, but modern advertising has been carefully designed to increase consumer desire. It does so in part by inducing social comparison with idealized images and by raising consumers' expectations about what ought to be in their own lives, particularly with respect to consumer goods. For many, the result of these processes is dissatisfaction and a desire for increased consumption.

Increases in consumer desire can have positive economic consequences, at least in the short run, by raising the consumer expenditures that help sustain economic growth and that contribute to the profitability of those firms that effectively satisfy consumers. The longer run negative consequences of superfluous consumer desire are, however, often overlooked. These negative consequences, including a personal sense of dissatisfaction, neglect of social relationships in the pursuit of things, excessive debt, environmental damage, and the premature depletion of nonrenewable resources, have been described by several observers (Belk, 1988b; Durning, 1992; Fromm, 1976; Hirsch, 1976; Meadows et al., 1972; Worster, 1993).

Although advertising using idealized images can be criticized for contributing to consumer discontent, among other negative consequences, it must be recognized that many consumers *like* such advertising, just as they enjoy movies and television programs that encourage escape and fantasy. In addition, such advertising is frequently successful in selling products. Thus, it simply is not plausible to suggest that advertisers abandon the use of idealized images in the interests of furthering social contentment. Some actions are possible, however, to mitigate some of the undesirable effects of these idealized images.

To blunt the impact of such images Neil Postman, among others, has argued that consumers need to be educated in the interpretation of the images of advertising. Just as school children are taught the standards of knowledge creation so they can evaluate the truth and falsity of statements, so too do people need to learn how to interpret the meaning and potential influence of advertising images. Although the effects of such training have not been empirically examined, the idea is sufficiently provocative to deserve further investigation.

Though this chapter has focused on the role of idealized advertising images in fostering discontent, it must be recognized that these images are not the only, and probably not the most potent, cause of dissatisfaction. It can be argued that discontent is an inherent condition of humankind, and some people seem to experience unhappiness whatever their circumstances and regardless of the advertisements they see (Costa & McCrae, 1980; Heady & Wearing, 1989). When people are discontented, however—whether this stems from their nature, their circumstances, or their perceived inferiority in comparison to idealized media images—they look about themselves to determine how they can make themselves happier and how they can improve their lot. The discontented person asks, "What should I strive for to make myself happy?" The answer provided by advertising, encountered at every turn, is "more stuff." In a capitalistic society possessing the benefit of free speech, that answer will not go away.

What is needed is a greater *variety* of answers about what brings happiness. Research shows that feelings of well-being are influenced by a variety of factors; the ability to buy things, in and of itself, appears to have little bearing on the happiness of individuals, except where income is relatively modest (Diener, Sandvik, Seidlitz, & Diener, 1993; Veenhoven, 1991). Family, friends, and other interpersonal connections play a much greater role (Argyle, 1987; Campbell, Converse, & Rodgers, 1976). Media representations that remind consumers of the other factors that contribute to happiness may encourage at least some individuals to place less emphasis on the desire to buy and more emphasis on other factors such as interpersonal relationships. For instance, television programming could more frequently depict, in ways that have both appeal and impact, the notion that connecting, giving, and helping are important routes to happiness; these messages should be as vivid, appealing, and well-executed as the messages that tell consumers that *goods* are the route to happiness. Although a few advertising campaigns have done this effectively (e.g., AT&T's "Reach out and touch someone" advertising campaign for long-distance telephone service and commercials for Hallmark greeting cards), the selling proposition inherent in advertising may render advertising ineffective for this purpose, serving instead to convince consumers that they need more *things* to achieve interpersonal and other nonmaterial satisfactions (e.g., "My friends would *really* like me if I owned a sports car").

Instead, media other than advertising may be more effective in presenting alternatives to "getting more" as a route to happiness. News features and television programming that positively portray real people and fictional characters who achieve happiness without undue emphasis on material possessions can remind people, without moralizing, of the importance of interpersonal and other satisfactions in achieving happiness. To be effective, such programming should be integrated into regular programming schedules (rather than introduced as "special presentations") and have the same high production values as programs that are more materialistic. Social judgment theory suggests that these portrayals would be most effective if they focused on individuals somewhat like the typical American rather than on those who lead lives remarkably devoid of material concerns, such as Mother Teresa. The latter type of role model, though inspiring, leads lives that are so different from the daily concerns and aspirations of most Americans that they tend to be perceived as admirable but irrelevant role models.

Public policy can also be useful in helping citizens achieve a greater sense of satisfaction with their lives, using sources other than consumption. Murray (1988) has provided an extensive analysis of the ways in which government may fulfill what he sees as the government's primary obligation to its citizens—to enable their pursuit of happiness.

Twentieth-century America possesses a consumer culture, and even without idealized advertising images the desire for more would, no doubt, flourish. But given increasing demands on economic and environmental resources due to population increases and other factors, it is useful to think of ways in which the well-being of the populace can be maintained through means other than ever-increasing consumption.

References

Anderson, N. H. (1975). On the role of context effects in psychophysical judgment. *Psychological Review, 82,* 462-482.

Anderson, N. H. (1981). *Foundations of information integration theory.* New York: Academic Press.

Argyle, M. (1987). *The psychology of happiness.* London: Methuen.

Belk, R. W. (1983). Worldly possessions: Issues and criticisms. In R. P. Bagozzi & A. M. Tybout (Eds.), *Advances in consumer research* (Vol. 10, pp. 514-519). Ann Arbor, MI: Association for Consumer Research.

Belk, R. W. (1988a). Possessions and the extended self. *Journal of Consumer Research, 15,* 139-168.

Belk, R. W. (1988b). Third world consumer culture. In E. Kumcu & A. F. Firat (Eds.), *Marketing and development: Toward broader dimensions* (pp. 103-127). Greenwich, CT: JAI.

Belk, R. W., & Pollay, R. W. (1985). Materialism and magazine advertising during the twentieth century. In E. Hirschman & M. Holbrook (Eds.), *Advances in consumer research* (Vol. 12, pp. 394-398). Provo, UT: Association for Consumer Research.

Bredemeier, H. C., & Toby, J. (1960). *Social problems in America: Costs and casualties in an acquisitive society.* New York: John Wiley.

Buunk, B. P., Collins, R. L., Taylor, S. E., & Van Yperen, N. W. (1990). The affective consequences of social comparison: Either direction has its ups and downs. *Journal of Personality and Social Psychology, 59,* 1238-1249.

Campbell, A., Converse, P. E., & Rodgers, W. L. (1976). *The quality of American life: Perceptions, evaluations, and satisfactions.* New York: Russell Sage Foundation.

Campbell, C. (1987). *The romantic ethic and the spirit of modern consumerism.* New York: Basil Blackwell.

Carlson, J. M. (1993). Television viewing: Cultivating perceptions of affluence and support of capitalist values. *Political Communication, 10,* 243-257.

Carver, C. S., & Scheier, M. F. (1981). *Attention and self-regulation: A control-theory approach to human behavior.* New York: Springer.

Costa, P. T., & McCrae, R. R. (1980). Influence of extraversion and neuroticism on subjective well-being: Happy and unhappy people. *Journal of Personality and Social Psychology, 38,* 668-678.

Crosby, F. (1976). A model of egoistical relative deprivation. *Psychological Review, 83,* 85-113.

de Tocqueville, A. (1954). *Democracy in America.* New York: Vintage. (Original work published 1835)

Diener, E., Sandvik, E., Seidlitz, L., & Diener, M. (1993). The relationship between income and subjective well-being: Relative or absolute? *Social Indicators Research, 28,* 195-223.

Dittmar, H. (1992). *The social psychology of material possessions: To have is to be.* New York: St. Martin's.

Durning, A. T. (1992). *How much is enough?: The consumer society and the future of the earth.* New York: Norton.

Duval, S., & Wicklund, R. A. (1972). *A theory of objective self-awareness.* New York: Academic Press.

Duval, T. S., Duval, V. H., & Mulilis, J.-P. (1992). Effects of self-focus, discrepancy between self and standard, and outcome expectancy favorability on the tendency to match self to standard or to withdraw. *Journal of Personality and Social Psychology, 62,* 340-348.

Easterlin, R. A., & Crimmins, E. M. (1988). Recent social trends: Changes in personal aspirations of American youth. *Sociology and Social Research, 72,* 217-223.

Easterlin, R. A., & Crimmins, E. M. (1991). Private materialism, personal self-fulfillment, family life, and public interest: The nature, effects, and causes of recent changes in the values of American youth. *Public Opinion Quarterly, 55,* 499-533.

Englis, B. G. (1992). The willing suspension of disbelief and its importance in understanding advertising effects. In C. T. Allen et al. (Eds.), *Marketing theory and applications* (pp. 203-208). Chicago: American Marketing Association.

Eugeni, F. (1993). Consumer debt and home equity borrowing. *Economic Perspectives, 17*(2), 2-13.

Ewen, S. (1988). *All consuming images: The politics of style in contemporary culture.* New York: Basic Books.

Festinger, L. (1954). A theory of social comparison processes. *Human Relations, 7,* 117-140.

Fox, R. W., & Lears, T.J.J. (1983). *The culture of consumption: Critical essays in American history, 1880-1980.* New York: Pantheon.

Fox, W. S., & Philliber, W. W. (1978). Television viewing and the perception of affluence. *Sociological Quarterly, 19,* 103-112.

Freedman, J. L. (1964). Involvement, discrepancy, and change. *Journal of Abnormal and Social Psychology, 69,* 290-295.

Fromm, E. (1976). *To have or to be?* New York: Harper & Row.

Gardner, J. (1983). *The art of fiction.* New York: Knopf.

Gerbner, G., Gross, L., Signorielli, N., & Morgan, M. (1980). Aging with television: Images on television drama and conceptions of social reality. *Journal of Communication, 30,* 37-47.

Gerbner, G., & Signorielli, N. (1982). The world according to television. *American Demographics, 4,* 14-17.

Goethals, G. R. (1986). Social comparison theory: Psychology from the lost and found. *Personality and Social Psychology Bulletin, 12,* 261-278.

Goethals, G. R., & Darley, J. M. (1977). Social comparison theory: An attributional approach. In J. M. Suls & R. L. Miller (Eds.), *Social comparison processes: Theoretical and empirical perspectives* (pp. 259-278). New York: John Wiley.

Hawkins, R. P., & Pingree, S. (1981). Using television to construct social reality. *Journal of Broadcasting, 25,* 347-364.

Heady, B., & Wearing, A. (1989). Personality, life events, and subjective well-being: Toward a dynamic equilibrium model. *Journal of Personality and Social Psychology, 57,* 731-739.

Helson, H. (1947). Adaptation-level as frame of reference for prediction of psychophysical data. *American Journal of Psychology, 60,* 1-29.

Higgins, E. T. (1987). Self-discrepancy: A theory relating self and affect. *Psychological Review, 94,* 319-340.

Hirsch, F. (1976). *Social limits to growth.* Cambridge, MA: Harvard University Press.

Hoch, S. J., & Loewenstein, G. F. (1991). Time-inconsistent preferences and consumer self-control. *Journal of Consumer Research, 17,* 492-507.

James, W. (1890). *The principles of psychology.* New York: Holt.

Jordan, B., & Bryant, K. (1979, April 28). *The advertised couple: The portrayal of the couple and their relationship in popular magazine advertisements.* Paper presented at the Popular Culture Association and American Culture Association meetings, Pittsburgh.

Karlins, M., Coffman, T. L., & Walters, G. (1969). On the fading of social stereotypes: Studies in three generations of college students. *Journal of Personality and Social Psychology, 13,* 1-16.

Kisielius, J., & Sternthal, B. (1986). Examining the vividness controversy: An availability-valence interpretation. *Journal of Consumer Research, 12,* 418-431.

Kruglanski, A. W., & Mayseless, O. (1990). Classic and current social comparison research: Expanding the perspective. *Psychological Bulletin, 108,* 195-208.

Lewicki, P. (1986). *Nonconscious social information processing.* New York: Academic Press.

Lewicki, P., & Hill, T. (1987). Unconscious processes as explanations of behavior in cognitive, personality, and social psychology. *Personality and Social Psychology Bulletin, 13,* 355-362.

McCracken, G. (1986). Culture and consumption: A theoretical account of the structure and movement of the cultural meaning of consumer goods. *Journal of Consumer Research, 13,* 71-84.

Meadows, D. H., Meadows, D. L., Randers, J., & Behrens, W.H.B., III. (1972). *The limits to growth: A report for the Club of Rome's project on the predicament of mankind.* New York: Universe Books.

Miller, A., & Nayyar, S. (1994, September 26). Ads of our lives. *Newsweek* pp. 48-50.

Moog, C. (1990). *"Are they selling her lips?": Advertising and identity.* New York: William Morrow.

Murray, C. (1988). *In pursuit of happiness and good government.* New York: Simon & Schuster.

Nisbett, R., & Ross, L. (1980). *Human inference: Strategies and shortcomings of social judgment.* Englewood Cliffs, NJ: Prentice Hall.

Olson, J. M., & Hazlewood, J. D. (1986). Relative deprivation and social comparison: An integrative perspective. In J. M. Olson, C. P. Herman, & M. P. Zanna (Eds.), *Relative deprivation and social comparison, The Ontario Symposium* (Vol. 4, pp. 1-15). Hillsdale, NJ: Lawrence Erlbaum.

Parducci, A. (1968). The relativism of absolute judgments. *Scientific American, 219,* 84-90.

Pettigrew, T. F. (1967). Social evaluation theory: Convergences and applications. In D. Levine (Ed.), *Nebraska Symposium on Motivation, 1967* (pp. 241-315). Lincoln: University of Nebraska Press.

Pollay, R. W. (1986). The distorted mirror: Reflections on the unintended consequences of advertising. *Journal of Marketing, 50*(April), 18-36.

Potter, W. J. (1986). Perceived reality and the cultivation hypothesis. *Journal of Broadcasting and Electronic Media, 30,* 159-174.

Rassuli, K. M., & Hollander, S. C. (1986). Desire—Induced, innate, insatiable? *Journal of Macromarketing, 6,* 4-24.

Richardson, J. T. E. (1980). *Mental imagery and human memory.* New York: St. Martin's.

Richins, M. L. (1987). Media, materialism, and human happiness. In M. Wallendorf & P. Anderson (Eds.), *Advances in consumer research* (Vol. 14, pp. 352-356). Provo, UT: Association for Consumer Research.

Richins, M. L. (1991). Social comparison and the idealized images of advertising. *Journal of Consumer Research, 18,* 71-83.

Richins, M. L., & Dawson, S. (1992). A consumer values orientation for materialism and its measurement: Scale development and validation. *Journal of Consumer Research, 19,* 303-316.

Roper Starch Worldwide. (1994). *Survey of America's inner financial life.* New York: Author.

Rudmin, F. W., & Kilbourne, W. E. (in press). The meaning and morality of voluntary simplicity: History and hypotheses on deliberately denied materialism. In N. Dholakia & R. W. Belk (Eds.), *Consumption and marketing: Macro dimensions.* Northridge, CA: PWS-Kent Publishing.

Salovey, P., & Rodin, J. (1984). Some antecedents and consequences of social-comparison jealousy. *Journal of Personality and Social Psychology, 47,* 780-792.

Schudson, M. (1984). *Advertising, the uneasy persuasion.* New York: Basic Books.

Sherif, C. W., Sherif, M., & Nebergall, R. E. (1965). *Attitude and attitude change: The social judgment-involvement approach.* Philadelphia: W. B. Saunders.

Sherif, M., & Hovland, C. I. (1961). *Social judgment: Assimilation and contrast effects in communication and attitude change.* New Haven, CT: Yale University Press.

Shrum, L. J., O'Guinn, T., Semenik, R. J., & Faber, R. J. (1991). Processes and effects in the construction of normative consumer beliefs: The role of television. In R. H. Holman & M. R. Solomon (Eds.), *Advances in consumer research* (Vol. 18, pp. 755-763). Provo, UT: Association for Consumer Research.

Siero, F. W., & Doosje, B. J. (1993). Attitude change following persuasive communication: Integrating social judgment theory and the elaboration likelihood model. *European Journal of Social Psychology, 23,* 541-554.

Smith, R. H., Diener, E., & Garonzik, R. (1990). The roles of outcome satisfaction and comparison alternatives in envy. *British Journal of Social Psychology, 29,* 247-255.

Taylor, S. E., & Lobel, M. (1989). Social comparison activity under threat: Downward evaluation and upward contacts. *Psychological Review, 96,* 569-575.

Thibaut, J. W., & Kelley, H. H. (1959). *The social psychology of groups.* New York: John Wiley.

Tversky, A., & Kahneman, D. (1973). Availability: A heuristic for judging frequency and probability. *Cognitive Psychology, 5,* 207-232.

Veenhoven, R. (1991). Is happiness relative? *Social Indicators Research, 24,* 1-34.

Wachtel, P. L. (1983). *The poverty of affluence: A psychological portrait of the American way of life.* New York: Free Press.

Wood, J. V. (1989). Theory and research concerning social comparisons of personal attributes. *Psychological Bulletin, 106,* 231-248.

Worster, D. (1993). *The wealth of nature.* New York: Oxford University Press.

8

Portrayals of African, Hispanic, and Asian Americans in Magazine Advertising

CHARLES R. TAYLOR
JU YUNG LEE
BARBARA B. STERN

THE SIZE OF the three largest minority groups in the United States—African Americans, Hispanic Americans, and Asian Americans—makes them attractive target markets. The 1990 census reveals that more than 30 million African Americans and 23.3 million Hispanic Americans currently reside in the United States. Furthermore, the Asian American population, now at 7.3 million, is the fastest growing minority on a percentage basis. Thus, more than 60 million people are both the subjects and the objects of advertisements targeted to one or more minority groups.

The importance of minority groups is reflected in the number of studies since the 1960s focusing on minority portrayals. This research has, for the most part, focused on three issues—frequency of representation, valence of portrayal (positive or negative depictions), and changes in portrayals over time. Notably, more controversy than

133

conclusive evidence has been the outcome of prior research. One major unresolved problem is conflicting findings on frequency of minority portrayals, for the percentage found has differed widely from study to study (Zinkhan, Qualls, & Biswas, 1990). Another problem is the difficulty in pinning down the components of positive versus negative valence, a result of using different variables and different samples. Still a third problem is the singular focus of most earlier studies, which, in dealing with one minority group alone, do not allow for comparison of similarities and differences in portrayals.

The purpose of the present study was to address the above problems by means of rigorous content analysis. It began with the basic issue of numerical representation of minority portrayals in mainstream magazine advertising. This was a counting task that measured the incidence of male and female African, Hispanic, and Asian American models in terms of the percentage of advertisements in which they appeared. In addition, the analysis included an assessment of prominence or importance of minority models in the aforementioned advertisements. Next, the study used social and contextual variables to discern the positive and negative context of these portrayals. Last, the study used the frequency and valence data to compare the portrayals of one group versus another.

Note here that one limitation of content analysis is the implicit assumption of homogeneity of each minority group. For example, in counting Asian Americans as a group, the study overlooked differences between Korean Americans and Vietnamese Americans. Nonetheless, aggregate counting does provide a barometer of the numerical representation of a minority group in proportion to its representation in the population. Furthermore, it enables comparisons between percentage representation in advertising versus percentage representation in the population. This is not simply a measurement issue but one that carries implications for the societal valuation of minorities, for when a segment of the population is found to be underrepresented in advertising, the covert message may be that the societal majority is indifferent or hostile to the minority.

The study began with measurement, but it moved beyond counting to deal with the meanings that advertising attaches to minority status by including contextual and societal variables not covered in most previous studies. These address the issues of the type of products that minorities are shown using; settings that feature minorities; and personal relationships in which minorities are shown to engage. The rationale for including these variables as indexes of positive/negative valence with social impact will now be discussed.

Impact of Advertising Portrayals on Minority Groups

Negative stereotypical depiction of minorities or their exclusion from advertisements in mainstream media has been found to have harmful social effects. Expectancy theory (Jussim, 1990) describes the influence of negative expectations, for insofar as advertising portrayals build or reinforce such expectancies, they influence social reality. This may contribute to social problems such as prejudice and inequities in educational and occupational opportunities by encouraging self-fulfilling prophecies. For example, because Hispanic Americans are often stereotyped as uneducated (Czepiec & Kelly, 1983), Hispanic American children may feel that it is socially permissible to drop out of school earlier than other Americans. Similarly, if African Americans are often depicted as athletes or entertainers, children may see role models whose achievements are not realistic for most of the population. To the extent that minorities are invisible in advertising, group members may experience the dominant culture as unwilling to embrace them as full participants in a range of human and social activities.

PRIOR RESEARCH ON PORTRAYALS
OF MINORITIES IN ADVERTISING

Perhaps the most widely investigated issue is minority visibility, in terms of the percentage of advertisements in which minority models appear. Generally, African Americans have been found to be portrayed more frequently in television advertising than in magazines. Kassarjian's (1969) study of magazine advertisements in 1965 found that less than 1% of the sample contained African American models. Dominick and Greenberg's (1970) study of television commercials in 1969 found the percentage to be 11%, and Zinkhan et al.'s (1990) study of magazine and television commercials in 1986 reported figures of 4.4.% and 16.0%, respectively. The latter study reviewed earlier ones and found an upward trend in portrayals of African Americans in both magazine and television advertising. This trend is supported by Wilkes and Valencia (1989), who found that 26% of a sample of prime-time television commercials in 1984 that used live models included African Americans. Thus, the frequency of portrayals still appears to be clouded by controversy, indicating that more research is needed.

Controversy also surrounds the nature of portrayals of African Americans, for though negative stereotyping was found for the first half of this century, changes in a more positive direction have occurred since the 1960s. Pettigrew (1965), one of the first researchers to evaluate the portrayal of African Americans in the mass media, found that as far back as the 1930s, African Americans were relegated to three roles: entertainers, athletes, and servants. In a content analysis of a large sample of magazine advertisements in 1965, Kassarjian (1969) found that African Americans were depicted in low-status positions and rarely shown as equals to whites. Cox (1970), however, rebutted this finding in a study that found African Americans portrayed in more prominent roles. In current studies tracking change, African Americans' roles in advertisements have been found to evidence higher status (Zinkhan et al., 1990).

The frequency issue also occupied early studies of Hispanic Americans, for whom infrequent media appearances tended to be the norm. For example, Hispanic American characters accounted for only 1.5% of the speaking parts in the three seasons of network TV programming during the late 1970s (Greenberg & Batista-Fernandez, 1980). In magazine advertising (Czepiec & Kelly, 1983), only 3 (1.5%) advertisements out of a 1982 sample of 206 contained Hispanic models. Television advertisements fared somewhat better in the incidence of Hispanic models (Wilkes & Valencia, 1989); Hispanics appeared in 6% of 1980s commercials. These models tended to occupy background roles in crowd scenes, however, as opposed to central ones figuring prominently in product use.

As far as the portrayal of Asian Americans in advertising, there is virtually no data, for no major published study has examined the frequency or nature of portrayals of this group. Given their rapid growth as a percentage of the population, the Asian group has been quite understudied. We now attempt to rectify the gap by providing additional insights on Asian Americans as well as by comparing portrayals of the three groups.

Research Questions: Frequency, Valence, Stereotyping

FREQUENCY OF PORTRAYAL

The first research question deals with the frequency of representation of minority groups in magazine advertisements. In evaluating frequency, the study used the proportionality criterion, which states that a minority's representation should approximately equal its proportion of the U.S. population (Faber, O'Guinn, & Meyer, 1987). Frequency in relation to proportion of the population provides data on the visibility in society. The current percentages of African Americans, Hispanic Americans, and Asian Americans in the American population are 12.1%, 9.4%, and 3.3%, respectively.

> Question 1: Is the proportion of magazine advertisements portraying each minority group higher or lower than its proportion of the U.S. population?

A second and related question concerns the prominence of minority models when they appear. If a group is fairly and fully represented in advertising, its members should be depicted in starring as well as background roles. Conversely, consistent portrayal of a minority group in the background is evaluated as underrepresentation, for the minority is shown to be peripheral rather than central to social life.

> Question 2: When minority models are present in a magazine advertisement, do they appear most frequently in major roles, minor roles, or background roles?

NATURE OF PORTRAYALS: VALENCE AND STEREOTYPING

Turning from frequency to valence, the next two research questions investigate the use of stereotypes to portray minority groups in magazine advertising. Before stating the questions, let us define the term *stereotype* and examine the relevant ones. A *social stereotype* (Branthwaite & Pierce, 1990) is a prevailing and frequently used image of one group as uniform (rather than as individually differentiated) used to categorize all members of the group on a limited number of dimensions. Prior research has indicated that advertising has historically perpetuated social stereotypes of African Americans as uneducated, low-status members of society in low-status roles. The only exceptions are entertainers or athletes (Pettigrew, 1965). Advertising has tended to reinforce stereotypes of Hispanic Americans as uneducated blue-collar workers who are not well assimilated into mainstream American culture and who have large, close-knit families (e.g., Faber et al., 1987). Although there is little information about advertising portrayals of Asian Americans, they are socially stereotyped as technically competent, hardworking, serious, and well assimilated (Cohen, 1992).

These stereotypes have implications for the product categories and magazine types in which minority models are likely to appear. For example, if African Americans or Hispanic Americans are stereotypically portrayed as uneducated, they are not likely to be depicted frequently in publications with highly educated readers, such as *Scientific American* or *Business Week*. On the other hand, if Asian Americans are stereotypically portrayed as technically oriented, they are likely to be more frequently represented in these publications. In reference to products, a group perceived as uneducated is unlikely to be frequently portrayed as users or purchasers of technologically sophisticated products, such as electronic diaries or computer systems. In contrast, a group perceived as hardworking is not likely to be shown in usage situations in which fun is the object. The following research questions assess the reflection of stereotypes in magazine vehicles and product categories:

Question 3: In what types of magazines are minority models likely to be portrayed?

Question 4: With what types of products are minority models likely to be shown?

Two questions related to stereotyping deal with settings and personal relationships. Insofar as stereotypes of Hispanic Americans promulgate their predilection for close-knit families, they are likely to be shown in home settings with family relationships prominent. In contrast, stereotypes of Asian Americans depicting their high education and work ethic suggest that they are likely to be shown in business settings and work relationships more frequently than either Hispanic or African Americans. Questions 5 and 6 assess the reflection of these aspects of stereotyping:

Question 5: In what types of settings are minority models likely to be depicted?

Question 6: In what types of interpersonal relationships are minority models likely to be portrayed?

The Study: Methodology

SAMPLE

A content analysis of advertisements from four types of magazines was conducted, following recommended guidelines (Kolbe & Burnett, 1991) for enhancing the reliability and objectivity of the data set. The categories were the business press (*Business Week, Fortune*); women's magazines (*Vogue, Good Housekeeping*); general interest magazines (*Time, Newsweek*); and technical publications (*Scientific American, Popular Science, Popular Mechanics*). These categories were chosen to represent a cross section of mainstream magazines that contain the types of advertisements to which Americans are typically exposed.

Sampling frames for each of the general categories were developed by examining the *Advertising Age* 300, a list of the largest magazines in terms of dollars spent on advertising, for 1992 (Endicott, 1993). Only those publications ranking in the top 10 in the four categories were considered, and specific publications were chosen randomly from an alphabetized list of each category's top 10, using a table of random digits. Table 8.1 shows the publications chosen to represent each category and the number of advertisements analyzed in each publication.

A quota sampling procedure was employed so that approximately the same number of advertisements from each publication category could be analyzed. Issues from September 1992 through August 1993

TABLE 8.1 Total Number and Percentages of Advertisements With
Minorities, by Publication

Publication	Total Advertisements With Models	Percentage of Advertisements With Minorities
Popular Business Press		
Business Week	197	25.9
Fortune	216	25.5
Technical Publications		
Scientific American	93	31.2
Popular Science	111	15.3
Popular Mechanics	80	7.5
Women's Magazines		
Good Housekeeping	212	9.9
Vogue	278	5.4
General Interest Magazines		
Time	205	17.6
Newsweek	224	25.4
Total	1,616	

were randomly selected, and in each of the weeks and the months
chosen, all advertisements of one or more full pages were included.
When the sample advertisements included models, those with minority models were identified by the researchers, and only the latter were
content analyzed. The number of advertisements with only white
models was recorded, however, so that data on the percentage of
appearance of each minority group relative to the appearance of any
human models in the advertisements could be reported.

CODING AND VARIABLES ANALYZED

To ensure reliability, two coders independently content analyzed
20% of the sample, and disagreements were resolved in consultation
with the researchers. The coders were then assigned to code half of
the advertisements in the sample, and trained by the researchers to
use the codebook that contained operational definitions of each
variable (see chapter Appendix). Items measured were the presence
of African, Hispanic, and Asian American models; their perceived
importance in the advertisement; the setting; and the relationship
among the characters. The coders were also asked to classify the
product category according to a list of 21 codebook categories, later

aggregated into two groups. These were "technology-based" products, such as automobiles, electronics, banking and financial services, and telecommunications and transportation services; and "nontechnology-based" products, all others such as food, cosmetics, and furniture. Presence of minority models was recorded as a simple number. Perceived importance was recorded in terms of whether these models tended to be central to the advertisements or whether they appeared in minor roles. To assess this, coders were asked to specify whether the most prominent model from each group played a major, minor, or background role (see Appendix).

Setting and relationships among characters were also recorded. Setting was recorded based on the coding scheme shown in the Appendix. Relationships were recorded based on the assessment of the relationship between the most prominent minority model and any other people shown.

Results

RELIABILITY

Percentage agreement figures for all reported items are in excess of the 85% agreement standard recommended for figures not corrected for chance (Kassarjian, 1977). When the figures are corrected for chance agreement (Hughes & Garrett, 1990), they are as follows (measured by Cohen's kappa): presence of African American models, 96.7%; presence of Hispanic American models, 76.0%; presence of Asian American models, 94.9%; setting, 91.5%; relationship among models, 86.4%; and product category, 92.2%.

Question 1: Incidence of Minority Models

The sampling procedure resulted in a total of 1,616 advertisements with human models. Of these, 287 (17.8%) contained at least one minority model. Table 8.1 shows the percentage of minority models by publication. In the sample, 184 advertisements (11.4%) included African American models, 76 (4.7%) included Hispanic American models, and 65 (4.0%) included Asian American models. The difference

TABLE 8.2 Incidence of Minority Models as Compared to U.S.
Population Representation

	Asian Americans	African Americans	Hispanic Americans
U.S. Population			
In millions	7.3	30.0	22.3
Percentage of population	3.3	12.1	9.0
Representation in Advertisements			
Actual number	65	184	76
Percentage of sample	4.0	11.4	4.7
Difference[a]	+0.7%	–0.7%	–4.3%

NOTE: a. Calculated as percentage of U.S. population minus percentage of sample.

in relative frequency of minority group representation was statistically significant (chi-square = 80.1; $p < .001$).

Based on the proportionality criterion, African Americans (11.4% of the sample vs. 12.1% of the population) were slightly underrepresented, and Hispanic Americans were considerably underrepresented. As Table 8.2 indicates, the 4.7% representation of Hispanic Americans in the sample was considerably lower than the 9.0% figure that they represent in the overall U.S. population. In contrast, Asian Americans are slightly overrepresented, for they are present in 4.0% of the advertisements in the sample, a figure higher than the 3.3% of the population they represent.

Question 2: Perceived Importance of Characters

Table 8.3 indicates that African American models were depicted in major roles in 37.0% of the advertisements in which they appeared; Hispanic American models, in 47.4%; and Asian American models, in 50.8%. When African Americans were not in major roles, they appeared in minor roles 30.3% of the time and in background roles 29.9% of the time. In comparison to the other minority groups, then, African American models appear to be underrepresented in the category of major roles and overrepresented in the category of background roles. Hispanic American models scored at an average level on the perceived importance dimension (47.4% major, 30.3% minor, 22.4% background). Asian Americans were the least likely to be

TABLE 8.3 General Characteristics of Advertisements Featuring Minorities

Characteristic	Asian Americans	African Americans	Hispanic Americans
Number of minorities	65	184	76
Mean number of minority			
Number per advertisement	1.12	1.17	1.42
Total number of models	72	261	88
Sex of model			
Percentage male	61.1	59.8	63.6
Percentage female	38.9	40.2	36.4
Perceived importance in advertisement			
Major role	50.8%	37.0%	47.4%
Minor role	36.9%	33.2%	30.3%
Background role	12.3%	29.9%	22.4%

portrayed in background roles; only 12.3% of the advertisements containing Asian American models were in this category.

Questions 3 and 4: Magazine Type and Product Category

Table 8.4 shows that representation of Asian Americans was highly skewed toward the business press and technical publications as opposed to women's and general interest magazines. The finding for both African and Hispanic Americans showed a more even split. Just over one half (53.8%) of the African American models appeared in women's and general interest magazines, compared to 46.2% in the other two types. Similarly, Hispanic Americans were represented only slightly more often in the women's and general interest category (51.3%) than in the popular business and technical publications (48.7%). The above differences in minority group representation were statistically significant (chi-square = 32.4; $p < .01$).

Table 8.5 presents the data on minority models and product categories. Here, African American models were underrepresented in advertisements for technology-based products, appearing in only 34.6% of those advertisements. In contrast, Hispanic American models were evenly split between the advertisements for technical and nontechnical products. Asian Americans, however, were quite overrepresented in advertisements for technical products, with more than 75% of

TABLE 8.4 Number of Advertisements Containing Minorities, by
Publication

Publication	Asian Americans		African Americans		Hispanic Americans		Total	
Popular Business Press								
Business Week	15	(23.1)	34	(18.5)	9	(11.8)	58	(17.8)
Fortune	18	(27.7)	31	(16.8)	11	(14.5)	60	(18.5)
Technical Publications								
Scientific American	11	(16.9)	10	(5.4)	4	(5.3)	25	(7.7)
Popular Science	3	(4.6)	7	(3.8)	9	(11.8)	19	(5.8)
Popular Mechanics	0	(0.0)	3	(1.6)	4	(5.3)	7	(2.2)
Women's Magazines								
Good Housekeeping	8	(12.3)	19	(10.3)	13	(17.1)	40	(12.3)
Vogue	1	(1.5)	8	(4.3)	8	(10.5)	17	(5.2)
General Interest Magazines								
Time	2	(3.1)	29	(15.8)	6	(7.9)	37	(11.4)
Newsweek	7	(10.8)	43	(23.4)	12	(15.8)	62	(19.1)
Total	65		184		76		325	

NOTE: Percentages of total advertisements for each minority group are in parentheses.

TABLE 8.5 Percentages of Minority Groups in Technical Versus
Nontechnical Categories

Category	Asian Americans	African Americans	Hispanic Americans
Technical	75.4	34.8	50.0
Nontechnical	24.6	65.2	50.0

appearances falling into this category. Differences in minority group
representation were statistically significant (chi-square = 13.54; $p < .01$).

Questions 5 and 6: Setting and Relationships Between Characters

Table 8.6 shows the settings in which each minority group was
depicted. Excluding the "other" category, African Americans were
shown most frequently in business settings (34.8%), followed by
outdoor settings (25.5%), social settings (5.4%), and home settings
(3.2%). Compared to the other two groups, African Americans were
midway in representation in business settings (less than Asian Americans but more than Hispanic Americans) and were slightly overrepre-

TABLE 8.6 Percentages of the Setting of Advertisements, by Minority Group

Settings	Asian Americans	African Americans	Hispanic Americans
Business	60.0	34.8	30.2
Home	4.1	3.2	6.6
Outdoors	14.5	25.5	21.0
Social	4.1	5.4	5.2
Other (includes studio setting)	17.3	31.1	37.0
Total	100.0	100.0	100.0

sented in outdoor settings (25.5% vs. 21.1% for Hispanic Americans and 4.5% for Asian Americans). African Americans also ranked first in representation in social settings.

Hispanic Americans were also shown most frequently in business settings (30.2%) and outdoor settings (21.0%), followed by home settings (6.6%) and social settings (5.2%). Overall, Hispanic Americans appeared in more advertisements with a business setting than any other setting, but compared to the other two minority groups, they are shown less frequently as professionals in business settings. In fact, Hispanic Americans appeared to be somewhat underrepresented in business settings (30.2% vs. 34.8% for African Americans and 60.0% for Asian Americans) and slightly overrepresented in home settings (6.6% vs. 3.2% for African Americans and 4.1% for Asian Americans).

Excluding the "other" category, Asian American models were portrayed in business settings in 81.2% of the advertisements in which they appeared. Asian Americans were rarely portrayed in outdoor, home, or social settings. In all cases, differences in the settings by minority group were statistically significant (chi-square = 23.82; $p < .01$).

Table 8.7 shows the relationships in which each minority group was depicted. Advertisements with only one model or with models in an impersonal context were excluded from consideration. In advertisements that were judged to show relationships, African Americans were most frequently shown in social relationships (41.2%), followed by business relationships (40.2%) and family relationships (18.8%). They were overrepresented in social relationships compared to the other minorities (41.2% vs. 27.7% for Hispanic Americans and 34.2% for Asian Americans) and underrepresented in business relationships

TABLE 8.7 Percentages of Relationships Depicted Between Characters, by Minority Group

Relationship	Asian Americans	African Americans	Hispanic Americans
Family	5.7	18.8	24.1
Social	34.2	41.2	27.7
Business	60.0	40.2	48.2

NOTE: This table includes only those advertisements that depicted relationships. For Asian Americans, $n = 35$; for African American, $n = 101$; and for Hispanic Americans, $n = 29$.

compared to the other minorities (depicted as co-workers 40.2% of the time vs. 48.2% for Hispanic Americans and 60.0% for Asian Americans).

Hispanic Americans were shown most frequently in business relationships (48.2%), followed by social relationships (27.7%) and family relationships (24.1%). As the findings for settings suggest, Hispanic Americans were depicted in family relationships somewhat more frequently than African and Asian Americans. Among advertisements with Hispanic American models, a family relationship was depicted in 24.1% of cases, compared to 5.7% for Asian Americans and 18.8% for African Americans. Thus Asian Americans, although not frequently depicted in relationships (there were only 35 such cases), were most commonly shown as co-workers. Although these differences were provocative, we note that they were not statistically significant (chi-square = 4.44).

Discussion and Conclusion

The findings suggest that some stereotypes are powerful, whereas others seem to be fading. The settings in which the minority model appears to reflect a change in the stereotyping of African Americans as either stars or outcasts, for they frequently appear as professionals in business settings. Settings continue, however, to perpetuate the stereotype of Asian Americans as "all work, no play" and the stereotype of Hispanic Americans as family oriented, because they appear more frequently in family settings and relationships than other groups.

Appearance in technical versus nontechnical product categories is stereotypical, in that the underrepresentation of Asian Americans in nontechnical product categories and underrepresentation of African Americans in technical product categories are consistent with what one might expect. Because Asian Americans are stereotyped as being uniformly hardworking, well educated, and talented in math and science, it is not surprising to see Asian American models well represented in technical product categories.

Although African Americans are not quite as underrepresented in technical categories as Asian Americans are in nontechnical categories, their greater representation in nontechnical product advertisements also confirms the stereotype of a poorly educated group. In failing to show African Americans using complex and scientifically advanced products, the implication is that they either do not understand or are not interested in learning about this product type.

To sum up, this study spotlights problem areas in the portrayals of Asian Americans, African Americans, and Hispanic Americans in magazine advertising. Perhaps the most striking finding is a consistently stereotypical portrayal of Asian Americans as an "all work, no play" group. They tend to be portrayed in advertisements for technology-related products, in business and technical magazines, and in business settings and relationships. This one-sided portrayal makes an implicit social comment by making invisible family life, social life, or both. In addition to reinforcing majority stereotypes of this minority group, the portrayals may also encourage expectancies of career success that put pressure on Asian Americans to excel in business and technological fields. At the same time, these expectancies diminish expectations of achieving rich social relationships or self-actualization. To correct for these possible negative impacts, advertisers should include Asian Americans in a variety of nonbusiness settings and personal relationships in advertisements for food, clothing, leisure activities, and other nontechnical products.

Whereas African Americans are only slightly underrepresented, a major concern is the severe underrepresentation of Hispanic Americans. Currently, Hispanics represent 9.0% of the U.S. population, but only 4.7% of our sample contained a Hispanic model. Hispanic Americans are the most underrepresented of the three minority groups in magazine advertising, which sends a subtle signal about their lack of full acceptance in mainstream society (Jussim, 1990). To correct for the potentially negative interpretation, advertisers should portray Hispanic Americans more frequently and in settings, product use, and relationships not determined by family orientation.

Although the data suggest that portrayals of African Americans may be less blatantly stereotypical (servants or inferiors) than in the 1960s, some concerns still remain. The large number of appearances of African Americans in minor and background roles and the converse—their relative infrequency of appearance in major roles—suggest an unwelcome tokenism. Furthermore, the underrepresentation of African Americans in technical product categories seems to sustain stereotypes related to educational and occupational status.

APPENDIX

Operational Definitions Pertaining to Perceived Importance of Characters, Setting, and Relationships

I. Perceived Importance of Minority Characters

Major Role—A character who is very important to the advertising theme or layout, shown in the foreground or shown holding the product.

Minor Role—A character who is of average importance to the advertising theme or layout. Generally, these characters are not spotlighted in the advertisement and do not hold the product, but they are not difficult to find in the advertisement when casually looking at it.

Background Role—A character who is difficult to find in an advertisement and who is not important to its theme or layout.

II. Setting

Business Setting—Factories, sales or office rooms, and retail settings in which consumers are depicted inside.

Home, Indoor or Outdoor—Recognizable as a residence, room, garage, yard, home or apartment, or driveway or parking space.

Outdoors and Natural Scenery—Includes forests, rivers, ocean, fields, or sky as well as streets, public roads, sidewalks, or pathways. Does not include outdoor settings at individuals' homes or outdoor social settings.

Social Setting Outside Home—Includes public places, auditoriums, restaurants, movie theaters, places where people meet for social purposes.

Other—Includes artificial settings and any other settings not listed above.

III. Relationship to Others in the Advertisement

Family Context—Includes husband and wife and any relationship among relatives, including children as well as extended family, such as aunts and uncles, grandparents, grandchildren, adopted children, foster children.

Social Context—Includes friends or any other two people depicted in a social setting, with the exception of family members depicted in a social context.

Business Context—The depiction of members of or workers in the same company, those who are employed by the same company. Also, colleagues in the same profession or occupation, although they may be employed by different companies. Any relationship between employees or professionals who work together.

Impersonal Context—More than one character appears in the advertisement, but there is no apparent relationship between the characters.

Nobody Else in Advertisement—Choose this option when only one model appears in the advertisement.

Other Relationship—Any other than those listed above.

References

Branthwaite, A., & Pierce, L. (1990). The portrayal of black people in British television advertisements. *Social Behaviour, 5,* 327-344.

Cohen, J. (1992). White consumer response to Asian models in advertising. *Journal of Consumer Marketing, 9,* 17-27.

Cox, K. K. (1970). Social effects of integrated advertising. *Journal of Advertising Research, 10,* 41-44.

Czepiec, H., & Kelly, J. S. (1983). Analyzing Hispanic roles in advertising: A portrait of an emerging subculture. *Current Issues & Research in Advertising, 5,* 219-240.

Dominick, J. R., & Greenberg, B. S. (1970). Three seasons of blacks on television. *Journal of Advertising Research, 10,* 21-27.

Endicott, C. R. (1993, June 14). The Ad Age 300. *Advertising Age, 64,* S1-S14.

Faber, R. J., O'Guinn, T. C., & Meyer, T. P. (1987). Televised portrayals of Hispanics: A comparison of ethnic perceptions. *International Journal of Intercultural Relations, 11,* 155-169.

Greenberg, B. S., & Batista-Fernandez, P. (1980). Hispanic-Americans: The new minority on television. In *Life on television: Content analyses of U.S. drama* (pp. 202-223). Norwood, NJ: Ablex.

Hughes, M. A., & Garrett, D. E. (1990). Intercoder reliability estimation approaches in marketing: A generalizability framework for quantitative data. *Journal of Marketing Research, 27,* 185-195.

Jussim, L. (1990). Social reality and social problems: The role of expectancies. *Journal of Social Issues, 46,* 9-34.

Kassarjian, H. H. (1969). The Negro and American advertising, 1946-1965. *Journal of Marketing Research, 6,* 29-39.

Kassarjian, H. H. (1977). Content analysis in consumer research. *Journal of Consumer Research, 4,* 8-18.

Kolbe, R., & Burnett, M. S. (1991). Content analysis research: An examination of applications with directives for improving research reliability and objectivity. *Journal of Consumer Research, 18,* 243-250.

Pettigrew, T. F. (1965). Complexity and change in American racial patterns: A social psychological view. *Daedalus, 94,* 974-1008.

Wilkes, R. E., & Valencia, H. (1989). Hispanics and blacks in television commercials. *Journal of Advertising, 18,* 19-25.

Zinkhan, G. M., Qualls, W., & Biswas, A. (1990). The use of blacks in analysis of blacks in magazine and television advertising, 1946 to 1986. *Journalism Quarterly, 67,* 547-553.

PART IV

THE ONE TOPIC discussed in this book that has at least some historical precedent is legislative and social marketing issues. Discussions of deceptive advertising and the role of the Federal Trade Commission in the regulation of the advertising industry were popular in the late 1960s and the 1970s. Over time, the terrain has expanded beyond communications to include every aspect of the marketing mix. The chapters contained in this section examine some of the most critical problems faced by policy makers and social marketers today. Craig Andrews and Rick Netemeyer look at the impact of alcohol warning labels—mandated in 1989—on consumer behavior. Their chapter clearly demonstrates the limitations of current legislation. Jeff Stoltman and Fred Morgan use a similar approach to understanding the complex area of product safety and the limitations of warnings and product safety information. Finally, L. J. Shrum, Tina Lowrey, and John McCarty suggest a social marketing approach to increase recycling behavior.

Taken together, these works suggest that government is limited in its ability to change citizens' consumer behavior. As an alternative, private organizations and citizens must work with governmental bodies in shaping the directions of our consumption activities.

Additional Readings

Andrews, J. C., Netemeyer, R. G., & Durvasula, S. (1990). Believability and attitudes toward alcohol warning label information: The role of persuasive communications theory. *Journal of Public Policy & Marketing, 9*, 1-15.

Shrum, L. J., Lowrey, T. M., & McCarty, J. A. (1994). Recycling as a marketing problem: A framework for strategy development. *Psychology & Marketing, 11*, 393-416.

Stoltman, J. J., & Morgan, F. W. (1993). Psychological dimensions of (un)safe product usage. *AMA Winter Educators' Conference Proceedings*, pp. 143-150.

9

Alcohol Warning Label Effects

Socialization, Addiction, and Public Policy Issues

J. CRAIG ANDREWS
RICHARD G. NETEMEYER

IN 1988, the U.S. Congress enacted the Alcohol Beverage Labeling Act mandating that by November 18, 1989, the following two warnings be placed on all alcoholic beverage containers to be distributed and sold in the United States:

> GOVERNMENT WARNING: (1) According to the Surgeon General, women should not drink alcoholic beverages during pregnancy because of the risk of birth defects. (2) Consumption of alcoholic beverages impairs your ability to drive a car or operate machinery and may cause health problems.

AUTHORS' NOTE: A shorter version of this chapter appears as "The Effectiveness of Alcohol Warning Labels: A Review and Extension," in *American Behavioral Scientist*, *38*(4), February 1995, pp. 622-632. The authors gratefully acknowledge Ron Hill, Randy Rose, and Terry Shimp for their helpful comments and suggestions on an earlier draft of this chapter.

For further information, contact: J. Craig Andrews, Department of Marketing, Marquette University, 606 N. 13th Street, Milwaukee, WI 53233.

The legislation was motivated by a discussion of the staggering social costs of alcohol abuse, including testimony by the National Institute on Alcohol Abuse and Alcoholism (Gordis, 1988) and evidence provided by the Surgeon General's Workshop on Drunk Driving (1989).

Since the passage of the Alcohol Beverage Labeling Act, numerous studies have investigated a wide variety of topics with respect to the effectiveness of the warning labels (Hilton, 1993). One aspect of interest is that although younger and heavier drinkers are more aware of the specific risks associated with alcohol (Mazis, Morris, & Swasy, 1991), they tend to find the warning information to be less believable and less favorable than occasional or non-users of alcohol (Andrews, Netemeyer, & Durvasula, 1991). Similar findings of resistance have emerged from studies of targeted, "at-risk" population groups, such as pregnant drinkers from inner-city clinics (Hankin et al., 1993). Thus, it would be unfortunate if alcohol warning label information is being disbelieved or discounted by the very people who presumably need this information the most. In this sense, it would be instructive to explore the reasons *why* people might resist warning information, as well as to examine what methods can be used to enhance the internalization of such information.

Thus, the purpose of this chapter is first to review exactly how alcohol risk information has been communicated and processed in the context of the warning labels. Second, theoretical explanations for the resistance of warning information by at-risk groups is presented. This rationale is based on previous cigarette warning research, the fear appeal literature, psychological reactance theory, the persuasive communications field, the alcohol socialization process, and models of addictive behavior. Then, a variety of public policy alternatives will be discussed, including the enhancement of present alcohol warnings, as well as their integration with public service announcements and other educational efforts in building cognitive defenses, changing beliefs, and internalizing alcohol risk information.

What We Know From Alcohol Warning Label Research

Numerous studies on the efficacy of the federally mandated alcohol warning labels have appeared since 1989 from a wide variety of academic fields (see Hilton, 1993). One practical method of organizing the findings is to employ McGuire's (1980) Communication Persuasion Model, consisting of input (communication aspects) variables and output (response step or processing) variables. Communication aspects include the roles of warning source, message, channel (modality), receiver, and destination (i.e., immediate vs. delay; prevention vs. cessation) input variables.

COMMUNICATION ASPECTS

With the exception of research demonstrating that the words *Government Warning* improve alcohol warning detection times (Godfrey et al., 1991), surprisingly little research exists on the study of *source* effects associated with the alcohol warning labels. For example, does the inclusion of the words *Surgeon General* lend credibility to the subsequent processing of warning information? Or, based on research by Kelman (1961), can certain source factors be incorporated to enhance the internalization, identification, or compliance with alcohol warning information?

Studies of *message design* factors reveal that the noticeability of alcohol warning messages is improved by placing the message on the front label, in a horizontal position, with the words *Government Warning,* and by reducing surrounding clutter on the label (Godfrey et al., 1991; Laughery, Young, Vaubel, & Brelsford, 1993, Experiment #1). Furthermore, the use of pictorials, color, and signal icons is found to improve the noticeability of alcohol warning information, especially in combination with one another (Laughery et al., 1993, Experiment #2). Finally, in an innovative study employing eye-scanning equipment, mean response time in warning detection is found to be reduced by 49% with the inclusion of pictorial, icon, and color features (Laughery et al., 1993, Experiment #3). In sum, although Laughery et al. determined that the alcohol warning labels are not noticeable per se, the use of visual aids (icons, color, pictorial elements) can be quite effective in enhancing the noticeability of this warning information. Further message design research suggests that improving warning conspicuity (size and contrast) can increase recall of the alcohol warning information (Barlow & Wogalter, 1991). Moreover, alcohol warnings that contain fewer characters per inch, occupy a larger area, and are more isolated tend to be more noticeable than warnings without these message design features (Swasy, Mazis, & Morris, 1992).

Studies of *message content and destination* issues have examined topics such as the explicitness of conveying severity information in the alcohol warnings (Laughery, Rowe-Halbert, Young, Vaubel, & Laux, 1991). Results from Laughery et al. (1991) show that when the severity of the potential hazard is substantial (e.g., with birth defects), only explicit information (e.g., "If you drink while you are pregnant, your child may be born with fetal alcohol syndrome and need institutionalization") conveys the severity information adequately. Similarly, Beltramini (1988) has found that cigarette warning labels noting specific risk outcomes (e.g., lung cancer, heart disease, emphysema, fetal injury, premature birth) are significantly more believable than labels suggesting remedial action (e.g., quitting smoking) or harmful contents (e.g., carbon monoxide). In the case of alcohol warnings, many other message-related factors can be explored (Andrews, Netemeyer, & Durvasula, 1993, p. 60), such as the type of risk indicated (health, safety, and/or social), message valence (positive, neutral, negative), and degree of personal consequences of risk communicated.

Research studies on *modality* (channel issues) have shown that audio-only and audiovisual formats tend to produce significantly greater recall of warnings embedded in alcohol ads than video-only formats (Ducoffe, 1990). In general, Barlow and Wogalter (1991) have found that warning information about the hazards of alcohol consumption can also be communicated effectively in an advertising format. Finally, targeted alcohol warning posters have been found to enhance the exposure, awareness, and knowledge of alcohol warning information (Fenaughty & MacKinnon, 1993; Kalsher, Clarke, & Wogalter, 1993).

Perhaps the most neglected area of alcohol warning label research is the examination of *receiver effects*. Specifically, issues of receiver initial position and receiver motivation, ability, and opportunity to process warning information are important and often-studied aspects of marketing communication (Petty & Cacioppo, 1981). Yet beyond efforts to study alcohol consumption behavior of at-risk groups exposed to the warnings (Hankin et al., 1993), relatively few studies examine such receiver characteristics. Regarding receiver initial position, Andrews, Netemeyer, and Durvasula (1990) have found that those with more favorable attitudes toward alcohol consumption tend to disbelieve specific-instance warnings (e.g., birth defects, driving impairment, drug combination), while only disliking longer-term risks of alcohol consumption (e.g., hypertension, liver disease, addiction, cancer). One likely explanation is the role of psychological reactance based on subject *experiences* (see Brehm, 1966; Fazio, 1990). For example, negative outcomes of drinking cited in the warnings (e.g., birth defects, DWI, drug interactions) may be inconsistent with positive drinking behaviors salient in one's memory and are, therefore, readily discounted. The lack of experience with longer-term risks of consumption offers less information for immediate counterarguments to the warnings.

Outside of the alcohol warning context, certain message design factors (e.g., shape and color) have been found to increase the salience of warning information, as measured by retention of label details, label compliance, and perceived danger of the warning information (Rodriguez, 1991).

PROCESSING RESEARCH

Many alcohol warning label studies focus on processing measures or *response variables,* such as awareness levels, perceived risk, agreement with the warning information, and behavioral change. For instance, Mazis, Morris, and Swasy (1991) conducted a national survey in May 1989 (before the warnings) and in May 1990 (after and during the warnings) to examine changes in awareness of the label and specific risks of alcohol consumption. By May 1990, approximately 35% of their sample indicated that it was "very likely" or "somewhat likely" that the alcohol beverage containers contained a warning. The reported awareness was highest among younger adults (42%), and women displayed the largest awareness increase (14%) from 1989 to 1990. Approximately 11% of the sample were able to identify the specific warning for drinking during pregnancy—the highest awareness coming from younger adults and those who consume the most alcohol. Research by Scammon, Mayer, and Smith (1991; see also Mayer, Smith, & Scammon, 1991) suggests that the alcohol warning labels achieved a relatively high level of awareness by July 1989 (34.9%), yet did not influence specific risks attributable to alcohol consumption. A follow-up study by these authors (Scammon, Mayer, & Smith, 1992) indicates that the awareness of the alcohol warning labels may have peaked by April 1991, with recall of the driving impairment warning peaking earlier than that of the birth defects warning. Finally, Graves (1993) has found that by 1991, awareness of the warning label had increased to 27% in the United States and was especially recognized by men, younger adults, heavier drinkers, and those more educated.

Interestingly, although the above studies suggest that heavier drinkers are likely to be aware of and knowledgeable about the warnings, they may not necessarily be in *agreement* with such information. For example, Andrews et al. (1991) have found that frequent drinkers (i.e., those consuming alcohol more than once a week) perceived the warnings as significantly less believable and less favorable than occasional or nonusers of alcohol. The authors (Andrews et al., 1990) have also found that the birth defects and driving impairment warnings were significantly more believable than three warnings regarding hypertension, liver disease, and cancer; drug combinations; and addiction. The birth defects warning, in turn, was found to be significantly more favorable than the other warnings. Further research indicated, however, that cognitive responses (as measured by net support arguments) served to mediate 76% of the effect of the different warning labels on label attitudes (Andrews et al., 1993). These self-generated thoughts were found to be an important intermediate variable in the study of the persuasiveness of the alcohol warning information.

Many have argued, however, that the true measure of social marketing effort is *behavioral change* (Andreasen, 1994). Unfortunately, only one study (at this point) has focused on this issue by studying the effects of the warning label on at-risk pregnant drinkers from a prenatal clinic (Hankin et al., 1993). Hankin et al. discovered that 6 months following the appearance of the warning label, lighter drinkers reduced their drinking during pregnancy by a small yet statistically significant amount. Pregnant risk drinkers, however, did not significantly change their consumption of alcohol in this period. Similarly, a study of anti-drug and -alcohol abuse campaigns found greater impact in the form of ad recall, evaluation, and perceived effectiveness for nonusers than for those in stages of addiction (Bozinoff, Roth, & May, 1989).

Lessons From Cigarette Warning Research

Several excellent reviews on the regulation of cigarette advertising provide insight into the effectiveness of the dissemination of medical information (e.g., Sloan-Kettering and Surgeon General reports), package and advertising warnings, broadcast advertising bans, and the role of the Fairness Doctrine and public service announcements (PSAs) (cf. Schuster & Powell, 1987). Others have discussed the reality of trying to find causal linkages from advertising to behavior, especially in the aggregate (Cohen, 1990, pp. 237-241). One interesting aspect of the reviews is that, in comparison to cigarette package warnings (appearing in 1965), advertising warnings (appearing in 1984) and broadcast ad bans (beginning in 1970), counteradvertising and PSAs appear to have played an important role in facilitating a sharp reduction in total and per capita cigarette consumption (Schuster & Powell, 1987; Warner, 1977). Others have cautioned that it is difficult to estimate the magnitude of this effect due to other factors operating at the time (McAuliffe, 1988). Even so, it raises the question as to why the package and ad warnings were relatively unsuccessful in their effect on consumption.

Why People Resist Warnings

One argument for the ineffectiveness of the warnings is based on the theory of *perceptual defense* (McGinnies, 1949; Schuster & Powell, 1987). That is, consumers either ignore or do not attend to messages that are contrary to their own beliefs. Based on studies of *fear appeals*, this defensiveness (and subsequent increases in the individual's anxiety level) is especially present when warning processors are not provided with a method to cope or help solve the problem (Leventhal, Watts, & Pagano, 1967). Recent examinations of the Protection Model used in fear appeal research reveal that maladaptive coping responses (e.g., increased drinking) can occur in the process of assessing threat severity (e.g., birth defects), threat probability ("It won't happen to me"), the ability of the coping behavior to remove the threat (e.g., stopping or reducing alcohol consumption), and individual ability to carry out the coping behavior (Tanner, Hunt, & Eppright, 1991).

Leventhal, Singer, and Jones (1965) have demonstrated the difficulty of persuading high-risk groups to adopt appropriate coping responses. As argued by Tanner et al. (1991), strong maladaptive coping behaviors tend to exist for heavy users based on many previously-encountered threatening situations.

An additional argument for the relative futility found with the provision of federally mandated warning information (especially for at-risk groups) can be found in *psychological reactance theory* (Brehm, 1966; Mazis, 1975). According to Brehm, threatening to restrict or actually eliminating a person's freedom to act motivates the person to reestablish the lost or threatened behavior or attitude. Thus, when heavy drinkers are told that they should abstain in certain situations (e.g., when driving or if pregnant) or that long-term abuse is likely to create health problems, such drinkers may see their "freedom to drink" threatened. Petty and Cacioppo (1981), however, have reasoned that psychological reactance is lessened if the behavioral change is viewed as justified, if it is of lesser importance, if it is not totally eliminated, when similar alternatives exist, and if the individual feels either inadequate or controlled by external events in the situation.

The *Elaboration Likelihood Model* posits that as one's likelihood of message elaboration increases, the quality of message-related arguments becomes more important in *objectively*-based persuasion (Petty & Cacioppo, 1981). Some variables, however, such as alcohol warning labels, may introduce a *systematic bias* in processing under high elaboration, especially for heavier drinkers. For example, forewarning a highly-involved audience of a message's persuasive intent tends to increase active resistance and counterarguing (Petty & Cacioppo, 1979). *Social judgement theory* has been advocated to help change addicted behavior and reorient the processing of risk information in a more objective fashion (Bandura, 1977; Petty, Baker, & Gleicher, 1991). This can be accomplished through the development of new skills, actions, and enhanced self-perceptions in the modeling of behavioral consequences.

Under lower levels of message elaboration, cue-driven processes such as automatic activation (Fazio, 1990), pain-pill-pleasure mentalities (Shimp & Dyer, 1979), or both are likely. In such situations, peripheral cues (e.g., likable peers who drink, positive feelings based on prior drinking) may come to mind negating processing of warning information. Still other peripheral cues (e.g., credible sources) may work to enhance identification and possible internalization of the warning message.

Beyond Alcohol Warning Labels

Given such resistance, a broader perspective on the provision and internalization of alcohol risk information beyond warning labels may be in order. Arguably, the alcohol warning label may represent a post hoc solution, at best, for which drinkers simply are provided with birth defects, driving impairment, and general health risk information—*if* the label is noticed and processed. Unfortunately, the presence of warning information *at this stage* in a heavy drinker's life may be too late to counter years of alcohol socialization and possible abuse. For example, common counterarguments of drinkers to the alcohol warning label information include: statements of denial ("Stupid—I'm aware of the contents of the beverage"), skepticism ("If drunk, the label is of little help"), and positive criticism ("There should be some literature on pregnancy and drinking—not just the warning") (Andrews et al., 1993).

Thus, the critical question is: Exactly how is the specific risk information learned and internalized throughout an individual's life? For example, to what extent do children and young adults understand and internalize alcohol risk information, such as driving impairment and birth defects? How is this information best conveyed? Are there other important risk factors that should be communicated? For instance, some proponents of the mandated birth defects and driving impairment warnings have also advocated warnings regarding alcohol addiction; dangers in combination with OTC (over-the-counter), prescription, and illicit drugs; and risks associated with hypertension, liver disease, and mouth and throat cancers ("Alcohol Warning: Impact Is Debated," 1989; Center for Science in the Public Interest, 1992; Gordis, 1988; Zanga, 1990). Others have argued for warnings of the risks associated with alcohol poisoning (Center for Science in the Public Interest, 1992). In general, it is likely that such risks are not as well-known or as believable as the driving impairment and birth defects risks (see Andrews et al., 1990).

An additional concern beyond the content of the warnings and personal context with which warnings are viewed is the reliance on a single communication format (i.e., labels). The warning label should therefore be viewed as simply one of many methods of communicating risk information, rather than an end in itself. There may be a need to consider the multitude of methods (counteradvertisements and PSAs, educational programs, the media, warning labels), and their inherent differences, in effectively communicating such risk information in early stages of alcohol socialization. As recently advocated by the use of integrated marketing communications, all efforts could be coordinated and targeted to "speak with one voice" (Schultz, Tannenbaum, & Lauterborn, 1992; Shimp, 1993). Even so, such comprehensive efforts in transmitting warning information may face formidable external socialization and cultural impediments. And if addicted, the individual may also need to conquer internal coping mechanisms as well.

The Alcohol Socialization Process

Approximately $2 billion are spent each year in the United States on alcohol advertising and promotional expenditures (Center for Science in the Public Interest, 1992). Hypothetically, children viewing a minimum of two alcohol promotions or information cues a day would be exposed to more than 15,000 alcohol messages by the time they could legally purchase alcohol. According to the U.S. Secretary of Health and Human Services (Bowen, 1989), an estimated 4.5 million young people are dependent on alcohol or are problem drinkers. Recent alcohol education efforts, however (in conjunction with enforcement and treatment programs), have been cited as helping to reduce substantially the number of alcohol-related traffic fatalities among drivers between the ages of 15 and 20 years (Fell, Hedlund, Vegega, Klein, & Johnson, 1994). Although such fatalities have declined by 20% for all age groups since 1990, approximately 17,700 alcohol-related traffic fatalities remain in the United States (Fell et al., 1994).

In general, *consumer socialization* is viewed as a process by which young people acquire skills, knowledge, and attitudes relevant to their functioning in the marketplace (Ward, 1981). This knowledge emanates from a variety of sources, including family and parental values, friends, and media influences (Solomon, 1994). In fact, children under 6 years of age are found to engage in approximately 25% of their television viewing during prime time (Adler et al., 1980) and have been shown to be affected by programs and commercials targeted toward adults (Gorn & Florsheim, 1985). Arguably, such repeated exposure to adult products (e.g., beer) via a variety of promotional stimuli is likely to engender a positive affect toward such products through enhanced familiarity (Zajonc, 1968; Zajonc & Markus, 1982).

In general, studies of *aggregate* relationships, such as overall alcohol advertising expenditures and consumption, have shown mixed results (Schuster & Powell, 1987). This is not that surprising given the limitations of such aggregate research efforts (Cohen, 1990). A variety of studies, at the *individual* level, have controlled for demographic and normative influences, and have found effects of alcohol advertising on drinking knowledge, beliefs, and intentions among children (e.g., Atkin, Neuendorf, & McDermott, 1983; Grube & Wallack, 1994; Resnick, 1990). For example, pre-drinking children who were more aware of beer ads were found to hold more favorable beliefs about drinking, intended to drink more frequently as adults, and had greater knowledge of beer brands and slogans (Grube & Wallack, 1994). These effects were maintained even when reciprocal knowledge, belief, and intention relationships with awareness were included in the model. An interesting finding by Grube and Wallack was that alcohol advertising awareness was unrelated to beliefs about the *negative* aspects of drinking. This may point to the difficulty that PSAs and counteradvertisements face in "competing" with alcohol promotion (and other cultural cues) in the formation of beliefs in the socialization process.

Consumer behavior research has found that children aged 3-5 have marked difficulties in understanding the selling intent of commercials (Macklin, 1987) and, on average, appear to acquire such knowledge only by age 8 (Brucks, Armstrong, & Goldberg, 1988). As indicated by Brucks et al., however, children who understand the selling intent of commercials do not necessarily apply "cognitive defenses" to persuasion attempts. Also, according to Piaget (1954), children do not operate as abstract thinkers until approximately age 11, due to a primary reliance on recognition skills and reactions to symbols that need to be physically present in the child's perceptual field. Thus, it is not that surprising that recent studies of young children have found strong brand recognition effects for adult product symbols, such as cigarette logos (Fischer, Schwartz, Richards, Goldstein, & Rojas, 1991). Analogously, alcohol recognition statements from young children, such as "that's beer" or "cowboys drink beer," are not uncommon. Recently, the alcohol socialization process of U.S. college students, also known as a "rite of passage," has come under greater scrutiny. This past year, a comprehensive study of alcohol use by college students reported a dramatic increase in binge drinking reaching "epidemic proportions" (Center on Addiction and Substance Abuse, 1994). The report cites that:

- In a 2-week reporting period, 42% of all college students engaged in binge drinking (i.e., five or more drinks at a time) versus 33% of non-college counterparts.
- One in three college students now drinks primarily to get drunk. This includes 35% of college women, more than 3 times the average (of 10%) reported in 1977.

As a result, campuses have reported dramatic increases in alcohol-related deaths, sexually transmitted diseases, poor academic performance, and violent crime, all linked to alcohol (Center on Addiction and Substance Abuse, 1994, p. 2).

In sum, the socialization process may help promote alcohol consumption as an acceptable behavior for certain groups via peer pressure, rites of passage, and media advertising. In fact, one prominent model of the addiction process is socialization based. This, and a variety of addiction models from other disciplines, are now presented to provide greater insight into the behavior of heavier drinkers who are likely to discount alcohol warning information.

Alcohol Addiction

ADDICTION DEFINITIONS

There are several definitions of *addiction* in the medical, psychiatric, clinical psychology, and social science literatures. For example, Jacobs (1989) defines addiction as a dependent state acquired over an extended period of time by a predisposed person in an attempt to correct a chronic stress condition. Marlatt, Baer, Donovan, and Kivlahan (1988) view addiction as "a repetitive habit pattern that increases the risk of disease and/or associated personal and social problems" (p. 224). Peele (1985) describes addiction as an adjustment by the individual in coping with his or her environment, psychological traits, and biological functions, where individuals who become addicted develop a tolerance for the behavior and have difficulty in ceasing the behavior.

Regardless of the definition, most researchers would agree that addictive behaviors are characterized by a loss of control where the behavior continues to occur despite attempts to stop, immediate gratification in the short term, long-term deleterious effects, and a high rate of relapse. Furthermore, the existence of co-morbidity (i.e., problems with other compulsive and/or addictive behaviors) and commonalities across different addictive behaviors has been well documented (Hirschman, 1992; Jacobs, 1989; Krych, 1989; Marlatt et al., 1988; Orford, 1985; Peele, 1985). Others have argued that addictive behaviors are often initiated by persons as methods of self-medicating or coping with emotional and mental anxiety experienced as a result of preexisting mental disorders (Hirschman, 1995). As such, alcohol addiction clearly falls into the general category of addictive behaviors.

MODELS OF ADDICTION

There are a number of approaches that attempt to model the etiology of addictive behaviors. The following discussion will briefly outline the more prevalent models as they relate to alcohol addiction.

Medical/Disease Model. An early approach in the study of alcoholism was the medical model, which took the perspective that alcoholism was a disease (e.g., Marlatt et al., 1988). Most recent advocates of the medical/disease model hypothesize an underlying disease process with an emphasis on physical dependency, genetic predispositions, and the progressive nature of the disease. Critics of this approach, however, suggest that it does not consider the commonalities in behaviors across addictions, it negates the influence of the situational context, and that the model suggests the individual is not responsible for the disease or changing his or her behavior (e.g., Marlatt et al., 1988; Orford, 1985). Still, this model has contributed to our understanding of the addiction process.

Biological/Genetic Model. In a review of the alcoholism literature, Schuckit (1987) found that there was consistent evidence for a biological/genetic component in the development of addiction. Schuckit found that sons of alcoholics had a "decreased intensity of reaction to modest doses of ethanol" (1987, p. 307), which may put them at greater risk of alcohol abuse than sons of nonalcoholics. Other research suggests that addictions are manifestations of traits that are passed on from generation to generation. Results show that children of alcoholics are up to 4 times more likely to develop alcoholism as compared to children of nonalcoholics (Marlatt et al., 1988).

Personality Model. With regard to alcohol abuse, several personality correlates have been identified, including impulsivity, nonconformity, and reward seeking (Cox, 1987). One study discovered six different clusters or profile types of alcoholics when using the MMPI (Minnesota Multiphasic Personality Inventory) as a measurement instrument (Graham & Strenger, 1988). Other studies, however, suggest that no one personality type can be traced to alcoholism (Sutker & Allain, 1988). Still, the personality approach has uncovered insights into the etiology of addiction.

Psychological Model. Several researchers suggest that addiction may be the result of psychopathology. *Psychopathology* refers to a dysfunction of the mental processes, where psychological adaptations are the consequences of ego deficiencies, such as a lack of maternal attention during childhood. Studies have shown a relationship between addictive behaviors and psychopathy of depression. For example, Jones, Chesire, and Moorhouse (1985) found a higher level of depression in alcoholics than that found in the general population. These findings have been replicated across numerous other addictive behaviors, including compulsive spending and pathological gambling (e.g., Raviv, 1993). Other widely studied psychopathological variables in relation to addiction are anxiety and self-esteem. Links between these two variables and alcoholism have been consistently found (Jacobs, 1989; Marlatt et al., 1988).

Sociological Model. The sociological view contends that addictive behavior is learned and is the result of adaptation to meet internal and external needs over time (Peele, 1985). This approach suggests that addiction may be the result of socialization in which the behaviors and attitudes of one's family, peers, and environment are integral in the development of the behavior. In terms of alcohol abuse, there is some evidence to suggest that individuals acquire beliefs and expectations about alcohol well before they begin to drink (Marlatt et al., 1988). For example, Goldman, Brown, and Christianson (1987) noted three potential sources in the formation of expectations: causal attributions, vicarious learning, and classical conditioning. Causal attributions suggest the individual may have experienced an event and a related outcome with respect to the addictive behavior. Vicarious learning does not require the actual experience of the individual, rather, the individual may have formed a relationship merely from observation. Goldman et al. also note that expectations formed in this way may be the result of exposure to mass media. In fact, some have cited symbolic appeals in beer advertising commonly focusing on escapism; "male-bonding"; and beer as a reward in overcoming challenges, such as losing poise and control (Strate, 1991). In a similar sense, the relationship between OTC drug advertising and the tendency for a pain-pill-pleasure mentality has been examined (Shimp & Dyer, 1979). Others have explored the role of alcohol marketing communication as a cue in engendering trial and relapse behavior in stages of alcohol addiction and cessation behavior (DePaulo, Rubin, & Milner, 1987). Thus, the sociological model advocates that the role played by society and culture may be a contributing factor behind individuals developing addictions.

In sum, many models designed to study the etiology of addiction have been proposed and recognize that addiction is likely to have multiple determinants. As such, several investigators are now considering various combinations of the models discussed above as contributing factors to addiction, including genetics, biological dysfunction, family environment, cultural impact, and personality (Jacobs, 1989; Marlatt et al., 1988; Peele 1985). This approach appears promising and has become known as the "biopsychosocial approach" (Marlatt et al., 1988). Thus, these many potential factors and approaches represent important theoretical contexts for the study of the provision and internalization of alcohol risk information, especially in the case of more frequent and heavier drinkers. Clearly, in the case of alcohol addiction, such risk information is likely to be incorporated into specific treatment programs, with goals of positive behavioral and lifestyle changes. More generally-applied, public policy alternatives for the provision and internalization of alcohol warning information are now examined.

Alternatives for Public Policy

A wide variety of public policy alternatives exist for alcohol information provision and regulation. Many such options are recommended by the Advertising and Marketing and the Education Panels of the Surgeon General's Workshop on Drunk Driving (1989, pp. 27-32, 37-46; see also Mazis, 1990). One recommendation from the Education Panel of the Workshop is to expand the [existing] alcohol warning labels. In this regard, a variety of *message design and content* improvements are argued to enhance the noticeability and comprehension of the warnings. For example, variations in cigarette warning presentation formats and ad type (textual ad vs. pictorial ad) are shown to impact warning message comprehension (Bhalla & Lastovicka, 1984). Thus, many have advocated the rotation of warning label information and the presentation of new and specific information in order to reduce processing habituation and inattention.

A second recommendation of the Workshop is for the warnings appearing on alcohol beverage containers to be required—in a clear and conspicuous manner—in *all* alcohol advertising. This option has been translated in the "Sensible Advertising and Family Education Act of 1993" (S. 674 and H.R. 1823), sponsored by Senator Strom Thurmond and Representative Joseph Kennedy (Colford, 1993). The proposed bill contained a series of seven rotating health and safety messages for both broadcast and print media. The messages for print media were more comprehensive and included a toll-free number for information. Given strong political opposition, however, Senator Thurmond withdrew the legislation from the Senate Subcommittee on Commerce, Science, and Transportation before its vote (Colford, 1994). The threat of ad warnings has generated promises of an increased number of PSAs, however, including some addressing fetal alcohol syndrome (Colford, 1993).

A third recommendation of the Workshop is to match the level of alcohol advertising with *equivalent* exposure of pro-health and safety messages. In fact, approximately 60% of consumers favored this alternative in a survey conducted at the time of the dissemination of the alcohol warning labels (Freedman, 1989). Such an equivalency, however, may present difficult (yet possibly not insurmountable) funding requirements to match approximately $1 billion in alcohol advertising a year. For example, the *entire* budget for one major sponsor of PSAs, the Ad Council (an arm of the National Association of Broadcasters), is approximately $1 billion per year (Colford, 1993). Recent ideas for increasing public alcohol PSA funding include the application of alcohol tax funds, special appropriations to the Department of Health and Human Services, and setting aside funds from state and federal substance abuse programs (see Center for Science in the Public Interest, 1992; Grube & Wallack, 1994; Resnick, 1990). Although other private sponsors exist (e.g., NCAA/TEAM), some have argued that equivalent exposure would crowd out spots for AIDS, education, highway safety, and crime ("Big Win for Ad Council," 1993). Also, the 1967 Fairness Doctrine called for *reasonable* access for differing viewpoints on cigarettes (cf. Mazis, 1990). As it turned out, the Federal Trade Commission estimated that for every 4.4 cigarette ads, there was 1 antismoking ad (Schuster & Powell, 1987).

Four other Surgeon General recommendations specified restrictions when a significant proportion of the audience is under the legal drinking age. When such an audience is likely, these restrictions would cover the promotion of alcohol on college campuses, in certain public events (e.g., concerts), the use of celebrities, and sponsorship of athletic events. These specific promotional instances have received the scrutiny of the Federal Trade Commission (Rose, 1991) and the issuance of several consent agreements. For example, Canandaigua Wine Company agreed to stop misrepresenting Cisco as a low-alcohol product and from encouraging retailers to display it next to wine coolers (*Canandaigua Wine Company*, 1991).

Based on the present review of the warning, socialization, and addiction literatures, and arguments elsewhere (Mazis 1990), perhaps one of the more fruitful avenues to explore is the goal of increasing not only the number, but the effectiveness, of alcohol counteradvertising and PSAs. Existing attempts by alcohol manufacturers could be viewed as helpful, yet perhaps sending mixed messages (e.g., abstention to young adults, yet at age 21, drinking is promoted as a normal part of one's life). In general, some recent PSA success stories include anti-drug ads that incorporate coping and cognitive defense strategies, as well as modeled behavior. For example, in a recently-aired PSA sponsored by the Partnership for a Drug-Free America (1994b), a drug pusher approaches a young child and his friends on the schoolyard and asks him, "What do you need?" Suddenly, the boy's face becomes angry and larger than life when he shouts back at the pusher a multitude of positive alternatives to using drugs (e.g., "I need friends, a job, peace . . . "). The rehearsal of such counterargumentation is likely to aid in a balancing of alcohol ad messages *if* young children can be taught such coping strategies (Brucks et al. 1988). On average, such cognitive defenses may be appropriate for children aged 8 and older (Brucks et al., 1988), and identification and compliance processes (Kelman, 1961) may be more appropriate for younger children. Other strategies include the use of modeling behavior in recent PSAs with the theme, "if you use drugs, your kids will too" (Partnership for a Drug-Free America, 1994a). Coping behaviors, alternative solutions, social risk appeals, and inoculation strategies are important ingredients in such PSAs, as well as providing attractive executional features (Goldberg, Gorn, & Gibson, 1978; Pechmann & Ratneshwar, 1994).

Efforts at warning label redesign and PSA campaign activity are most effective as part of a coordinated and targeted integrated marketing communication (IMC) program (Schultz et al., 1992). Such programs are customized to each relevant group (e.g., pregnant women, young adults), attempt to speak with a single voice, and ultimately are focused on affecting behavioral change. For example, an IMC program for pregnant women might make coordinated use of direct mail brochures, circulars available in doctors' offices, and targeted messages in magazines, all in conjunction with the warning label message. Such preventive efforts may help reduce the future discounting of alcohol warning label information, especially for those who need the information the most.

References

Adler, R., Ward, S., Lesser, G., Meringoff, L., Robertson, T., & Rossiter, J. (1980). *The effects of television advertising on children: Review and recommendations.* Lexington, MA: Lexington Books.

Alcohol warning: Impact is debated. (1989, November 15). *New York Times,* pp. C1, C6.

Andreasen, A. R. (1994). Social marketing: Its definition and domain. *Journal of Public Policy & Marketing, 13*(1), 108-114.

Andrews, J. C., Netemeyer, R. G., & Durvasula, S. (1990). Believability and attitudes toward alcohol warning label information: The role of persuasive marketing communications theory. *Journal of Public Policy & Marketing, 9,* 1-15.

Andrews, J. C., Netemeyer, R. G., & Durvasula, S. (1991). Effects of consumption frequency on believability and attitudes toward alcohol warning labels. *The Journal of Consumer Affairs, 25*(2), 323-338.

Andrews, J. C., Netemeyer, R. G., & Durvasula, S. (1993). The role of cognitive responses as mediators of alcohol warning label effects. *Journal of Public Policy & Marketing, 12*(1), 57-68.

Atkin, C., Neuendorf, K., & McDermott, S. (1983). The role of alcohol advertising in excessive and hazardous drinking. *Journal of Drug Education, 13,* 313-325.

Bandura, A. (1977). *Social learning theory.* Englewood Cliffs, NJ: Prentice Hall.

Barlow, T., & Wogalter, M. S. (1991). Alcohol beverage warnings in print advertisements. In *Proceedings of the Human Factors Society-35th Annual Meeting* (Vol. 1, pp. 451-455). Santa Monica, CA: Human Factors Society.

Beltramini, R. F. (1988). Perceived believability of warning label information presented in cigarette advertising. *Journal of Advertising, 17*(1), 26-32.

Bhalla, G., & Lastovicka, J. L. (1984). The impact of changing cigarette warning message and format. In T. Kinnear (Ed.), *Advances in consumer research* (Vol. 11, pp. 305-310). Provo, UT: Association for Consumer Research.

Big win for ad council. (1993, October 4). *Advertising Age,* p. 32.

Bowen, O. R. (1989). Secretary of Health and Human Services. Opening remarks. In *Surgeon General's Workshop on Drunk Driving: Proceedings* (pp. 9-11). Rockville, MD: U.S. Department of Health and Human Resources.

Bozinoff, L., Roth, V., & May, C. (1989). Stages of involvement with drugs and alcohol: Analysis of the effects of drug and alcohol abuse advertising. In T. K. Srull (Ed.), *Advances in consumer research* (Vol. 16, pp. 215-220). Provo, UT: Association for Consumer Research.

Brehm, J. W. (1966). *A theory of psychological reactance.* New York: Academic Press.

Brucks, M., Armstrong, G. M., & Goldberg, M. E. (1988). Children's use of cognitive defenses against television advertising: A cognitive response approach. *Journal of Consumer Research, 14*(4), 471-482.

Canandaigua Wine Company. (1991, July 2). Consent agreement [Federal Trade Commission Docket No. C-3334]. Washington, DC: Federal Trade Commission.

Center for Science in the Public Interest. (1992). *Mad at the ads! A citizens' guide to challenging alcohol advertising practices.* Washington, DC: Author.

Center on Addiction and Substance Abuse. (1994, June). *Rethinking the rites of passage: Substance abuse on America's campuses.* New York: Columbia University, Center on Addiction and Substance Abuse.

Cohen, J. B. (1990). Charting a public policy agenda for cigarettes. In P. Murphy & W. Wilkie (Eds.), *Marketing and public policy: The Federal Trade Commission in the 1990s* (pp. 234-254). Notre Dame, IN: University of Notre Dame Press.

Colford, S. W. (1993, September 27). NAB corks up threat of alcohol warnings in ads. *Advertising Age*, p. 8.

Colford, S. W. (1994, March 23). Thurmond retreats on alcohol ad health warnings. *Advertising Age*, p. 50.

Cox, W. M. (1987). *Why people drink: Parameters of alcohol as a reinforcer.* New York: Gardner.

DePaulo, P. J., Rubin, M., & Milner, B. (1987). Stages of involvement with alcohol and heroin: Analysis of the effects of marketing on addiction. In M. Wallendorf & P. Anderson (Eds.), *Advances in consumer research* (Vol. 14, pp. 521-525). Provo, UT: Association for Consumer Research.

Ducoffe, S. J. (1990). The impact of product usage warnings in alcohol beverage advertisements. *Journal of Public Policy & Marketing, 9,* 16-29.

Fazio, R. H. (1990). Multiple processes by which attitudes guide behavior: The MODE model as an integrative framework. In M. Zanna (Ed.), *Advances in experimental social psychology* (Vol. 23, pp. 75-109). New York: Academic Press.

Fell, J. C., Hedlund, J., Vegega, M. E., Klein, T. M., & Johnson, D. (1994). Reduction in alcohol-related traffic fatalities-United States, 1990-1992. *Journal of the American Medical Association, 271*(2), 100.

Fenaughty, A. M., & MacKinnon, D. (1993). Immediate effects of the Arizona alcohol warning poster. *Journal of Public Policy & Marketing, 12*(1), 69-77.

Fischer, P. M., Schwartz, M. P., Richards, J. W., Goldstein, A. O., & Rojas, T. H. (1991, December 11). Brand logo recognition by children aged 3 to 6 years: Mickey Mouse and Old Joe the Camel. *Journal of the American Medical Association, 266,* 3145-3148.

Freedman, A. M. (1989, November 14). Rebelling against alcohol, tobacco ads. *Wall Street Journal*, pp. B1, B11.

Godfrey, S. S., Laughery, K. R., Young, S. L., Vaubel, K. P., Brelsford, J. W., Laughery, K. A., & Horn, E. (1991). The new alcohol warning labels: How noticeable are they? In *Proceedings of the Human Factors Society-35th Annual Meeting* (Vol.1, pp. 446-450). Santa Monica, CA: Human Factors Society.

Goldberg, M. E., Gorn, G. J., & Gibson, W. (1978). TV messages for snack and breakfast foods: Do they influence children's preferences? *Journal of Consumer Research, 5*(2), 73-81.

Goldman, M. S., Brown, S. A., & Christianson, B. A. (1987). Expectancy theory: Thinking about drinking. In H. T. Blaine & K. E. Leonard (Eds.), *Psychological theories of drinking and alcoholism* (pp. 181-226). New York: Guilford.

Gordis, E. (1988, August 10). *Highlights of scientific evidence regarding the proposed warning labels: Testimony before the Subcommittee on the Consumer, Senate Commerce, Science, and Transportation Committee* (100th Congress, 2d Session) (pp. 24-26). Washington, DC: Government Printing Office.

Gorn, G. R., & Florsheim, R. (1985). The effects of commercials for adult products on children. *Journal of Consumer Research, 11*(4), 962-967.

Graham, J. R., & Strenger, V. E. (1988). MMPI characteristics of alcoholics: A review. *Journal of Consulting and Clinical Psychology, 56*(2), 197-205.

Graves, K. L. (1993). An evaluation of the alcohol warning label: A comparison of the United States and Ontario, Canada in 1990 and 1991. *Journal of Public Policy & Marketing, 12*(1), 19-29.

Grube, J. W., & Wallack, L. (1994). Television beer advertising and drinking knowledge, beliefs, and intentions among schoolchildren. *American Journal of Public Health, 84*(February), 254-259.

Hankin, J. R., Firestone, I. J., Sloan, J. J., Ager, J. W., Goodman, A. C., Sokol, R. J., & Martier, S. S. (1993). The impact of the alcohol warning label on drinking during pregnancy. *Journal of Public Policy & Marketing, 12*(1), 10-18.

Hilton, M. E. (1993). An overview of recent findings on alcohol beverage warning labels. *Journal of Public Policy & Marketing, 12*(1), 1-9.

Hirschman, E. C. (1992). The consciousness of addiction: Toward a general theory of compulsive consumption. *Journal of Consumer Research, 19*(2), 155-179.

Hirschman, E. C. (1995). Professional, personal, and popular culture perspectives on addiction. *American Behavioral Scientist, 38*(4), 537-552.

Jacobs, D. F. (1989). A general theory of addictions: Rationale for and evidence supporting a new approach for understanding and treating addictive behaviors. In H. J. Shaffer, S. A. Stein, B. Gambino, & T. N. Cummings (Eds.), *Compulsive gambling: Theory, research, and practice.* Lexington, MA: D. C. Heath.

Jones, D. A., Chesire, N., & Moorhouse, H. (1985). Anorexia nervosa, bulimia, and alcoholism: Associations of eating disorders and alcohol. *Journal of Psychiatric Research, 19*(2-3), 377-380.

Kalsher, M. J., Clarke, S. W., & Wogalter, M. S. (1993). Communication of alcohol facts and hazards by a warning poster. *Journal of Public Policy & Marketing, 12*(1), 78-90.

Kelman, H. C. (1961). Processes of opinion change. *Public Opinion Quarterly, 25*(Spring), 57-78.

Krych, R. (1989). Abnormal consumer behavior: A model of addictive behavior. In T. K. Srull (Ed.), *Advances in consumer research* (Vol. 16, pp. 745-748). Provo, UT: Association for Consumer Research.

Laughery, K. R., Rowe-Halbert, A. L., Young, S. L., Vaubel, K. P., & Laux, L. F. (1991). Effects of explicitness in conveying severity information in product warnings. In *Proceedings of the Human Factors Society-35th Annual Meeting* (Vol. 1, pp. 481-485). Santa Monica, CA: Human Factors Society.

Laughery, K. R., Young, S. L., Vaubel, K. P., & Brelsford, J. W. (1993). The noticeability of warnings on alcoholic beverage containers. *Journal of Public Policy & Marketing, 12*(1), 38-56.

Leventhal, H., Singer, R. P., & Jones, S. (1965). Effects of fear and specificity of recommendation upon attitudes and behavior. *Journal of Personality and Social Psychology, 2,* 20-29.

Leventhal, H., Watts, J. C., & Pagano, F. (1967). Effects of fear and instructions on how to cope with danger. *Journal of Personality and Social Psychology, 6*(3), 313-321.

Macklin, M. C. (1987). Preschoolers' understanding of the informational function of television advertising. *Journal of Consumer Research, 14*(2), 229-239.

Marlatt, G. A., Baer, J. S., Donovan, D. M., & Kivlahan, D. R. (1988). Addictive behaviors: Etiology and treatment. *Annual Review of Psychology, 39,* 223-252.

Mayer, R. N., Smith, K. R., & Scammon, D. L. (1991). Evaluating the impact of alcohol warning labels. In R. H. Holman & M. R. Solomon (Eds.), *Advances in consumer research* (Vol. 18, pp. 706-714). Provo, UT: Association for Consumer Research.

Mazis, M. B. (1975). Antipollution measures and psychological reactance theory: A field experiment. *Journal of Personality and Social Psychology, 31,* 654-660.

Mazis, M. B. (1990). The marketing of alcohol: A spirited debate. In P. Murphy & W. Wilkie (Eds.), *Marketing and advertising regulation* (pp. 221-233). Notre Dame, IN: University of Notre Dame Press.

Mazis, M. B., Morris, L. A., & Swasy, J. L. (1991). An evaluation of the alcohol warning label: Initial survey results. *Journal of Public Policy & Marketing, 10*(1), 229-241.

McAuliffe, R. (1988). The FTC and the effectiveness of cigarette advertising regulation. *Journal of Public Policy & Marketing, 7,* 49-64.

McGinnies, E. (1949). Emotionality and perceptual defense. *Psychological Review, 56,* 244-251.

McGuire, W. J. (1980). The communication-persuasion model and health risk labeling. In L. A. Morris, M. B. Mazis, & I. Barofsky (Eds.), *Product labeling and health risks: Banbury report 6* (pp. 99-122). Cold Spring Harbor, NY: Cold Spring Harbor Laboratory.

Orford, J. (1985). *Excessive appetites: A psychological view of addictions.* New York: John Wiley.

Partnership for a Drug-Free America. (1994a). *Parents who use drugs* [Public service announcement]. New York: Author.

Partnership for a Drug-Free America. (1994b). *What I need* [Public service announcement]. New York: Author.

Pechmann, C., & Ratneshwar, S. (1994). The effects of antismoking and cigarette advertising on young adolescents' perceptions of peers who smoke. *Journal of Consumer Research, 21*(2), 236-251.

Peele, S. (1985). *The meaning of addiction: Compulsive experience and its interpretation.* Lexington, MA: Lexington Books.

Petty, R. E., Baker, S. M., & Gleicher, F. (1991). Attitudes and drug abuse prevention: Implications of the elaboration likelihood model of persuasion. In L. Donohew, H. E. Sypher, & W. J. Bukoski (Eds.), *Persuasive communications and drug abuse prevention* (pp. 71-90). Hillsdale, NJ: Lawrence Erlbaum.

Petty, R. E., & Cacioppo, J. T. (1979). Effects of forewarning of persuasive intent on cognitive responses and persuasion. *Personality and Social Psychology Bulletin, 5,* 173-176.

Petty, R. E., & Cacioppo, J. T. (1981). *Attitudes and persuasion: Classic and contemporary approaches.* Dubuque, IA: William C. Brown.

Piaget, J. (1954). *The construction of reality in the child.* New York: Basic Books.

Raviv, M. (1993). Personality characteristics of sexual addictions and pathological gamblers. *Journal of Gambling Studies, 9*(Spring), 17-30.

Resnick, M. D. (1990). Study group report on the impact of televised drinking and alcohol advertising on youth. *Journal of Adolescent Health Care, 11,* 25-30.

Rodriguez, M. A. (1991). What makes a warning label salient? In *Proceedings of the Human Factor Society-35th Annual Meeting* (Vol. 2, pp. 1029-1033). Santa Monica, CA: Human Factors Society.

Rose, L. (1991, September 23). FTC has surprises for you. *Advertising Age,* p. 22.

Scammon, D. L., Mayer, R. N., & Smith, K. R. (1991). Alcohol warnings: How do you know when you have had one too many? *Journal of Public Policy & Marketing,* *10*(1), 214-228.

Scammon, D. L., Mayer, R. N., & Smith, K. R. (1992). The morning after: Have consumers learned anything from the alcohol warning labels? In P. N. Bloom & R. G. Starr, Jr. (Eds.), *Proceedings of the Marketing and Public Policy Conference* (pp. 93-103). Chicago: American Marketing Association.

Schuckit, M. A. (1987). Biological vulnerability to alcoholism. *Journal of Consulting and Clinical Psychology, 55,* 301-309.

Schultz, D. E., Tannenbaum, S. I., & Lauterborn, R. F. (1992). *Integrated marketing communications.* Lincolnwood, IL: NTC Publishing Group.

Schuster, C. P., & Powell, C. P. (1987). Comparison of cigarette and alcohol controversies. *Journal of Advertising, 16*(2), 26-33.

Shimp, T. A. (1993). *Promotion management & marketing communications* (3rd ed.). Fort Worth, TX: Dryden.

Shimp, T. A., & Dyer, R. F. (1979). The pain-pill-pleasure model and illicit drug consumption. *Journal of Consumer Research, 6*(1), 36-46.

Solomon, M. (1994). *Consumer behavior* (2nd ed.). Boston: Allyn & Bacon.

Strate, L. (1991). The cultural meaning of beer commercials. In R. Holman & M. Solomon (Eds.), *Advances in consumer research* (Vol. 18, pp. 115-119). Provo, UT: Association for Consumer Research.

Surgeon General's Workshop on Drunk Driving: Proceedings. (1989). Rockville, MD: U.S. Department of Health and Human Services.

Sutker, P. B., & Allain, A. N. (1988). Issues in personality conceptualizations of addictive behaviors. *Journal of Consulting and Clinical Psychology, 56*(2), 172-183.

Swasy, J. L., Mazis, M. B., & Morris, L. A. (1992, May). *Message design characteristics affecting alcohol warning message noticeability and legibility.* Paper presented at the Marketing and Public Policy Conference, Washington, DC.

Tanner, J. F., Jr., Hunt, J. B., & Eppright, D. R. (1991). The protection motivation model: A normative model of fear appeals. *Journal of Marketing, 55*(3), 36-45.

Ward, S. (1981). Consumer socialization. In H. Kassarjian & T. Robertson (Eds.), *Perspectives in consumer behavior* (pp. 380-396). Glenview, IL: Scott, Foresman.

Warner, K. E. (1977). The effects of the anti-smoking campaign on cigarette consumption. *American Journal of Public Health, 67*(7), 645-650.

Zajonc, R. B. (1968). The attitudinal effects of mere exposure. *Journal of Personality and Social Psychology, 9,* 1-27.

Zajonc, R. B., & Markus, H. (1982). Affective and cognitive factors in preferences. *Journal of Consumer Research, 9*(2), 123-131.

Zanga, J. R. (1990, July 18). *Testimony on H.R. 4493: A bill requiring health warnings to be included in alcohol beverage advertisements before the U.S. House of Representatives, Subcommittee on Transportation and Hazardous Materials, Committee on Energy and Commerce.* Washington, DC: Government Printing Office.

10

Expanding the Perspective on Consumer Product Safety

JEFFREY J. STOLTMAN
FRED W. MORGAN

THE PRESENT LEVEL of consumer safety in the United States has been achieved over several decades. This society enjoys a relatively high level of safety, yet problems persist. Severe instances of a threat to safety can result in death or disability, and it is these outcomes that attract the most attention. The safety problem is reflected in a range of more frequently occurring and less serious consequences, however, including abrasions, lacerations, minor trauma, and temporary discomfort. Because the economic and personal costs can be significant, marketers, policy makers, and consumer researchers have been interested in understanding and raising the level of consumer safety. Avoidance is a preferred goal, and consumer information programs seem to be the most popular mechanism for accomplishing this goal. This chapter provides an examination of these programs and, in evaluating the dominant policy issues, promotes an expanded discussion of consumer safety—one that places far greater emphasis on usage behavior itself.

Overview

Public policy makers address both seller and consumer aspects of the safety problem via the development of design standards, the issuance of product recalls and bans, and various information remedy programs such as labels, warnings, and other educational efforts. Consumer safety is also affected by legal developments, particularly safety regulations and product liability litigation. Legal goals are both preventive (e.g., aimed at averting harmful situations) and compensatory (i.e., redressing those who suffer harm).

Although some policy initiatives are focused on the sellers' side of the safety problem, others are aimed specifically at buyers. Programs designed to provide certain information to consumers on product packaging (i.e., warnings and labels) often place the onus on sellers. They also presume consumers will make proper use of this information. Federal and state agencies participate by mandating certain information requirements, as well as through their own consumer education programs. Public interest and consumer advocacy groups also affect the level of safety by way of their consumer education efforts and their involvement on the legal front.

Consumer researchers have primarily contributed through their efforts to study the comprehension and use of risk information (see Bettman, 1975; Bettman, Payne, & Staelin, 1986; Mazis & Staelin, 1982; Mazis, Staelin, Beales, & Salop, 1981; Wright, 1979). It is basically assumed that consumers will use the information being provided, and the expertise that is usually brought to bear concerns the optimal design of information displays. These displays primarily affect the prepurchase and purchase activities of consumers. This research has helped inform both private sector and regulatory efforts intended to provide consumers with the information needed to make safe choices. Safety is achieved if consumers refer to this information prior to and during actual product use, storage, and disposal.

The primary purpose of this chapter is to focus greater attention on usage itself. We argue that the information programs are a necessary but not sufficient basis for improved consumer safety. Further increases in the level of consumer safety will depend upon how much attention we give to the basic fallibility of human behavior. Our premise is that safety problems arise even when neither the manufacturer nor the consumer act negligently. The products being used—products that produce many benefits—and the way they are used combine to produce the possibility of a mishap. Risk is ubiquitous and may thus be discounted. Moreover, people simply make mistakes. But the risks can be better understood, and the reasons for these mistakes can be understood, even predicted. If consumer researchers make a greater effort to examine when, where, and how consumers use products, then new ways of thinking about the safety problem can emerge, and a new set of safety initiatives will follow. The need for a fresh approach is apparent. Accidents continue to occur despite the measures being taken by manufacturers and despite the regulations that exist.

A general discussion of the thrust and the limitations of the predominant perspective on consumer safety is presented next. We then offer an expanded view of product, situational, and consumer dimensions of the product safety problem. This expanded perspective is then used to make recommendations for improving the level of product safety and for conducting future research in the area.

Information Remedies and Consumer Safety

Bettman et al.'s (1986) significant effort to create symbol-based, user-friendly labeling information is a notable example of the conventional perspective on consumer safety. These authors stress the need to use multiple information sources (e.g., point-of-sale, labels, inserts, etc.) and the need to accommodate the limitations and biases of the consumer effort to process such information. Their position reflects widely accepted principles of consumer behavior. They note, too, that information-based solutions to safety problems are much preferred over product bans because of fewer constraints on individual freedom to assume risk (see also Hadden, 1991; Russo & Leclerc, 1991).

Bettman et al. (1986) discuss a large number of stimulus characteristics that need to be managed if a label or warning is to be effective. The complexity and importance of these characteristics is such that this area of research has been the primary emphasis of most of the published research on consumer safety. This type of research has so dominated that other critical issues have been overlooked. Upon closer examination, there are a number of reasons to question the efficacy and sufficiency of the information remedy perspective.

Despite the duty to warn, there is reason to question whether the necessary information is, in fact, being provided. Andreasen (1991) observes that consumers can be poorly informed because manufacturers simply do not provide the necessary information. Manufacturers can be preoccupied with the competitive and legal ramifications of disclosure, or they may simply decide the information is not necessary. Certainly, the timely receipt of important information can be critical to consumers. Regulations are meant to address this problem, but there are many political and economic issues related to this course of action. Considerations include the size of the affected market, the type of consumer who is most at risk, and the type of risk that is presented.

Information programs can be designed for the largest affected segment or for those who would suffer the most severely (see Bettman et al., 1986). Normative and utilitarian approaches often guide these programs, and these approaches tend to lose sight of the individual accidents that produce population statistics. An aggregate view of the market and the cost-benefit calculus that dominates discussions of policy regulations will tend to obscure individual costs (see Rubin, 1991). Markets may indeed be "efficient" in this context, as most economists assert. But we should not overlook the fact that, even in the best of circumstances, the market correction process does take time. In the interim, individuals pay the price for the trial-and-error learning that occurs. Greater attention should be given to the way consumers learn safe behavior and to whether or not markets are as efficient as presumed.

Hadden (1991) also observed that even though most consumers are enjoying the benefits of a wide range of "risky" products, certain groups (e.g., the immune-compromised, the elderly, and lower socioeconomic groups) may be systematically disadvantaged. She labeled the effects of labeling programs "regressive" because they often do not address the special needs of these consumer segments. The elderly suffer from diminished physical ability that negatively affects their capacity for reading these warnings. Poorly educated consumers would have a harder time reading, comprehending, and acting upon the information provided. Therefore, attention also needs to be given to the way different consumers respond to safety issues, and researchers need to consider the replicability and generalizability of their findings.

In a very basic sense, what we know about how consumers will generally acquire, process, and apply information should cause us to question the adequacy of the information remedies perspective (see Mazis et al., 1981). The mere existence of safety information matters little if consumers do not make an effort to collect and use it. A number of studies report that consumer information search behavior is typically quite limited, particularly for frequently purchased products (see Srinivasan, 1990). An excessive amount of information may, in any format, make consumers less likely to read and use the information. Furthermore, a practical upper limit exists with regard to the amount of information that can be presented on a label (particularly true with many over-the-counter—OTC—products).

Package inserts and instruction manuals do not appear to be effective vehicles for presenting warnings (see Morris, Ruffner, & Klimberg, 1985). Beyond the problems that stem from a disinclination to use information, the legibility and comprehension of information provided in this format is open to question. Also, information presented in this manner can easily become separated from the product. For example, power tools are often used for many years and it is likely that many consumers will ignore and/or misplace the instruction manual over that period. Consumers are not likely to read and apply information that is spatially and temporally separated from the actual risk, and they may not feel the need to if they already have experience with the product (see Showers, Lust, & Celuch, 1992; Slovic, 1987; Slovic, Fischoff, & Lichtenstein, 1980). The significant activity in the informal sale of secondhand goods poses an additional problem because items may not be in good condition, and the original labels and operating instructions may no longer be available.

Safety problems can also occur because many consumers do not have the resources to purchase or maintain a product in top condition, nor do they have the level of experience or skill required for safe usage. Economic circumstances cause some consumers to rent rather than own, though people of all income levels rent equipment on an as-needed basis as well. Levy (1992) notes a surge in rental activity attributed to the high cost and limited need for certain items—a post-hole digger, for instance. Rental firms have learned that equipment must be in top working condition, and they must offer training to customers to encourage safe usage. Simply placing warnings on these products or providing an instruction booklet will not be enough.

The more we look, the more we see that there are numerous instances where the consumers' need for a product propels them to use it, perhaps with sufficient information and attention to safety, and perhaps not. Beyond instances of clear negligence, product misuse, and abuse, there are many common explanations for why consumers have accidents. Most consumers can figure out how to use a product, but they may not be able to figure out how to use it safely. There are important issues regarding consumer motivations and abilities that need to be addressed.

It may be that consumers systematically underestimate the level of risk that exists, or they may simply be unconcerned about the potential danger. The role advertising plays in minimizing perceptions of risk should be considered. Advertising often extols the benefits of products and pays scant attention to the risks involved (see Pollay, 1986). Information remedies may help to correct inaccurate perceptions of risk, but motivations that affect safe conduct will remain.

Stoltman and Morgan (1993) have argued that those who have already used a product may be more vulnerable than previously acknowledged; that is, the novice may actually be more vigilant and cautious. Reason (1983) has theorized that absent-minded errors and mistakes happen when a behavior becomes well learned; hence, the consumer proceeds without attending to specifics. If a product is inherently risky, then this absent-minded behavior significantly increases the probability of a negative outcome. Even without inherent risk, failure to monitor and control one's actions can significantly increase the chance that an accident will occur while using an otherwise "safe" item. This particular outcome is more likely when the course of events does not proceed in the typical fashion (e.g., some obstruction arises that is not properly managed).

A frequent problem may be that risk information is perceived but subsequently forgotten or neglected (see Rethans & Hastak, 1982). Because consumers may rely more on what they know than what can be known, it is important to examine what they know, how they acquired this knowledge, and how they apply it. The role of consumer knowledge is a puzzling one. Most authors seem to work from the premise that consumers use products incorrectly because they do not know any better. Labels and warnings presumably address this deficit; however, these programs are an insufficient solution because consumers continue to ignore the labels and warnings, either because of design limitations (a factor that can be addressed with current research programs) and/or because they find the information to be unimportant (a factor not so readily addressed). Consumer knowledge of safe use may be more illusory than real.

In general, consumers may not possess the "right" knowledge, and they may not use the knowledge they have. What consumers know they often acquire through incidental learning from exposure to the mass media and from everyday situations. Their knowledge may be very inadequate. On the other hand, consumers can "know" about the hazards and even "know" how to prevent them but still be injured. Product misuse and carelessness can produce injury, and labels seem unlikely to mitigate these problems. Advertising may exacerbate the situation by inadvertently promoting unsafe product use (see Pollay, 1986), leading to consumer injuries (see Honigwachs, 1987).

Consumer researchers have basically overlooked many of these issues, because they have overlooked product use itself. This oversight may stem from the fact that the vast majority of the work has focused on packaged goods (e.g., OTC products, alcoholic beverages, cleaning products). These products are not complex, though the amount of information regarding risk can be overwhelming and does not reflect behavioral problems that can surface as a consequence of repeated usage. It seems logical to assume that, with this type of product, alerting the consumer to potential danger is about all that can be done. Other issues come to the forefront, however, when we consider the potential downside of a well-learned behavior, consumer fallibility, and consumer motivation.

In the policy arena, one finds limited discussion of consumer education programs that address these dimensions of the product safety problem. Most of the discussion is not over the focus or the instruments of policy (i.e., labels and other information displays), but over specific characteristics of an information remedy program (e.g., the source of information provided, standardization and placement of the labels, etc.). The Consumer Product Safety Commission works with manufacturers to develop design standards, can issue recalls, and alerts the public to problems with specific products' dangers. The Commission works hard to provide consumers with information about specific dangers, but consumer education that addresses the various issues noted here is not within their mandate.

Although our discussion has focused on limitations of the information remedies perspective, we do not mean to suggest that these programs should be abandoned. To the contrary, we feel the information being provided is a necessary—though not sufficient—foundation for understanding and increasing the level of safety. The primary limitation of the dominant approach to consumer safety is that it does not go far enough. By leaving the problem at the point of purchase, the information remedy perspective overlooks other dimensions of the threat and the way consumers act in proximity to danger.

Product, Situation, and Consumer
Dimensions of the Safety Problem

Our position is that product safety must be treated as both an information processing problem and a behavior problem. Because the prevailing view of information remedies is so dominant, the efficacy of other options for achieving safety in the consumer environment has not been examined thoroughly. In order to facilitate such an examination, we have described a "problem space" that organizes the issues raised thus far (see Table 10.1). The framework identifies the implicit threat presented by some products, the role of the product use and use situations, and the role of consumer characteristics. The scheme offered in Table 10.1 extends beyond the typical focus on packaged goods and illustrates the scope of the threat to consumer safety. Following Andreasen (1991), the basic nature of the threat is defined in terms of the conventional categories of risk. Because of their economic and personal costs, nonphysical risks and risks posed to others are included.

Risks are not always experienced immediately. Many authors note that far less attention has been given to residual risks and the cumulative threats to safety or well-being (see Andreasen, 1991; Bettman et al., 1986; Hadden, 1991; Layden, 1992). The long-term consequences

TABLE 10.1 Elements of the Product Safety Problem Space

Threat Types and Sources

Risks
  Threats to the physical, financial, and psychological well-being of oneself, others,
    or both
  Presented immediately or at some later point, intermittently or continuously
Behavioral dimensions
  Single occasion usage
    Failure to proceed properly—wrong sequence
    Excessive quantity used
    Failure to store/safeguard properly
  Usage over multiple occasions
    High frequency increases failure to proceed properly
    Excessive use through high frequency or cumulative quantity
    Excessive quantity creates dependency or addiction
Contingency of risk attributes
  Unconditional
    Flammability, shock hazard, head trauma, fall, poison, laceration, abrasion,
      puncture, invasion (eye, ear), water hazard, suffocation, asphyxiation, radiation
  Conditional
    Consumer based: Asthmatics, visually impaired, functional illiterates
    Situation based: Fatigue, physical surroundings (weather, lighting, etc.), affective
      tone (fantasy and fun vs. safety or learning)
    Product based: Chemical interactions, design aspects that afford or constrain
      certain actions (particularly during key action stages of initiation, operation,
      and termination), design uniformity/conventions and standards, working
      condition/repair

Examples of Product Risks and Risky Usage Behaviors
  • Food products: additives, dating, nutritional content; overeating
  • Alcohol: drinking and driving; chronic abuse
  • Over-the-counter drugs: histamines, sedatives, suppressants, age limits; diet pill abuse[a]
  • Health and beauty care: toxins, sunblocks; failure to apply regularly
  • Household cleaning products: toxins; failure to store or use properly
  • Appliances: poor exhaust ventilation; starting and operation mistakes
  • Outdoor equipment: pesticides, mowers, trimmers, snowblowers, gas grills
  • Hardware and power tools: power saws, tools, nail guns, extension ladders
  • Rental equipment: post-hole digger, rototiller, scaffolding, power auger
  • Sports and camping equipment: pools, play sets, lawn darts, lanterns, canoes
  • Infant furniture and toys: bedding, changing tables; size, packaging
  • Motorized vehicles: seat belts, child restraints; safe driving speed
  • Accessories: batteries, tires; installation, maintenance

NOTE: a. The threat posed by some products can be seen in advertising. Print ads for anti-histamines, nicotine patches, and other pharmaceutical products include language regarding the incidence rate of significant problems under headings such as "Contraindications," "Warnings," "Precautions," and "Adverse Reactions." This information itself is provided in very small print, usually separated from the actual selling message.

of many consumer activities, such as cigarette smoking, are now being considered, whereas others are just emerging as potential issues, such as the use of chemical fertilizers for lawn care. Growing concerns with pollutants and various carcinogens provide one example of a "quality of life" aspect of the consumer safety problem space.

Before information remedies, consumer education programs, or mandated changes in products are proposed, the nature of the behavior problem must first be defined. The options presented in Table 10.1 provide a starting point. Little attention has been given to the various forms of unsafe behavior and the diversity of safety problems depicted here. Researchers must examine the frequency, consistency, interval between, and amount or extent of product consumption/usage (see Hendrix, 1984). We do not fully understand how a consumer acting "normally" might actually create the circumstance of unsafe product use. A more complete understanding is achieved by looking past the instances of willful neglect to the generic circumstances that raise the probability of unsafe product usage.

Product misuse has both intentional and unintentional qualities, and the intentional form is more difficult to reconcile. Our concern is that unintentional misuse is far more common but not well understood. Why do consumers fail to follow the proper sequence when using a product? Why do they use a product beyond some recommended level? Why do they fail to store or properly dispose of a product? Though one explanation is that they do not know any better, other explanations are plausible. It may be that the consumer cannot act differently. Those who are addicted abuse products, but not necessarily because they intend to become dependent or disabled. Those who cannot avail themselves of opportunities that others enjoy (i.e., lacking the resources to buy newer equipment) may overuse certain products, but not necessarily because they prefer to do so.

Ergonomics provides another approach to such questions. *Ergonomics* is the science of human performance (also called human factors engineering), where analysis focuses on both the design and operation of objects (see Gopher & Kimchi, 1989; McCormick & Sanders, 1982; Salvendy, 1987). Norman (1988) recently provided a direct link between this field, often focused on occupational safety, and everyday behavior.

From Norman's (1988) perspective, safe and unsafe behaviors would need to be studied in terms of the place an object holds in an action sequence, the nature of the action sequence, the context of this sequence, and in terms of the user's knowledge of the object and its usage. Norman (1988) and others work from the premise that the potential for human error is high because the cognitive resources required to avoid difficulty are often not allocated to the performance task. Action slips (deviations from a well-learned action sequence) and error proneness (a failure to be vigilant because an activity is well learned or due to temporary or chronic absent-mindedness) can provide useful explanations of consumer safety problems.

Threats to consumer safety occur within three distinct phases of an action sequence. During *initiation,* that is, when a sequence is triggered, consumers may mistakenly attempt to perform the wrong act. For example, a consumer may mistakenly turn a power tool on before properly aligning the tool. During *implementation,* consumers can be distracted or side-tracked and may mindlessly skip or reverse certain steps, or perform an act imprecisely. For example, while operating a hedge-trimmer, a consumer may casually reach to clear foliage located near the cutting edge of the tool. Finally, *termination* problems can arise. For example, after using the trimmer, a consumer may not immediately disengage the switch that keeps a steady flow of power to the tool.

The way that a consumer negotiates the three stages of action can be mitigated by product design. Safety, however, primarily depends on whether or not the consumer exercises cognitive and motivational control. The likelihood of a misstep increases when mental focus is lost or when goals conflict, for example, proceeding safely versus finishing quickly. Stoltman and Morgan (1993) assert that cognitive monitoring and motivational control are pivotal aspects of consumer safety. Through monitoring, individuals can discover a hazard as it is developing and thus avoid difficulty. Reason (1983) has argued that attentional processes are the key to this activity. Stoltman and Morgan (1993), extending the work of Heckhausen and Beckmann (1990), place greater emphasis on the concept of motivational control.

In *narrow span control,* the consumer acts intentionally and is mindful of the steps and hazards that are present. In *wide span control,* action is largely mindless and not in conscious control. Acts are taken; they are not intentional in the conventional sense. Though *intention* connotes both volition and awareness of one's actions and their consequences, wide span control allows the individual to act without this awareness. The action is intentional in that it is a well-learned action sequence. Thus, one can trim a hedge without being aware of each detail in the action sequence and even without careful attention to the action sequence.

Many safety problems seem to be the result of unintentional misuse stemming from wide span control. By analyzing these behavioral dimensions of product safety, policy makers would be in a better position to evaluate and develop effective programs for improving the level of safety in this country. Such programs would target attitudes toward safety and would promote awareness of the steps that need to be taken to maintain the appropriate level of control. Researchers can contribute by beginning to catalog and explain these various aspects of consumer behavior. In particular, we feel it is important to separate and explore the different reasons for intentional and unintentional errors.

As shown in Table 10.1, beyond the behavioral dimensions, distinctions should be made regarding the product and situational dimensions of product safety. Products and services can be sorted into categories of threat or hazard likelihood. For example, boats, extension ladders, and power tools could be regarded as riskier than most, even when properly used. This type of product requires constant vigilance by even the most experienced consumer. These products and the typical usage situation present an *unconditional* threat, that is, the risk is inherent in the nature of the product, though the magnitude of the risk, the immediacy of the threat, the size of the affected population, and other dimensions of the problem may vary across products and consumer segments.

Some important product safety issues are properly categorized as *conditional*—the risk is probabilistic and contingent on the manner of use, the quantity used, or based on the nature of the user. This, too, must be catalogued and explained. Based on Norman's (1988) theory, Stoltman and Morgan (1993) proposed that elements of the situation and the consumer's motivational state can either afford or constrain hazardous outcomes. We need to know much more about the role of various usage situations—how and when safe behavior is facilitated or thwarted.

We should begin to consider the extent to which certain situations, (i.e., where hedonic, pleasure-seeking, and experiential goals are operating) are more likely to involve unsafe behavior. A consumer focused on fantasy, fun, and feelings (see Holbrook & Hirschman, 1982) seems unlikely to be calculating the risks involved or carefully monitoring warnings and the consequences, particularly the long-term consequences of certain behaviors. Teen abuse of steroids and diet pills are examples of this problem.

Whether a risk should be regarded as conditional or unconditional would, in part, depend on specific risk attributes of a product. Recent print ads for prescription drugs (e.g., Seldane) provide some indication of other residual risks associated with certain products (Everett, 1991; Swagler & Ballenger, 1984). In some cases, residual risks are contingent upon certain levels or forms of use—drug interactions, for example, or use of an OTC product beyond a recommended limit. In other cases, the risks are higher for certain populations, such as those with certain chronic conditions.

Implications and Directions for Future Research

Increased consumer safety is presumably achieved when consumers are helped to weigh purchase options and helped in their decisions to approach or avoid the purchase of a potentially hazardous product. In addition, we must begin to consider product usage and we must widen the perspective and define the threat to safe use in terms of: (a) the nature of the risk involved (physical vs. nonphysical); (b) the magnitude of the risk; (c) the degree to which this risk is apparent, observable, and understandable; (d) how quickly the negative consequences will occur, and (e) the nature of the performance required to successfully avoid problems.

The complexity of the problem space presents ample opportunity for both descriptive and explanatory consumer research. Many "narrow escapes" represent a legitimate threat to consumer safety and these should begin to be examined. A rough analogy would be the oxymoronic "near miss" in the airline industry: The fact that a tragic air disaster nearly occurred often prompts detailed investigations and preventive measures. In consumer settings, the extremely negative cases command headlines, but how often are detailed investigations of everyday mishaps and near misses undertaken? Do consumers reevaluate the behaviors that place them in jeopardy? If so, do they adjust their next performance? How long does this adjustment last? For those who do not take pause, why don't they? Is there anything that can be done to promote reflection and the learning it permits? There are many such questions for researchers to take up.

More should be done with respect to the ways product risk information is provided (see Andrews, Netemeyer, & Durvasula, 1990; Bettman et al., 1986; Gardner & Levine, 1982; Hadden, 1991; Russo & Leclerc, 1991; Wright, 1979). We need to improve labels, warnings, and other devices intended to affect product choice behavior (see Russo & Leclerc, 1991). But even this research can be expanded to consider whether an impact on use can be achieved.

Consumer education programs (see Hadden, 1991) represent a fraction of the regulated policy effort made to improve safety. These programs have primarily focused on choice behavior (see Mowen, 1990). Most of what has been achieved has been through design and manufacturing standards or through labeling initiatives that are educational to some degree. The viability of consumer education programs must be explored because of the postpurchase dimensions of the safety problem. The education solution is an attractive one in light of Russo and Leclerc's (1991) discussion of the effectiveness of market forces, such as newspapers and other media. We know very little, however, about how these programs should be designed. In our view, product use should be the issue.

Marketing representations, including advertising, can have a positive impact on consumer safety. The Advertising Council and the National Safety Council have advanced the consumer safety agenda for years. Private companies have contributed as well, as in the case of the beer company that admonishes consumers to know when to say when. Advertising can present specific role-playing situations and behavior strategies to help consumers avoid excessive drinking and drinking-and-driving problems (see Ducoffe, 1990). Public relations literature distributed by pediatricians and at some retail outlets by Fisher-Price, along with a national advertising campaign, warned parents of various situations that pose threats to children, and, again, provided strategies for managing risks. Various magazines run features that provide advice regarding safety, and there are other examples of marketing activities that focus on product usage problems.

These representations extend well beyond the banal "Parental Supervision Is Recommended" warning. Realistic and useful information that is intended to change consumer attitudes and practices is often the cornerstone of this type of program. Researchers can make a contribution both by providing direction as to what should be portrayed and by providing basic research that examines the efficacy of various approaches, messages, and channels for communication.

We need to accept that people are going to continue to use many potentially unsafe products. The emphasis should therefore be on safe usage, not safe product choice. Often the motivations and activities of consumers are such that they know, but do not adequately control, the specific actions that must be managed for safe conduct. Thus, warnings and labels may not significantly change things. However, educational campaigns that focus on these motives and practices may prove to be very effective. Much like the discovery that "being green" can be good for business, we believe that marketers can discover the competitive advantage of promoting consumer safety.

Russo and Leclerc (1991) found little reason to recommend programs that will remind consumers to use information. They argue that this knowledge has already been gained and the impact on behavior has already occurred. Hadden (1991) opines that the ubiquity of the reminders and the familiarity of the products can actually produce indifference. Human factors researchers have arrived at the same conclusion. In a review of human factors safety research over a 15-year period, Ayres, Gross, Horst, and Robinson (1992) concluded that, "we cannot rely on existing warnings standards or guidelines to tell us if or in what form warnings might be effective" (p. 501).

But other approaches hold great promise. These efforts might include goal-setting strategies that encourage consumers to define the behaviors they wish to change (see Russo & Leclerc, 1991). Approaches that have proven to be successful in worker safety programs (see Altman, 1964; Gopher & Kimchi, 1989; McCormick & Sanders, 1982) may be adapted. Training and retraining programs can help remind consumers of the steps needed to achieve and practice safety. Many newly purchased products come with some level of instruction, if only by videotape. Retailers in the do-it-yourself industry hold frequent "how to" clinics that could be used as a basis for promoting safety. Here we have something much stronger than "always wear protective eye-wear" in mind. Whatever effort is made must not be piecemeal, and it must address the conditions conducive to safe usage.

Educational programs should begin to embrace the issue of control and help provide consumers explicit instructions with regard to the three general stages of action. For each potential hazard, research is needed to describe the specific types of actions that are prone to mistakes, and also the most effective way to offer instruction. In this effort, we should remember that many actions are not under conscious control. Thus, as we begin to address the problem where and when it happens, our methods must rely on a combination of self-report, controlled laboratory studies, and behavioral measures and observational methods. The ethnography of consumer safety is an equally important area for future researchers to consider.

Efforts to improve product design would benefit from this research and would typically require some consumer education component as well (see Norman, 1988). For example, though consumers can probably be better trained to install child passenger restraint systems, the NHTSA is encouraging auto companies to build these restraints into their vehicles. This addresses some of the recurring problems, but it does not ensure that consumers will use the restraints. Yet this behavioral problem may be effectively changed through consumer education programs that focus on the relevant attitudes and perceptions of consumers or through a number of other methods of intervention (see Mowen, 1990). By isolating the types of problems that surface during identifiable stages of product usage, consumer researchers can better inform public policy efforts.

An emphasis on behavior itself offers a fresh approach to policies that develop and encourage consumer education. Although such programs have produced weak results in the past (see Andreasen, 1991; Mowen, 1990), a viable alternative arises from the framework introduced here. Educational programs should shift from an emphasis on the benefits of certain choice behaviors and instead emphasize the critical problem of behavioral control. Consumers can and do make adjustments to their behavior and can be persuaded to be more disciplined and more mindful of their actions. The annual coalition of government and media to alert the public during "tornado season" provides a useful model. These programs are often very specific in terms of motivation and behavior control; they are also well timed, and the messages are repeated frequently throughout the season. Similar programs have begun to appear for "sun-tanning season," and the model could be extended to include hedge trimming, mowing, and snowblowing "seasons," to name a few. Other alternatives that follow from a focus on behavior could involve applications of behavioral modification principles (see Nord & Peter, 1980) and diffusion models that can be used to help promote adoption of new behaviors over a period of time (see Rogers & Shoemaker, 1971). In addition, a number of individual difference factors are deserving of research, including the concept of error-proneness and monitoring skills (see Reason, 1983).

Concluding Comments

Safety problems can be reduced somewhat when products are (re)designed for safety, when unsafe products are removed from the marketplace, and when their distribution is tightly controlled. Problems are mitigated when consumers are properly warned of the inherent or potential risks. Safety also improves when consumers are educated and reminded of proper product use and care so they can avoid making mistakes once a product has been acquired. We believe too little attention is being given to what happens with products once consumers begin using them. It as if there is nothing more that can be learned or gained from examining consumer usage. It is not surprising, therefore, that novel educational approaches have been few and far between, and not surprising that the approaches adopted by the private sector, public interest groups, and government agencies have been unimaginative and largely ineffective. At present, consumers must acquire their knowledge of proper use through the haphazard and regressive process of consumer socialization. Much more can and should be done.

The perspective introduced here identifies various types of consumer behavior, the factors influencing and giving rise to these behaviors, and the degree of inherent risk posed by various products. We argue that the basic fallibility of human behavior must be taken into account. This fallibility is not a chance occurrence; it is a dimension of consumer behavior that can be explained and, to some extent, predicted. Further study of this phenomenon will provide a basis for increasing the level of consumer safety. The key to understanding the significance of human fallibility is to pay much greater attention to product usage, where the fallibility of the consumer is most apparent. The actual hazard arises in the kitchen or in the hedgerow, not in the store. This is where our research focus must be placed.

References

Altman, J. W. (1964). Improvements needed in a central store of human performance data. *Human Factors, 6*(6), 681-686.

Andreasen, A. R. (1991). Consumer behavior research and public policy. In H. Kassarjian & T. Robertson (Eds.), *Handbook of consumer research* (pp. 459-506). Englewood Cliffs, NJ: Prentice Hall.

Andrews, J. C., Netemeyer, R. G., & Durvasula, S. (1990). Believability and attitudes toward alcohol warning label information: The role of persuasive communications theory. *Journal of Public Policy & Marketing, 9,* 1-15.

Ayres, T. J., Gross, M. M., Horst, D. P., & Robinson, J. N. (1992). A methodological taxonomy for warnings research. *Proceedings of the Human Factors Society, 36,* 499-503.

Bettman, J. R. (1975). Issues in designing consumer information environments. *Journal of Consumer Research, 2*(December), 169-177.

Bettman, J. R., Payne, J. W., & Staelin, R. (1986). Cognitive considerations in designing effective labels for presenting risk information. *Journal of Public Policy and Marketing, 5,* 1-28.

Ducoffe, S. J. (1990). The impact of product usage warnings in alcoholic beverage advertising. *Journal of Public Policy & Marketing, 9,* 16-29.

Everett, S. E. (1991). Lay audience response to prescription drug advertising. *Journal of Advertising Research, 31*(April/May), 43-49.

Gardner, M. P., & Levine, R. S. (1982). Truth and consequences: The effects of disclosing possibly harmful effects of product use. In B. J. Walker (Ed.), *1982 Educator Conference Proceedings, Series No. 48* (pp. 39-42.) Chicago: American Marketing Association.

Gopher, D., & Kimchi, R. (1989). Engineering psychology. *Annual Review of Psychology, 40,* 431-455.

Hadden, S. G. (1991). Regulating product risk through consumer information. *Journal of Social Issues, 47*(1), 93-105.

Heckhausen, H., & Beckmann, J. (1990). Intentional action and action slips. *Psychological Review, 97*(January), 36-48.

Hendrix, P. E. (1984). *Product/service consumption: Key dimensions and implications for marketing.* Working Paper, Emory University, Atlanta, GA.

Holbrook, M. B., & Hirschman, E. C. (1982). The experiential aspects of consumption: Consumer fantasies, feelings, and fun. *Journal of Consumer Research, 9*(September), 132-140.

Honigwachs, J. (1987). Is it safe to call something safe? The law of puffing in advertising. *Journal of Public Policy & Marketing, 6,* 157-170.

Layden, W. M. (1992). Food safety: A patchwork system. *The GAO Journal,* 8(Spring/ Summer), 48-59.

Levy, C. (1992, April 19). Persuading people to rent more than just videos. *New York Times,* p. C8.

Mazis, M. B., & Staelin, R. (1982). Using information-processing principles in public policymaking. *Journal of Public Policy and Marketing,* 1, 3-14.

Mazis, M. B., Staelin, R., Beales, H., & Salop, S. (1981). A framework for evaluating consumer information regulation. *Journal of Marketing,* 45(Winter), 11-21.

McCormick, E. J., & Sanders, M. S. (1982), *Human factors in engineering and design.* New York: McGraw-Hill.

Morris, L. A., Ruffner, M., & Klimberg, R. (1985). Warning disclosures for prescription drugs. *Journal of Advertising Research,* 25(October-November), 25-32.

Mowen, J. C. (1990). *Consumer behavior* (2nd ed.). New York: Macmillan.

Nord, W. R., & Peter, J. P. (1980). A behavior modification perspective on marketing. *Journal of Marketing,* 44(Spring), 36-47.

Norman, D. A. (1988). *The psychology of everyday things.* New York: Basic Books.

Pollay, R. W. (1986). The distorted mirror: Reflections on the unintended consequences of advertising. *Journal of Marketing,* 50(April), 18-36.

Reason, J. T. (1983). Absent-mindedness and cognitive control. In J. E. Harris & P. E. Morris (Eds.), *Everyday memory, actions, and absent-mindedness* (pp. 113-132). New York: Academic Press.

Rethans, A. J., & Hastak, M. (1982). Representation of product hazards in memory. *Advances in Consumer Research,* 9, 487-493.

Rogers, E. M., & Shoemaker, F. (1971). *Communication of innovations.* New York: Free Press.

Rubin, P. H. (1991). Why regulate consumer product safety, *Regulation—The Cato Review of Business and Government,* 14(Fall), 58-63.

Russo, J. E., & Leclerc, F. (1991). Characteristics of successful product information programs. *Journal of Social Issues,* 47(1), 73-92.

Salvendy, G. (1987). *Handbook of human factors.* New York: John Wiley.

Showers, L., Lust, J., & Celuch, K. (1992). A descriptive study of consumers' use of product owner manuals. In P. Bloom & R. Starr (Eds.), *Proceedings of the 1992 Marketing and Public Policy Conference* (pp. 49-62). Chapel Hill: University of North Carolina.

Slovic, P. (1987). Perceptions of risk. *Science,* 236, 280-285.

Slovic, P., Fischoff, B., & Lichtenstein, S. (1980). Informing people about risk. In L. Morris, M. Mazis, & I. Barofsky (Eds.), *Product labeling and health risks* (pp. 165-181). Cold Spring Harbor, NY: Cold Spring Harbor Laboratory.

Srinivasan, N. (1990). Pre-purchase external search for information. In V. Zeithaml (Ed.), *Review of marketing* (Vol. 4, pp. 153-189). Chicago: American Marketing Association.

Stoltman, J. J., & Morgan, F. W. (1993). Psychological dimensions of (un)safe product usage. In R. Varadarajan & B. Jaworski (Eds.), *Marketing theory and applications* (Vol. 4, pp. 143-150). Chicago: American Marketing Association.

Swagler, R. M., & Ballenger, S. S. (1984). Providing patients with clinical information on prescription drugs: An analysis of patient package inserts and health care delivery. *Journal of Consumer Policy,* 7(December), 439-453.

Wright, P. L. (1979). Concrete action plans in TV messages to increase reading of drug warnings. *Journal of Consumer Research,* 6(December), 256-269.

11

Using Marketing and Advertising Principles to Encourage Pro-Environmental Behaviors

L. J. SHRUM
TINA M. LOWREY
JOHN A. McCARTY

EVERYONE SEEMS to be an environmentalist these days—at least when pollsters ask. Polls show that about 70% to 80% of Americans say they are concerned or very concerned about environmental problems (Hastak, Horst, & Mazis, 1994). Anywhere from 70% to 90% of respondents have indicated that they are concerned with or influenced by the environmental impact of their purchases (see Chase & Smith, 1992; Cramer, 1991). A J. Walter Thompson poll found that 82% of respondents indicated they would be willing to pay 5% more for a product that was environmentally friendly, up from 49% the previous year (Levin, 1990).

AUTHORS' NOTE: This chapter was supported by a Research Council Grant from Rutgers University awarded to the first author. Please address correspondence to L. J. Shrum, Rutgers University, Department of Marketing, 228 Janice Levin Building—Livingston Campus, New Brunswick, NJ 08903. E-mail may be addressed to shrum@everest.rutgers.edu.

Given this impressive array of public opinion results, one might be hard-pressed to determine precisely where the problem lies. Support for the environment appears to be nearly unanimous; consequently, solutions to environmental problems should be just around the corner. Yet that doesn't appear to be the case. Both social marketers (i.e., persons attempting to increase acceptance of environmental programs that require voluntary behavior) and traditional marketers (i.e., persons selling their products by emphasizing pro-environmental attributes) point to the fact that, poll results aside, both voluntary compliance and purchase of green products are not very impressive.

In other words, what people say and what people do don't always correspond. Of course, this is nothing new to anyone who studies human behavior. The relatively poor diagnosticity of attitudes (or any psychological construct) as predictors of behavior has puzzled social scientists for decades. More recent developments in attitude research, however, have focused on the *conditions* under which a greater attitude-behavior correspondence may be expected, and this line of research has yielded information that has direct implications for environmental issues. In addition, recent research has explicated other psychological and motivational variables that affect pro-environmental behaviors.

Such research has implications for both social marketers and traditional marketers. Clearly, both types of marketers must go beyond drawing conclusions from simple correlations (or lack thereof) between polling data and either voluntary behavior (e.g., recycling) or market behavior (e.g., buying green). With this in mind, our purpose for this chapter is to provide a synthesis of the vast amount of research that has implications, both directly and indirectly, for social and traditional marketers, and to provide suggestions for applying the research findings to solving household waste problems.

Our discussion is organized in the following way. First, space limitations preclude addressing research on all types of pro-environmental behaviors. We have therefore confined our discussion to research pertaining to household waste management. For our purposes, this refers to recycling and particular types of green buying that relate to waste reduction, such as buying products in reduced packaging, buying products that are recyclable, and buying products made from recycled materials. Second, we have divided the discussion into two sections: issues and research that pertain to social marketing (e.g., selling a voluntary social concept such as recycling) and issues and research that pertain to traditional marketing (e.g., selling products based on pro-environmental attributes). We recognize, and in fact have argued elsewhere (Shrum, Lowrey, & McCarty, 1994; see also Geller, 1989), that there are many similarities between marketing a voluntary, social idea such as recycling and marketing a consumer product based on environmentally friendly attributes. Certainly, much of the research on recycling behavior has implications for marketers of green products, and we discuss this throughout this chapter. However, there are also important differences in objectives, strategies, and tactics. Because one of our goals is to translate previous research into market planning, we have chosen to provide a separate discussion of each.

Social Marketing

Kotler and Zaltman (1971) define *social marketing* as the "design, implementation, and control of programs calculated to influence the acceptability of social ideas and involving considerations of product planning, pricing, communication, distribution, and marketing research" (p. 5). That definition suggests that the marketing of social ideas (and the behaviors that relate to them) may employ many of the same techniques that firms traditionally use in marketing their products.

In relating social marketing to recycling, we have argued that community recycling programs are analogous to products (Shrum et al., 1994). The goal of the recycling programs is to sell a particular, voluntary behavior. In selling this behavior, just as with any product, the marketing mix must be managed, and each component of the marketing mix has a corresponding function in the recycling program. In the case of recycling, product issues relate to the complexity of the recycling program. For example, some programs may be very simple, requiring consumers to recycle newspapers, glass, and aluminum—whereas other programs may also accept various types of plastics; office paper only; any type of paper such as magazines, envelopes, junk mail, and so forth. Complexity may also differ as a function of whether and how the recyclables are to be presented for collection:

Some programs require complete source separation of, for example, plastics, colored glass, clear glass, aluminum, and steel, whereas other programs may allow mixing of the recyclables, which are sorted later at the recycling plant.

Price may be considered to be the cost to the individual in terms of time, inconvenience, and cognitive effort. *Distribution,* instead of referring to the way in which the product is delivered to the consumer, may be thought of as the method in which the consumer delivers the recyclables (e.g., curbside pickup or delivered to a drop-off site). This process has been referred to as "reverse distribution" or "backward channels" (Zikmund & Stanton, 1971). *Promotion* refers to any type of activity that communicates with the consumer, including advertising and other promotional activities such as contests, raffles, and sweepstakes.

Viewing recycling compliance as a marketing problem has two particular benefits. First, it becomes obvious that developing strategies for marketing the recycling concept in a community is actually a complex process. The concept of integrated marketing communications suggests that not only should all of the elements of the marketing mix work together toward a common goal, but strategies should be developed with all of these elements in mind. This is especially true for recycling, where a community asks consumers to perform behaviors that have very clear and tangible costs (time and inconvenience) but less tangible benefits (future considerations of a better environment). Moreover, community budgets for recycling programs are quite often underfunded. It is consequently imperative that whatever synergies can occur from creative integration of the different marketing functions be realized, lest the program fail because enough funds were not available for any one function to reach a critical mass of effectiveness.

The second benefit of viewing recycling in terms of the different aspects of the marketing mix is that it allows for a useful categorization of the vast amount of recycling research and application of that research to specific components of a recycling program. All marketing research, regardless of the type (i.e., pricing, promotions, etc.), is typically for the purpose of aiding in strategy development, both for the strategy of the particular mix component, as well as the overall marketing strategy. Since recycling became a prominent environmental issue in the early 1970s, there has been an extensive amount of research conducted. Making sense of this research, much less applying it, is difficult without an organizational framework.

RECYCLING RESEARCH

Consumer Research

One of the most heavily researched areas of recycling deals with characteristics of the recycler. In marketing research, demographic and psychographic information guide the marketer in terms of to whom to talk (segmentation and targeting) and how to talk to them (communication strategies). Research on the relation of demographic variables (e.g., age, income, education, gender) to recycling appears ambiguous. Earlier studies found some relation between certain demographic variables and recycling. In particular, age was negatively correlated with recycling behavior and income was positively correlated with recycling. More recent studies, however, have often found little or no relation between demographic variables and recycling (for reviews see Schwepker & Cornwell, 1991; Shrum et al., 1994; Van Liere & Dunlap, 1980). This trend is not surprising in that, as recycling becomes diffused throughout a community, simple demographic differences may disappear. This is even more the case in states that have passed mandatory recycling statutes.

Psychographic information, unlike demographics, tells us about the *internal* makeup of individuals. This information is important to marketers because it allows them to understand the motivations of the consumer: that is, why they behave as they do. Research suggests that three broad psychographic constructs are important in understanding recycling behavior: attitudes, values, and traits.

Attitudes. Attitudes have often been characterized as relatively poor predictors of any behavior. As alluded to previously, this is consistent with the contentions of both marketers and pollsters that attitude and public opinion are not all that consistent with behavior: People say that the environment is important and that they want to buy green, but those attitudes are not reflected in community recycling programs or in the marketplace (see Cook & Berrenberg, 1981; Stern & Oskamp, 1987).

Recent developments in attitude research, and specifically in attitude research related to recycling, have provided new perspectives on the attitude-behavior relation. That research has focused on the conditions under which attitudes tend to drive behavior, and the results suggest that the simple valence of the attitude is not sufficient information. One also needs to know the *strength* of these attitudes: Strong attitudes tend to be better predictors of behavior than weak attitudes (see Fazio, 1989). Several studies have found this to be the case specifically for recycling behavior (Berger, 1993; Smith, Haugtvedt, & Petty, 1994).

Attitude research also indicates that the attitude-behavior correspondence is highest when the attitudes and behaviors are measured at the same level of specificity (Fishbein & Ajzen, 1974). In particular, specific attitudes (e.g., toward recycling) are more likely to be linked to specific recycling behaviors, but may not be linked to other pro-environmental behaviors (e.g., energy conservation). Similarly, general pro-environmental attitudes may not predict specific behaviors such as recycling, but when behavior is measured using multiple indicators of pro-environmental behavior (i.e., summing across participation in such things as energy conservation, water conservation, recycling, etc.), the attitude-behavior correspondence will typically be greater. This notion was in fact confirmed in studies by Weigel and Newman (1976) and Smith et al. (1994).

Values. A number of studies indicate that the different values people hold are related to recycling behavior. Values are different from attitudes in that they are more global, abstract beliefs and are not object- or situation-specific. Research has shown that the propensity to recycle is related positively to the importance of values such as helpfulness and accomplishment (Batson, Bolen, Cross, & Neuringer-Benefiel, 1986), frugal living (DeYoung, 1985-1986), self-actualization and aesthetics (Dunlap, Grieneeks, & Rokeach, 1983), and respect and achievement (McCarty & Shrum, 1993). In addition, McCarty and Shrum (1994a, 1994b) found that a collectivistic value orientation is related positively to recycling.

Traits. Traits, or stable characteristics of individuals, have been linked to pro-environmental behaviors. Specifically, locus of control has shown very consistent relations with environmental concern (Henion & Wilson, 1976) and green purchase intent (Schwepker & Cornwell, 1991; McCarty & Shrum, 1994a), with persons displaying a more internal locus of control (i.e., believing that they have control over events and that their actions make a difference) engaging in more pro-environmental behaviors. This relation is also supported by research on perceived consumer effectiveness, which is a domain-specific belief of individuals that their actions make a difference in particular situations. This research shows that higher perceived consumer effectiveness is related positively to pro-environmental behaviors (Berger & Corbin, 1992; Ellen, Wiener, & Cobb-Walgren, 1991; see also the research on self-efficacy and recycling, Taylor & Todd, in press).

Strategic Implications. The consumer research just discussed has a number of implications that relate to the development of a recycling strategy. First, if people want to assess attitudes in order to infer recycling behavior, it is clear that they should assess attitudes about *recycling*, rather than more general environmental attitudes, and make some attempt to determine the *strength* of the attitudes being measured. Second, the research on values and traits suggests that certain very stable beliefs are linked to pro-environmental behaviors in general and recycling in particular. As one might expect, persons who feel their actions make a difference are more likely to recycle, whereas persons who feel powerless are not. Clearly, promotional activities should emphasize, in very concrete terms, what effects recycling has. This can be accomplished on a very specific level by providing feedback on simple recycling performance of a community (e.g., we met our goal this month or this year). Such efforts may help combat the feelings of impotence that individuals may have regarding their contributions to problem solving (see Ellen et al., 1991).

Combating feelings of individual powerlessness and ineffectiveness can also be accomplished on a more general level by providing information on what recycling has accomplished on a city/state/national level. The research on personal values can be applied to promotional campaigns that stress how particular values are being fulfilled through recycling efforts. Again, we emphasize that these persuasive communications should be as specific as possible.

Pricing, Product, and Distribution Research

We conceptualize price as the cost to the individual. This includes issues of time, inconvenience, and cognitive effort. We think of the product as the type of recycling program offered, with programs differing in terms of what is recyclable and how the recyclables are to be presented for pickup. We view distribution as the means by which recycled materials are delivered from the consumer to the recycling facility. Examples are curbside pickup, central drop-off sites, and satellite drop-off sites. We have combined the pricing, product, and distribution functions because they are, in our view, inextricably entwined. The differences in recycling programs—in terms of what gets recycled, how the recyclables are prepared for delivery, and how delivery occurs—are directly related to time, inconvenience, and effort.

The research clearly shows that inconvenience is a major barrier to recycling behavior. For example, a study by Reid, Luyben, Rawers, and Bailey (1976) found that increasing the number of recycling bins (accompanied by an informational prompt regarding their presence) in an apartment complex resulted in an increase in the amount of deposits. Jacobs, Bailey, and Crews (1984) found that providing containers to help residents separate recyclables was effective in increasing recycling participation. Several studies also looked at consumer *perceptions* of inconvenience, and these studies found that persons who perceive more inconvenience or effort tend to recycle less (Dahab, Gentry, & Su, in press; DeYoung, 1988-1989; McCarty & Shrum, 1993, 1994b).

Strategic Implications. Two things are worth noting from this research. First, it appears that there is a "critical mass" that level of convenience must attain to overcome inconvenience as a significant barrier to participation. The issue of curbside pickups versus community drop-off points is a good example. It seems intuitive that it is important to provide consumers with a recycling program that is basically as convenient as a disposal program. This notion is confirmed from interviews we conducted with coordinators of community recycling programs. Second, the results of research indicating that *perceived* inconvenience is a barrier to recycling has implications for promoting recycling. Most of the studies that have found this result were conducted on samples in which participants were at the same general level in terms of objective difficulty (i.e., they did not differ in terms of the means in which they were required to recycle). Thus, given the same required behavior, some persons considered recycling more inconvenient than others. It is thus possible that these perceptions are just that: perceptions, not necessarily reality. One clear strategy, then, would be to induce trial, however temporarily, so that these perceptual barriers may be overcome.

Finally, the issue of time and inconvenience as a function of cognitive effort is worth considering. Through informal conversations and interviews both with consumers and with directors of recycling programs, it is clear that the average consumer has a difficult time understanding what to recycle and what to dispose of in household garbage, and how to recycle in terms of source separation, removing labels, tying together newspapers or cardboard, and so forth. Moreover, the consumer is typically unaware of the *reasons* for all of the requirements, and often considers them a nuisance. Given all of the cognitive barriers to proper recycling, consumers may very well "just give up" and recycle little or not at all. This notion is supported by research that shows that recyclers tend to be more knowledgeable than nonrecyclers (DeYoung, 1988-1989; Hines, Hungerford, & Tomera, 1987; Pieters, 1991; Simmons & Widmar, 1990). Although there are a number of explanations for this relation (including a reverse causal direction), it is possible that the lack of knowledge of recycling specifics and the lack of a ready means of acquiring the knowledge are barriers to recycling behavior.

Promotion Research

Promotion refers to efforts to communicate information about the product or service, and consist of four major components (the promotions mix): advertising, sales promotions, personal selling, and publicity. Several studies have been conducted that we believe relate to those components, although the studies have typically not been conceptualized in marketing terms. These types of studies, often referred to as "applied behavior analysis," investigate the effects of intervention strategies and tactics aimed at increasing recycling behavior. Examples include informational fliers and prompts (i.e., advertising); lotteries, raffles, and contests (i.e., sales promotions); and door-to-door solicitations of verbal and written commitments (i.e., personal selling).

The results have been fairly consistent (for a review, see Shrum et al., 1994). Lotteries, raffles, and contests have generally been very successful in increasing recycling behavior; once the promotions cease, however, recycling levels often return to baseline levels (Couch, Garber, & Karpus, 1978-1979; Witmer & Geller, 1976). In addition, the cost of the incentives often outweighs the value of the recyclables (Jacobs & Bailey, 1982-1983; Jacobs et al., 1984). Advertising and informational fliers have been shown to increase recycling, but the effects have generally been quite small. Programs such as those featuring block leaders, where neighborhood volunteers talk face-to-face with residents and obtain verbal or written commitments to recycle, have been effective in increasing neighborhood recycling (Burn, 1991).

Strategic Implications. Although the evaluation of one type of promotion technique in isolation often yields small effects (this has been especially true for information and prompts), and particular programs alone may not be cost-effective, these results do not necessarily suggest that the programs are not potentially useful. From a marketing perspective, and especially from an integrated communications perspective, the entire marketing or promotional *package* is the important variable, not each component in isolation. For example, traditional marketers do not expect advertising to be overly effective in the absence of support from sales promotion and personal selling. Thus, a combination of the various promotional techniques may in fact yield significant gains in terms of recycling compliance. This has been supported in at least one study that has looked at the effect of various procedures to increase recycling as a total package (Jacobs et al., 1984). In that study, weekly pickup, door-to-door delivery of handbills and brochures, and provision of recycling bins with separate compartments resulted in an increase in recycling that was cost-effective.

Another issue relating to effects of promotional activities pertains to the assumption that the relationship between promotions and sales is linear. In the studies that have investigated effects of particular promotional techniques on recycling behavior, the data have been analyzed using statistical techniques that test for a linear relation. However, the relationship between promotions and sales (termed the sales response function) may in fact be S-shaped (Luchsinger, Mullen, & Jannuzzo, 1977). That is, at low levels of promotional expenditures, little effect on sales is noted, but at a particular critical mass, the expenditures start to exert a substantial effect. Then, at still higher levels of spending, the effects start to subside (i.e., diminishing returns). If this model of sales response to promotions is correct, it suggests that a certain level of promotional expenditures must be attained before promotions can be expected to increase sales at a justifiable rate. It is quite possible that the studies investigating the effect of promotional-type activities on recycling behavior may have been using levels of promotion that fell below the critical mass needed to be a cost-effective behavioral stimulus.

Overall, the results of past research suggest that a careful development of a promotional campaign, carried out over time, may prove beneficial. Periodic provision of information to explain recycling procedures (especially to new residents), participation in community events (e.g., Fourth of July celebrations, community festivals), periodic contests or raffles to increase interest and involvement, and organization of neighborhood volunteer groups may be effective in the long run.

DEVELOPING A RECYCLING STRATEGY
FOR A MODEL COMMUNITY

The previous discussion highlights the complexity of the problem of increasing recycling behavior. At any given point in time, many individual, normative, and situational factors may influence a person's decision to recycle. We argue that applying a marketing perspective to the problem helps categorize these factors and provides a framework for addressing each in a systematic manner. Toward this end, we present below a rough but flexible plan for developing a recycling program in a hypothetical community (see also Shrum et al., 1994).

The first objective should be to increase awareness. Awareness may be increased by distributing fliers or sending mailers announcing the impending start of the neighborhood recycling program. Research also indicates that knowledge of what to recycle and how to recycle is important, which mirrors the experience of traditional marketers. That is, in new product introductions, it is necessary to educate the consumer on how the product works, how the consumer might use it, and why the consumer would want to use it. Consequently, either through the initial announcement or as part of a subsequent effort, residents should be educated about the requirements and procedures of recycling. This could also be accomplished through door-to-door "personal selling."

After making residents aware of the program and providing information on how recycling works, a promotional effort may be instituted to launch the "product introduction." For example, a neighborhood party or festival that focuses on collective community efforts might be useful. Such a festival would also be a good opportunity for additional educational efforts and would provide the chance to enlist the help of the entire family. Local merchants might be enlisted to set up booths to display recycling-related products such as disposal bins, and environmental groups may be interested in distributing their promotional literature.

In conjunction with the festival, a personal selling effort aimed at getting oral or written commitments from citizens may be instituted. Such a festival provides a convenient and efficient forum to obtain personal commitments by having residents come to a central location. After the festival, those citizens who did not attend may then be contacted in an attempt to obtain their personal commitment to recycle. It is important to note, however, that simply asking residents for a commitment to recycle is unlikely to be enough. In any selling situation, salespeople must persuade, which means they must clearly explain the attributes and benefits of the product and overcome any barriers to purchase. The research on characteristics of the recycler may be helpful in this regard. For example, appeals may be designed to address aspects of inconvenience. The sales pitch should also demonstrate how recycling can be empowering and consistent with personal values of the recycler.

After community residents have been made aware of the recycling program and interest in it has been generated, incentives for participation may be used to further encourage participation. Incentives could take the form of raffles or contests associated with recycling. For example, contest officials might conduct a random check of residents' trash when it is put out for collection; if the trash is free of recyclable material, the resident would win a cash prize. This type of promotion could be run for several weeks or months.

Another important part of the promotions mix is publicity. Local print and broadcast news would be useful in generating interest and participation in the recycling program, and if the program is successful, news stories reporting on the success may serve to increase community pride in the recycling program.

After a reasonable period of time has passed, managers of the program should step back and take stock of both the program's accomplishments and failures. The manager might consider using a survey at this point to find out what residents think about the program and to pinpoint what is working and what is not.

It is important for persons in charge of the program to understand that a good marketing effort is continuous. Thus, such things as periodic incentives, annual parties, and follow-up surveys should be an ongoing part of the program. One of the initial objectives of a promotional effort is to elicit cooperation and a community spirit, but such cooperation may dissipate over time. Consequently, providing a continuous marketing effort is important.

We understand that the program we have suggested is extensive and may require more funds than a typical budget would allow. We stress that such a program is a comprehensive example of what might be done under *ideal* conditions. As with any good marketing program, it is flexible. If funds are minimal, some of the promotions may be modified or eliminated. Moreover, many of the suggestions rely on recruitment of volunteers to help administer the program.

The point we have tried to make thus far is that recycling research suggests many avenues for increasing recycling participation. Often, however, the research is aimed at determining which type of promotional effort works better: personal selling, advertising, sales promotions, and so forth. It is our contention that "Which is better?" is the wrong question. Instead, we should investigate how disparate research findings might be integrated and used in developing the most effective program. We have drawn an analogy to the marketing of typical products, and we have suggested that viewing recycling as a product to be marketed makes strategies for increasing recycling compliance more apparent. It is our hope that communities can use these principles to make their programs more successful.

Buying Green and Closing the Loop

Most environmentalists realize that recycling is only a partial solution to the solid waste problem. In fact, it addresses a symptom of the problem (how to reduce solid waste disposal given a large amount of waste material) rather than the problem itself (we generate too much solid waste). Green buying addresses both.

We define *green buying* as the purchase of a product or service in which the purchase decision is based wholly, or in part, on the extent to which the purchaser considers particular attributes of the product or service to be good for the environment.

For the purposes of this discussion, we have confined green buying to the purchase of products based on attributes that relate to the reduction of solid waste. Such product attributes would include being made out of recyclable materials, using reduced packaging, and being returnable.

Buying green is extremely important for at least two reasons. First, buying products that are packaged using a minimal amount of material and buying products that are packaged in reusable or returnable containers reduces solid waste disposal, apart from recycling. Second, and just as important, buying products that are made from recycled materials "closes the loop."

Closing the loop refers to the fact that the recycling concept only works if there is a market for the recycled materials. Thus, recycling compliance represents only one part of the recycling "loop." It is one thing to remove materials from landfill designation and put them into the recycling stream, but quite another thing to get companies to use the recycled materials. If companies have no incentive to use the recycled materials when "re-manufacturing" products and packaging, then the recyclables will accumulate, and the end result will be that we have simply created two places to store solid waste (landfills and recycling centers) rather than achieving any net reduction in solid waste. On the other hand, if consumers demand products that use recycled materials and/or are recyclable, then economic theory assures us that companies will supply such products.

Figure 11.1 depicts how "closing the loop" works. After consumers purchase, use, and recycle the qualifying materials, the materials must

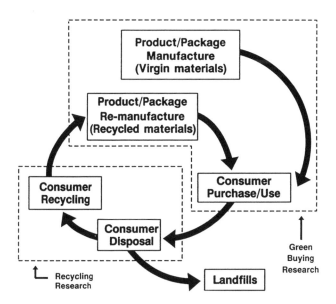

Figure 11.1. Closing the Recycling Loop: How Virgin and Recycled Materials Pass Through the Materials Life Cycle

then be used to manufacture new products in order to reenter the consumer purchase/use-disposal-recycle loop. If this does not occur, the loop remains open. Clearly, the manufacturer must have incentives to use recycled materials in making new products. The incentive may come from consumer demand, as consumers "pull" the product through the distribution channel, or it may come from regulatory measures that mandate the use of recycled materials in product manufacture, thereby "pushing" the product through the distribution channel.

Note also in Figure 11.1 that recycling research and green buying research are concerned with different parts of the loop. Each is important in understanding how to promote the behavior involved in a particular part of the loop.

The previous discussion pertained strictly to recycling research and its implications for increasing recycling compliance. We now provide a review and synthesis of research on the green buying component of the loop.

GREEN BUYING RESEARCH

Several studies have looked at the relationship of demographic and psychographic variables with green buying behavior. As one might expect, the results of those studies are similar to the results discussed previously when the dependent variable was recycling. Perceived consumer effectiveness has been found to be positively related to the propensity to buy green (Berger & Corbin, 1992; Ellen et al., 1991), attitude strength moderates the relation between environmental attitudes and intention to purchase environmentally friendly products (Berger, 1993; Smith et al., 1994), and attitudes and locus of control discriminate between consumers who have high and low intentions to purchase ecologically packaged products (Schwepker & Cornwell, 1991).

In a departure from the typical psychosocial variables that have been investigated, Shrum, McCarty, and Lowrey (1995) looked at the relation between green purchase intent and variables that are more directly related to buyer behavior. That study found that persons who indicate a greater propensity to buy products in biodegradable packaging consider themselves to be opinion leaders, are more careful shoppers who are price conscious and actively seek out product information (including information from advertising), and indicate more interest in new products, compared to persons indicating less propensity to buy green. No differences in brand loyalty were found, and demographics showed little or no relation to green buying.

Additional findings in the Shrum et al. (1995) study have at least tangential relevance to the lack of correspondence between attitudes and behavior. The study found that persons who are more concerned with buying green products are also more skeptical of advertising, compared to persons indicating less concern with buying green. Specifically, green purchasers tend to agree more with such statements as, "Advertising insults my intelligence," and "I refuse to buy a brand whose advertising I dislike," compared to non-green buyers. Thus, it appears that green buyers are for the most part distrustful of advertising. This may explain why advertisers are complaining that consumers are not following through on their expressed pro-environmental attitudes by buying their green products: It may not be the products the consumers dislike, but the (misleading) advertising that accompanies the products.

There is ample evidence that consumers' distrust of advertising is well founded. A number of studies have shown that consumers often misunderstand product claims referring to "recyclable" and "recycled" (e.g., Morris, Hastak, & Mazis, 1994; for a review, see Mayer, Scammon, & Gray-Lee, 1994). That is, when marketers claim that a product or package is recyclable, consumers often assume that it is recyclable in their community, when in fact that may not be the case. Similarly, when marketers claim that a product or package is made out of recycled materials, consumers often assume that most, if not all, of the package is made of recycled materials; in fact, in many cases, the recycled content of a package or product may be quite low. Although inducing confusion may not be the goal of advertisers, knowledgeable and experienced green buyers may understand the vague and misleading characteristics of many green claims and simply ignore or avoid products with such claims. In fact, requests for regulatory guidelines have been made by advertisers themselves (along with pressure from environmental activist groups), resulting in the issuance of guidelines by the Federal Trade Commission in 1992 (Mayer et al., 1994; Mayer, Scammon, & Zick, 1992; Scammon & Mayer, 1995).

Although we can only speculate, it may also be the case that consumers committed to buying green may resent marketers who use green claims without having any true pro-environmental commitment. Examples include making pro-environmental claims for a product (e.g., no harmful chemicals) but at the same time using environmentally harmful packaging (e.g., excess packaging, not recyclable) and using environmentally friendly packaging for products that themselves are harmful to the environment.

One can probably think of several other examples of such practices. Indeed, it seems that many marketers have simply assumed that if people say they are pro-environmental, they will surely be persuaded by any pro-environmental claim, no matter how vague, misleading, or specious. We would simply like to point out that if marketers want to sell their products successfully using a green positioning strategy, they should remember that consumers are not stupid. In fact, the research indicates that persons who recycle and buy green are typically very knowledgeable, hold *strong* attitudes, are good consumers, and do not blindly listen to advertising messages, although they do pay attention to them.

An additional issue worth noting for marketers is that the majority of Americans are probably not committed to the environment *at the expense of all other issues.* For example, although they may desire environmentally friendly products, they would also like them to perform at a reasonable level. Put differently, consumers may indeed, as surveys indicate, be willing to pay a premium for green products, but they may not necessarily be willing to pay more *and* receive a product that is inferior to their initial choice.

Conclusion

In conclusion, rather than merely complaining that what consumers say and what they do don't always correspond, marketers should spend time trying to figure out why this discrepancy occurs, *just like they do with any product.* Perhaps marketers have been seduced by a match between overwhelming public opinion and product attributes that they perceive to be fairly simple to deliver, when in fact, as always, things are never as simple as they seem.

References

Batson, C. D., Bolen, M. H., Cross, J. A., & Neuringer-Benefiel, H. E. (1986). Where is the altruism in the altruistic personality? *Journal of Personality and Social Psychology, 50,* 212-220.

Berger, I. E. (1993). The relationship between environmental attitudes and behavior. *Canadian Journal of Marketing Research, 12,* 36-43.

Berger, I. E., & Corbin, R. M. (1992). Perceived consumer effectiveness and faith in others as moderators of environmentally responsible behaviors. *Journal of Public Policy & Marketing, 11*(2), 79-89.

Burn, S. M. (1991). Social psychology and the stimulation of recycling behaviors: The block leader approach. *Journal of Applied Social Psychology, 21,* 611-629.

Chase, D., & Smith, T. K. (1992, June 29). Consumers keen on green but marketers don't deliver. *Advertising Age,* pp. s2-s4.

Cook, S. W., & Berrenberg, J. L. (1981). Approaches to encouraging conservation behavior: A review and conceptual framework. *Journal of Social Issues, 37,* 73-107.

Couch, J. V., Garber, T., & Karpus, L. (1978-1979). Response maintenance and paper recycling. *Journal of Environmental Systems, 8,* 127-137.

Cramer, J. (1991, September 16). The selling of the green. *Time,* p. 48.

Dahab, D. J., Gentry, J. W., & Su, W. (in press). New ways to reach nonrecyclers: An extension of the model of reasoned action to recycling behaviors. In F. R. Kardes

& M. Sujan (Eds.), *Advances in consumer research* (Vol. 22). Provo, UT: Association for Consumer Research.

DeYoung, R. (1985-1986). Encouraging environmentally appropriate behavior: The role of intrinsic motivation. *Journal of Environmental Systems, 15,* 281-292.

DeYoung, R. (1988-1989). Exploring the difference between recyclers and non-recyclers: The role of information. *Journal of Environmental Systems, 18,* 341-351.

Dunlap, R. E., Grieneeks, J. K., & Rokeach, M. (1983). Human values and pro-environmental behavior. In W. D. Conn (Ed.), *Energy and material resources: Attitudes, values and public policy* (pp. 145-168). Boulder, CO: Westview.

Ellen, P. M., Wiener, J. L., & Cobb-Walgren, C. (1991). The role of perceived consumer effectiveness in motivating environmentally conscious behaviors. *Journal of Public Policy and Marketing, 10*(2), 102-117.

Fazio, R. H. (1989). On the power and functionality of attitudes: The role of attitude accessibility. In A. R. Pratkanis, S. J. Breckler, & A. G. Greenwald (Eds.), *Attitude structure and function* (pp. 153-179). Hillsdale, NJ: Lawrence Erlbaum.

Fishbein, M., & Ajzen, I. (1974). Attitudes toward objects as predictors of single and multiple behavioral criteria. *Psychological Review, 81,* 59-74.

Geller, E. S. (1989). Applied behavior analysis and social marketing: An integration for environmental preservation. *Journal of Social Issues, 45,* 17-36.

Hastak, M., Horst, R. L., & Mazis, M. B. (1994). Consumer perceptions about and comprehension of environmental terms: Evidence from survey research studies. In D. Ringold (Ed.), *Proceedings of the 1994 Marketing and Public Policy Conference* (pp. 94-108).

Henion, K. E., & Wilson, W. H. (1976). The ecologically concerned consumer and locus of control. In K. E. Henion & T. C. Kinnear (Eds.), *Ecological marketing* (pp. 131-144). Austin, TX: American Marketing Association.

Hines, J. M., Hungerford, H. R., & Tomera, A. N.(1987). Analysis and synthesis of research on responsible environmental behavior: A meta-analysis. *Journal of Environmental Education, 18*(2), 1-8.

Jacobs, H. E., & Bailey, J. S. (1982-1983). Evaluating participation in a residential recycling program. *Journal of Environmental Systems, 12,* 141-153.

Jacobs, H. E., Bailey, J. S., & Crews, J. I. (1984). Development and analysis of a community-based resource recovery program. *Journal of Applied Behavior Analysis, 17,* 127-145.

Kotler, P., & Zaltman, G. (1971). Social marketing: An approach to planned social change. *Journal of Marketing, 35*(3), 3-12.

Levin, G. (1990, November 12). Consumers turning green: JWT survey. *Advertising Age,* p. 74.

Luchsinger, P. B., Mullen, V. S., & Jannuzzo, P. T. (1977). How many advertising dollars are enough? *Media Decisions, 12,* 59.

Mayer, R. N., Scammon, D. L., & Gray-Lee, J. W. (1994). *Consumer interpretations of environmental marketing claims: Meanings and inferences.* Unpublished manuscript, University of Utah, Salt Lake City.

Mayer, R. N., Scammon, D. L., & Zick, C. D. (1992). Turning the competition green: The regulation of environmental claims. In P. Bloom & R. Starr, Jr. (Eds.), *Proceedings of the 1992 Marketing and Public Policy Conference* (pp. 152-165).

McCarty, J. A., & Shrum, L. J. (1993). A structural equation analysis of the relationships of personal values, attitudes and beliefs about recycling, and the recycling of solid waste products. In L. McAlister & M. Rothschild (Eds.), *Advances in consumer research* (Vol. 20, pp. 641-646). Provo, UT: Association for Consumer Research.

McCarty, J. A., & Shrum, L. J. (1994a). *Cultural value orientations as antecedents of recycling attitudes, beliefs, and behaviors.* Unpublished manuscript, American University, Washington, DC.

McCarty, J. A., & Shrum, L. J. (1994b). The recycling of solid wastes: Personal and cultural values and attitudes about recycling as antecedents of recycling behavior. *Journal of Business Research, 30,* 53-62.

Morris, L. A., Hastak, M., & Mazis, M. B. (1994). *Consumer comprehension of environmental advertising claims.* Unpublished manuscript, American University, Washington, DC.

Pieters, R. G. M. (1991). Changing garbage disposal patterns of consumers: Motivation, ability, and performance. *Journal of Public Policy & Marketing, 10*(2), 59-76.

Reid, D. H., Luyben, P. D., Rawers, R. J., & Bailey, J. S. (1976). Newspaper recycling behavior: The effects of prompting and proximity of containers. *Environment and Behavior, 8,* 471-481.

Scammon, D. L., & Mayer, R. N. (1995). Agency review of environmental marketing claims: Case-by-case decomposition of the issues. *Journal of Advertising, 24*(2), 33-43.

Schwepker, C. H., & Cornwell, T. B. (1991). An examination of ecologically concerned consumers and their intention to purchase ecologically packaged products. *Journal of Public Policy & Marketing, 10*(2), 77-101.

Shrum, L. J., Lowrey, T. M., & McCarty, J. A. (1994). Recycling as a marketing problem: A framework for strategy development. *Psychology & Marketing, 11,* 393-416.

Shrum, L. J., McCarty, J. A., & Lowrey, T. M. (1995). Buyer characteristics of the green consumer and their implications for advertising strategy. *Journal of Advertising, 24*(2), 71-82.

Simmons, D., & Widmar, R. (1990). Motivations and barriers to recycling: Toward a strategy for public education. *Journal of Environmental Education, 22,* 13-18.

Smith, S. M., Haugtvedt, C. P., & Petty, R. E. (1994). Attitudes and recycling: Does the measurement of affect enhance behavioral prediction? *Psychology & Marketing, 11,* 359-374.

Stern, P. C., & Oskamp, S. (1987). Managing scarce environmental resources. In D. Stokols & I. Altman (Eds.), *Handbook of environmental psychology* (pp. 1043-1088). New York: John Wiley.

Taylor, S., & Todd, P. (in press). An integrated model of waste management behavior: A test of household recycling and composting intentions. *Environment and Behavior.*

Van Liere, K. D., & Dunlap, R. E. (1980). The social bases of environmental concern: A review of hypotheses, explanations and empirical evidence. *Public Opinion Quarterly, 44,* 181-197.

Weigel, R. H., & Newman, L. S. (1976). Increasing attitude-behavior correspondence by broadening the scope of the behavioral measure. *Journal of Personality and Social Psychology, 33,* 793-802.

Witmer, J. F., & Geller, E. S. (1976). Facilitating paper recycling: Effects of prompts, raffles, and contests. *Journal of Applied Behavior Analysis, 9,* 315-322.

Zikmund, W. G., & Stanton, W. J. (1971). Recycling solid wastes: A channels of distribution problem. *Journal of Marketing, 35,* 34-39.

Index

About the Authors

Linda F. Alwitt is Associate Professor in the Department of Marketing of the College of Commerce, DePaul University, and Coordinator of Societal Marketing Programs at DePaul's Kellstadt Center for Marketing Analysis and Planning. She received a Ph.D. in Experimental Psychology from the University of Massachusetts-Amherst. She organized a conference on "Marketing and the Poor" held in June 1994, and among her research interests are other topics related to not-for-profit marketing: consumer attitudes and actions about the environment; general attitudes to TV advertising; perceptions of fund-raising organizations. She is the editor of two volumes on consumer behavior, and her most recent publications concern attitudes to advertising, on-line evaluations of TV commercials, and perceptions of fund-raising organizations.

J. Craig Andrews is currently Associate Professor of Marketing with Marquette University, Milwaukee. He received his Ph.D. in marketing from the University of South Carolina. He recently served as a Consumer Research Specialist with the Federal Trade Commission in their Division of Advertising Practices. His research on alcohol warning labels, cross-cultural advertising, and advertising involvement processes

has appeared in *Journal of Consumer Research, Journal of Public Policy &
Marketing, Journal of Advertising,* and *The Journal of Consumer Affairs,*
among others.

Julia Bristor is Assistant Professor of Marketing at the University of
Houston. She received her B.S., M.B.A., and Ph.D. from the University
of Michigan. Her research interests include feminism and gender
issues in marketing, consumer research and management, postposi-
tivist research methods, and minority portrayals in the media. She has
recently published in the *International Journal of Research in Marketing,
Journal of Consumer Research,* and *Psychology & Marketing.*

Eileen Fischer is Associate Professor of Marketing at York University
in North York, Ontario, Canada. She received her Ph.D. in marketing
from Queen's University in Kingston, Ontario. She conducts research
on the gender socialization of consumers, feminist issues in consumer
research, hermeneutics, and experiential learning. Her work has been
published in *Journal of Consumer Research, Psychology and Marketing,
International Journal of Research in Marketing, Journal of Business Ventur-
ing, Journal of Small Business and Entrepreneurship, Journal of Small
Business Management, IEEE Transactions on Engineering Management,* and
in several edited volumes and conference proceedings.

James W. Gentry is Professor of Marketing at University of Nebraska-
Lincoln. He earned his bachelor's degree in Civil Engineering at
Kansas State University and his M.B.A. and D.B.A. degrees at Indiana
University. He has also taught at Kansas State University, Oklahoma
State University, and the University of Wisconsin-Madison. His recent
publications have appeared in *Journal of Business Research, Journal of
Public Policy & Marketing,* and *Advances in Consumer Research.* His
research interests include family decision making (especially during
transitional periods) and cross-cultural consumer decision making.

Cathy Goodwin is Associate Professor of Marketing at the University
of Manitoba. She earned her doctorate at the University of California
at Berkeley and has taught on the faculties at Georgia State University,
University of Alaska, and University of Manitoba. She has published
related work in *Journal of Economic Psychology, Journal of Services Marketing,* and *Journal of Public Policy & Marketing.* Her research interests
include marketing services and coping processes during times of
stress.

Ronald Paul Hill received his Ph.D. from the University of Maryland at College Park. He is Professor and Chairperson of Marketing, College of Commerce & Finance at Villanova University. His career has and continues to be dedicated to the study of social issues from marketing and consumer behavior perspectives. Previous and current topics of investigation include AIDS, political advertising, homelessness, consumer debt, juvenile delinquency, gun control, and abortion, as well as others. His work has been published in *Journal of Consumer Research, Journal of Marketing Research, Journal of Public Policy & Marketing, Journal of Advertising,* and *Journal of Health Care Marketing,* as well as additional outlets.

Elizabeth C. Hirschman is Professor of Marketing in the School of Business, Rutgers University. She is the author of more than 150 scholarly articles and papers. Her research interests include semiotics, interpretive consumer research, and philosophy of science. Most recently, she has coauthored *Postmodern Consumer Research* (Sage, 1993) and *The Semiotics of Consumption* (1994) with Morris Holbrook.

Ju Yung Lee is a graduate research assistant at Villanova University. Her research interests include minority portrayals in advertising and consumer behaviors of Asian Americans. Her publications have appeared in *Journal of Public Policy & Marketing* and conference proceedings.

Tina M. Lowrey received her Ph.D. from the University of Illinois. She is an Assistant Professor of Marketing at Rider University. Her research interests include ritualistic consumption, attitude functions, and the effects of syntactic complexity on advertising persuasiveness. Her work has recently appeared in *Journal of Consumer Research, Journal of Consumer Psychology,* and *Psychology & Marketing.*

John A. McCarty received his Ph.D. from the University of Illinois. He is Assistant Professor of Marketing at American University. His research interests include the influence of culture on consumption and the application of research to public policy issues. His work has recently appeared in *Journal of Advertising, Psychology & Marketing,* and *Journal of Business Research.*

Fred W. Morgan received his Ph.D. from Michigan State University. He is Director, School of Management at the University of Kentucky. He teaches in the areas of marketing strategy, sales management, and social issues in business. His research interests include the legal environment's impact on marketing and business strategy, distribution channel relationships, and sales force management issues. His research has been published in a number of journals, including the *Journal of Marketing, Journal of Consumer Research, Journal of Public Policy and Marketing, Journal of Retailing,* and the *Journal of Business.*

Jeff B. Murray is Associate Professor of Marketing. He received his doctoral degree from Virginia Polytechnic Institute and State University. His research interests are critical and postmodern theory, interpretive theories and methods, and the sociology of marketing and consumer research. His recent work with Julie L. Ozanne has appeared in the *Journal of Consumer Research,* and a chapter in *Research in Consumer Behavior* (1994; edited by Russell W. Belk and Janeen Costa).

Richard G. Netemeyer is Associate Professor of Marketing at Louisiana State University, Baton Rouge. He received his Ph.D. in marketing from the University of South Carolina. His major research interests include consumer behavior and public policy issues. His work has appeared in *Journal of Consumer Research, Journal of Marketing Research, Journal of Marketing, Journal of Public Policy & Marketing,* and elsewhere.

Julie L. Ozanne is Associate Professor of Marketing. She received her doctoral degree from the University of North Carolina at Chapel Hill. Her interests are in critical and interpretive theories and methods, and in social marketing. Her recent work with Jeff B. Murray has been published in *Journal of Consumer Research* and in a chapter in *Research in Consumer Behavior* (1994; eds. Russell W. Belk and Janeen Costa).

Marsha L. Richins is Professor of Marketing at the College of Business and Public Administration at the University of Missouri, Columbia. She has written many articles on consumer behavior, particularly dealing with materialism and other aspects of consumption. Her articles have appeared in the *Journal of Consumer Research, Journal of Consumer Psychology, Journal of Economic Psychology,* and elsewhere.

Debra Jones Ringold is Associate Professor of Marketing at the Atkinson Graduate School of Management, Willamette University. Her research has appeared in *Journal of Marketing, Journal of Public Policy & Marketing, Advances in Public Policy and Marketing, Psychology and Marketing,* and numerous conference proceedings, including *Advances in*

Consumer Research. She received her Ph.D. in marketing from the University of Maryland, College Park.

L. J. Shrum received his Ph.D. from the University of Illinois. He is Assistant Professor of Marketing at Rutgers University. His research interests pertain to effects of mass media on both cognitive representations and socialization processes, as well as the application of research to issues of public policy. His work has recently appeared in *Communication Research, Journal of Advertising,* and *Psychology & Marketing.*

Barbara B. Stern is Professor of Marketing at Rutgers University. She has recently published in *Journal of Advertising* and *Journal of Current Issues and Research in Advertising,* as well as other publications. Her research incorporates literary criticism into the study of marketing, consumer behavior, and advertising. She has analyzed advertisements, research text, and consumer-generated text from the perspective of narrative structure and figurative language. She has also focused on gender issues by using feminist deconstruction to analyze values encoded in advertising text and in research accounts of consumer preference-formation.

Jeffrey J. Stoltman received his Ph.D. from Syracuse University. He is Associate Professor of Marketing at Wayne State University. He teaches in the areas of marketing policy, marketing strategy, consumer behavior, and marketing research. His research interests include public policy and consumer behavior, motivational and situational influences, shopping behavior and patronage dynamics, and relationship management. His research has appeared in a number of journals, including the *Journal of Marketing, Journal of Advertising,* and the *Journal of Business Research.*

Charles R. Taylor is Assistant Professor of Marketing at Villanova University. His research areas include international advertising, marketing to minority groups, and public policy issues in marketing. Recent publications have appeared in *Journal of Public Policy & Marketing, Journal of Current Issues and Research in Advertising, Journal of International Marketing, Journal of Macromarketing,* and numerous other journals and conference proceedings.